Looking through a Glass Bible

# Biblical Interpretation Series

VOLUME 125

*The titles published in this series are listed at brill.com/bins*

# Looking through a Glass Bible

## Postdisciplinary Biblical Interpretations from the Glasgow School

*Edited by*

A. K. M. Adam and Samuel Tongue

BRILL

LEIDEN · BOSTON
2014

Library of Congress Cataloging-in-Publication Data

Looking through a glass Bible : postdisciplinary Biblical interpretations from the Glasgow School / edited by A. K. M. Adam and Samuel Tongue.
   pages cm. — (Biblical interpretation series, ISSN 0928-0731 ; VOLUME 125)
   Includes index.
   ISBN 978-90-04-25907-2 (hardback : alk. paper)—ISBN 978-90-04-25909-6 (e-book) 1. Bible—Criticism, interpretation, etc. 2. Postmodernism—Religious aspects—Christianity. I. Adam, A. K. M. (Andrew Keith Malcolm), 1957– editor of compilation.

   BS511.3.L66 2013
   220.6—dc23

                                                                                    2013029433

This publication has been typeset in the multilingual "Brill" typeface. With over 5,100 characters covering Latin, IPA, Greek, and Cyrillic, this typeface is especially suitable for use in the humanities. For more information, please see www.brill.com/brill-typeface.

ISSN 0928-0731
ISBN 978-90-04-25907-2 (hardback)
ISBN 978-90-04-25909-6 (e-book)

This book is printed on acid-free paper.

MIX
Paper from
responsible sources
FSC® C109576

Printed by Printforce, the Netherlands

The editors and authors dedicate these essays
to the
glorious history of biblical studies
at the
University of Glasgow:
to a storied past,
a vigorous present,
and a future yet to come.

CONTENTS

# ILLUSTRATIONS

*Adam*

*Sharmanka*

PREFACE

In the Memorial Chapel of the University of Glasgow, a window represent-ing the study of Theology looks down at the elevated stalls reserved for the Chancellor and the Principal. The window depicts a scholar deliber-ating over a thick book—perhaps a Bible?—and an encouraging angel, both limned in shades of blue, grey, and brown (shades unusual in the depiction of transcendent beauties); but of this it is difficult to be certain, in part because of the modern style of arranging the panes of the window, in part because of the murky palette of colours, and in part because years of exposure to Glasgow's industrial atmosphere have coated the windows with a layer of grime. The Theology depicted among the other Arts in the chapel's window is a business of puzzling out interpretations from a semi-opaque Bible, in uncertain colours, with precious few unambiguous clarities.

In these ways and more, the Theology window stands as a fitting emblem of the Glasgow School of biblical scholarship. The work of interpretation displayed in these pages challenges the imagination with varying degrees of transparency, with unexpected colours, with industrial exertion, with stained panes and angelic encouragement, and here and there with some outright dirty bits. The glass way, *der Glasweg*, allows as well for polished lambency, even magnification, and for disconcerting refractions. The *Glas-wegeschule* takes up the Bible as one pane in a variegated panorama of a culture's luminous fabric, sometimes examining the Bible's location in its more expansive contexts, sometimes considering the shifting appearance of the Bible as its environmental conditions change, sometimes attend-ing to the tracery that connects the panes, sometimes peering through to tease out clues concerning the conditions beyond the Bible, sometimes analysing the constitution of the medium, sometimes taking the images as a point of departure toward far-flung associated notions, sometimes seek-ing illumination by the diffuse light the window transmits. Practitioners of this *Glasweg* of interpretation move freely among interpretive discourses, attending at this moment to history, at that to aesthetics, at another to politics, at another to popular media, at yet another to reception history, and at another to literature—honouring such theoretical traffic laws as suit their imaginative purposes, accepting the risk of transgressing in the service of more expansive imaginative horizons than the safely insular interpretations. So as editors, we did not ask our colleagues to show their licence and insurance, nor did we enforce any specified approach to the contributions in this collection. Rather, we invited essays that permitted the authors' own sense of speaking from this academic, rough-edged, hard-working, sometimes undisciplined city, with results that exemplify the industrial-strength, sometimes murky, other times brilliantly-lambent light of biblical interpretation seen through the *Glaswegeschule* window.

For instance, while much work currently endeavours to define the terms and boundary markers of 'reception history', it may be said (without too much posturing from the Weegies amongst us) that Yvonne Sherwood's *A Biblical Text and Its Afterlives: The Survival of Jonah in Western Culture*[1] has to be one of the *ur-texts* of what has become a burgeoning field.[2] Sherwood's influence may certainly be discerned in some of her current and former students here, but each perspective glues together different theories and bible readings in new forms, rather like the Sharmanka kinemats that appear in Sherwood's own co-authored piece at the end of this collection.

The *Glasweg* of textual illumination proceeds fully aware that a series of warnings is attached to such palimpsestuous[3] reading techniques. It is never a matter of just setting up 'Bible and...' (literature, art, politics, theory, etc.) and expecting all parties to be in full agreement with the arranged match. Such pairings can be very complex, demanding a highly skilled and wide-ranging scholarly acumen. In a certain sense, the *Glaswegeschule* offers some traditional Scottish hospitality, inviting strangers over the threshold, into the home (even as many of the scholars here would argue against hasty assumptions about which side of which threshold constitutes a 'home'). And yet such an interdisciplinary invitation brings danger with it; indeed, as Derrida warns, "hospitality is the

---

[1] Yvonne Sherwood, *A Biblical Text and Its Afterlives: The Survival of Jonah in Western Culture* (Cambridge: Cambridge University Press, 2000).

[2] On the New Testament side, our colleague John Riches has heightened awareness of the history of the interpretation with his monographs on Galatians and on twentieth-century New Testament criticism among other works: *Galatians Through the Centuries*, Blackwell Bible Commentaries (Wiley-Blackwell, 2007); *A Century of New Testament Study* (Cambridge: Lutterworth Press, 1993).

[3] Gerard Genette takes this term form Philip LeJeune and then paraphrases it thus: "To put it differently... one who really loves texts must wish from time to time to love (at least) two together." Gerard Genette, *Palimpsests: Literature in the Second Degree*, trans. Channa Newman and Claude Dubonsky (Lincoln: University of Nebraska Press, 1997), p. 399.

deconstruction of the at-home [...].⁴ Hospitality is demanding and dangerous; as Derrida notes, in the code of hospitality that invites the stranger into the home "is inscribed... the very meaning [*valuer*] of stranger, foreign, or foreigner [*étranger*], that is to say what is foreign to the proper, foreign and not proper to, not close to or proximate to. The stranger is a digression that risks corrupting the proximity to self of the proper."⁵ The necessary hermeneutic danger of inviting a stranger over the threshold lies with the guest who may, in fact, be an enemy, a *hostis*, who might take more than is given, instilling distrust in systems of truth-telling corrupting the proper, and opening up a gap in the current economy (*oikos*) of the 'at-home'. Inviting different thinkers and artists into the University Chapel to gaze up at the Theology window, we get more than we bargained for. All of the essays collected below invite guests into the 'at-home' of biblical studies—or gate-crashers from biblical studies occupying other discourses!—guests who are sometimes wild and unruly, sometimes respectful and reverent, but all of whom rejuvenate and refresh what we think we mean by the Bible and the biblical. It's just that someone (probably the editors) may need to clean up afterwards.

We may need to scrub the wainscoting when Benjamin Morse's opening essay splatters us with a hermeneutic that mixes psalmodic lament and Jackson Pollock's 'anti-art'. By hanging Psalm 13 alongside Pollock's *Cathedral*, Morse argues that the painting becomes a visual map of a protesting consciousness, paralleling the dramatic style of a psalm of lament. He is able to offer an extraordinary diagrammatic rendition of how the psalm works on a reader's consciousness, emphasising how words are always doing more than we think, that the emphases and flow and stylistics of text are always more than syntactical order.

From Pollock's Long Island studio to the Firth of Clyde, Hugh Pyper's translation of Jonah brings the seafaring prophet to an unfamiliar port: Glasgow, like Tarshish, like Tarsus, no mean city. Pyper's Jonah MacAmity rises to challenge the imperious hegemony of English-language translations. This Scots Jonah eschews sentimental indulgence in quaint biblical Tartan tat in favour of wresting an unfamiliar, vivid vernacular from vernacular Hebrew. In so doing, Pyper draws attention to the Hebrew, to the Scots, and especially to the arresting literary imagination that brings

---

⁴ Jacques Derrida, "Hospitality," in *Acts of Religion*, ed. Gil Anidjar (New York and London: Routledge: 2002), p. 364.
⁵ Ibid., p. 402.

Jonah to life before our ears and eyes; with this publication, we gladly honour the prophet in Hugh's own country.

Hannah Strømmen's essay turns to another narrative about another prophet away from home. She examines the Book of Daniel and the question of how the human subject understands herself in relation to animals (often upheld as symbols of natural otherness in the sustained and tactical forgetfulness of the animality of the human), and the archive, most resolutely represented in our cultural imaginaries around 'the Bible'. As a cultural archive, the Bible has had a major part to play in our understanding of the sovereignty of the human; how does the Book of Daniel play with and perhaps overturn this extra-animal sovereignty, within the biblical archive itself?

Alastair Hunter takes the opportunity to forward a radical proposal for understanding the Book of the Covenant from Exodus 19–24; rather than attempting to find here a collection of sources for historical events or even treating the text as a repository of redacted traditions, Hunter argues that a better question to ask is 'what is/was this text for?', concluding that Exodus actually displays a *liturgical* function, perhaps linked with a number of festivals, of which *Pesach* is but one. With such work, he raises problems with the ways in which history/historiography have been linked in various ways in biblical history—particularly, the idea that historical reference is supposed to have the final say over the possibilities of meaning—at the same time as admitting that this search for a 'biblical history' has always been an addictive quest. Hunter encapsulates some of the key tensions that continue to animate biblical studies.

Sketching an intellectual history of modern biblical scholarship, Jonathan Birch's contribution takes this problem of historical reference in a different direction. He notes how the hunt for non-canonical and extra-canonical texts that critique received orthodoxy displays an urge to crack the glass that sequesters the canon, to include more and more texts that offer different perspectives on the origins and constitutions of early Christianities. Illustrating his case with the Secret Gospel of Mark promulgated by Morton Smith and the Gospel of Barnabas promoted by Glasgow's own John Toland, Birch argues that this potentially provocative non-canonicity is doomed to failure once the novelty of another 'new gospel' has worn off.

Utilising non-canonical literature (in both the biblical and literary senses) provides Anna Fisk with the foundations to address questions of canonicity and identity politics from a different intellectual trajectory. She focuses on feminist biblical scholarship that attempts to recover the lost stories of the women who merit only a fleeting mention in narratives mostly concerned with a male God's dealings with human males; these women's silence in the biblical versions of their stories takes her into the realms of extra-canonical literary retellings. Drawing on feminist scholarship and contemporary women's imaginative writing, this essay explores the various ways in which readings of Hagar and Sarah, as paradigmatic biblical women, speaks to contentious issues of contemporary identity politics. A number of issues then come into play: What status does literary imagination have in relation to the exegetical procedures of biblical scholarship? What of the conflicted sisterhood between Hagar and Sarah which has been deployed to symbolize the relationship between white feminism and black womanism? Fisk's work heightens her readers' awareness of how certain marginalised feminist perspectives can also be deemed as speaking from a position of privilege.

Many of the contributors take their lead from literary concerns. Samuel Tongue offers a reading of what Roland Barthes identified as the 'Babel-complex' to examine how biblical texts and tropes become part of an urban signifying practice; the construction of tall towers that irrecoverably alter the city's skyline and, in so doing, alter and complicate the ways in which the city can be read. The Babel story from Genesis 11: 1–9 has a long cultural history, most notably in studies of the origins of linguistic difference. Here, Tongue is particularly interested in how such textual constructions as the Tower/City of Babel live on as an imaginative blueprint in the commentary around architectural feats such as the Eiffel Tower and The World Trade Center, moving between the textual rendering of Babel, the psycho-social discourse around the meaning of such towers, and their material construction and destruction.

The *Glaswegeschule* we are tracing here has always been interested in engaging the impact and interpretation of the Bible wherever it may be found, often analysing how 'religion' (that increasingly problematic and indefinite term) is regularly constructed in relation to how the Bible is used. A. K. M. Adam's essay is concerned with how biblical texts become iconic talismans, often only tenuously linked with the content and context of the biblical material itself. He begins by demonstrating how the Ten Commandments (themselves explicitly aniconic) have become such a significant part of American civil religion, before exploring how the U.S. flag itself exists as sacred totem with constitutional protection; desecrating an American flag draws heavy penalties. But, as Adam demonstrates, the connotations of being able to *desecrate* such a symbol shows the explicit link between patriotism and a national religion. Adam names this fusion of Christian religion and political nationalism *Sacramerica*. By reading a Sapolio soap advert from the 1880s that displays the tagline 'A clean nation has ever been a strong nation', Adam is able to foreground how Sacramerica names a signifying practice, a repertoire of premises and, especially, actions that express, affirm, reinforce, and disseminate particular sorts of meaning. This work takes biblical studies in a much broader direction; the *Glaswegeschule* is particularly interested in how desecration (of biblical texts, of 'sacred values') leads into debates around religion, the sacred, and how the Bible both upholds and undermines certain contemporary sacralities. Ideas of what constitutes or institutes 'the sacred'[6] go well beyond the often staid and adversarial positioning of the 'religious' and the 'secular'.

The networked registers of religion and the secular interweave in different ways in Abigail Pelham's examination of Job. On one hand, the Book of Job (and God's casual wager with *hassatan*) concern nothing other than theology; and on the other, Pelham illumines the resolutely religious narrative by juxtaposing it with Elaine Scarry's critical discourse on pain, Kurt Vonnegut's fictive allotopian discourse in *Galápagos*, and an advertising trope associated with voice actor Don LaFontaine. Where somber academics often insist that their favoured disciplines—usually grammar, lexicography, and history—are necessary for the legitimate interpretations that shed true light on the biblical text, Pelham insouciantly relies on critical theory, fictional futurism, and film trailers to envision a world in which Job's story unexpectedly ends... as the Bible narrates it.

Eduard Bersudsky, sculptor-mechanic and Russian cultural refugee, along with theatre director Tatyana Jakovskaya, founded the unique art-performance experience *Sharmanka* in St. Petersburg in 1989. It relocated to Glasgow in 1996 and has been clanking, whirring, and creaking in a corner of the city ever since. The cultural-critical collective *Religart* offer multiple readings of these kinetic sculptures (or kinemats) that almost seem to defy narrative or textual description. Many specifically reference biblical themes, motifs, and images but this is something beyond textual exegesis; *Sharmanka* is a complex *articulation* of cultural references in all senses of the word and the collective, layered response of the contribu-

---

6 For much further nuance on the differences between 'sacred' and 'religious', see Gordon Lynch, *On The Sacred* (Durham: Acumen, 2012). As he argues, "far from entering an age of rational Enlightenment, society remains profoundly shaped by compelling moral, emotional identifications with symbolic representations of the sacred. Such sacred motivations are not simply the preserve of religious fundamentalists but woven throughout social life in forms that overwhelm rigid categories of the religious and secular." p. 9.

tors is one way to trace how art and artifice sustain such complexities in radical ways.

From active sculptural assemblages to action painting to adverts to archives to *owerset* agitators, these essays traverse a landscape of varied discourses without the sense—familiar from first-generation refugees from historical criticism's secure homeland—of a residual debt to the strictures that shaped earlier generations of scholars. Indeed, these essays lack also the self-congratulatory impudence that often marks newly-liberated interpreters. The contributors to this postdisciplinary collage vest the authority of their work less in vigilant obedience to legitimating rules (or jubilant transgression thereof) than in the quality of the interpretation itself: to what they show us about a text, a world, an image, a culture. These shards have cutting edges; they do not simply add up to some tidily integrated whole. Gathered in one place, they bespeak the readiness to move on from only regrinding the same methodological lenses over and over, in favour of putting to work the varieties of glass, coloured and clear, murky and scintillating, performing interpretive labour in a sort of active collage of fragmentary insights—without pretending to an authority that our fractured discourses could never fully warrant.

There may be a final, authoritative way to rearrange the bits of glass in the window; presumably Irenaeus would have insisted that the glass meant to portray a beautiful image of a king should not be rearranged to make them into the form of a dog or of a fox ('and even that but poorly executed'[7] *Adv, hær.* I.viii.1). Ah, but what of a *well-executed* image of a fox? What if the king had a vulpine demeanour? And what about interpreters who operate outwith Irenaeus's jurisdiction? Under the stained-glass sign of Theology (now sharing the bill with 'Religious Studies'), a studio of biblical interpreters has come together to read and imagine widely, colourfully, exploring a way of working with stained glass whose legitimation rests on the quality of the insights it produces. This studio, this school, is dispersing (as such studios do); some no longer work for Glas-wages, others will be departing soon, and others will linger. Their practice of non-anxious postdisciplinary biblical interpretation will continue, though, among scholars at the University of Glasgow and furth of the Firth of Clyde; the *Glasweg* leads on.

A. K. M. Adam & Samuel Tongue

---

7 Alexander Roberts, trans., in *The Ante-Nicene Fathers* vol. 1, ed. Alexander Roberts and James Donaldson. (Buffalo: The Christian Literature Publishing Company, 1885) 326.

# ABSTRACTION ON A LAMENT: PSALM 13 AS POURED PAINT

## Benjamin Morse

> ...David being not only pinched with extreme distress, but also over-whelmed with long and manifold miseries heaped one upon the other, calls upon God's faithfulness for help, which was the only remedy that remained for him...[1]

> ...like pictures painted on the inside walls of his mind... [Pollock's] work amounts to an invitation: Forget all, sever all, inhabit your white cell and—most ironic paradox of all—discover the universal in your self, for in a one-man world you are universal![2]

Liturgical (e)motions flow according to painterly aesthetics. To introduce an abstract reading of a rather generic individual lament (one Hermann Gunkel designated as "the model of a 'lament of the individual'... in which the individual components of the genre step forth most clearly"),[3] I begin with an art historical debate that will intertwine the biblical object and thinking surrounding it with interpretive twists not commonly found in exegesis. The polarized assessment of certain American painters of the 1940s and 1950s provides a basis on which to rethink a similar split found in the way people write about psalms. The added sensitivity of one critic to judgments he detected against style, subjectivity and interpretation further allows us to rehang Psalm 13 as a protest in poured paint.

The legacy of the so-called New York School[4] was for several decades determined by the battle to quantify the value—or failure—of Abstract Expressionism. As the artists' distinctive styles appeared to manifest mere individual preferences, the question of their work's ultimate relevance helped draw a bold line in the critical sand. One camp of critics, who

---

[1] John Calvin, *A Commentary on the Psalms of David* (first published in 1557; reprinted in London: Thomas Tegg, 1840), 121.

[2] John Berger, *Permanent Red* (London: Methuen & Co., 1960), 68–69.

[3] Hermann Gunkel, *Die Psalmen*, Handkommentar zum Alten Testament (Göttingen: Vandenhoek & Ruprecht, 1926), 46; cf. Craig C. Broyles, *The Conflict of Faith and Experience in the Psalms: A Form Critical and Theological Study*, (Sheffield: Sheffield Academic Press, 1989), 185.

[4] The name groups stylistically diverse post-War artists in New York—many of them expatriates—under a deceptively unifying banner.

insisted formal qualities alone gave art its meaning, regarded the work of
Jackson Pollock (1912–1956) and his 'drip' method as a particular triumph.
The opposing side regarded the physical act he conducted in his painting
to be important for reasons beyond the state of the paint; and so Pollock
helped introduce the concept of the event as art.

Clement Greenberg and Harold Rosenberg led the colours of these
theorist-troops via "some of the most vivid partisan writing in the history of criticism".[5] Greenberg celebrated Pollock's role as an *avant-garde*
artist who more than anyone surpassed painting's representational limits
by elevating the medium to a plane far above politics and the common
culture. John Berger found universal possibilities in Pollock's "one-man
worlds" (*supra*) but maintained Greenberg's focus on his formal achievements; passing over "the pretentious incantations written around the kind
of painting [Pollock] fathered", Berger contextualised the artist's canvases
according to their "colour, their consistency of gesture, [and] the balance
of their tonal weights".[6] Rosenberg on the other hand identified existential implications in the method revealed in Pollock's picture planes; he
saw the artist's action as a negotiation with the human condition. Equally
Leo Steinberg brought to light the social significance of Pollock's irrever-
ent style. Though the two critical traditions valued drip painting for different reasons, they never doubted its importance.

By 1979, Peter Fuller would discredit Pollock for failing to speak beyond
his own generation; he found the work "symptomatic of the courageous-
ness of what the Abstract Expressionists tried to do and of the enormity of
their failure." In attempting to realise a historical vision through his painting, Fuller alleged, "his vision became increasingly confined within the
universal imagery of psychosis and infantilism".[7] Donald Kuspit quickly
exposed Fuller's generalizations about American culture and his ill-
informed assumptions about Pollock's apparent political apathy. Asserting that Pollock's work transcends mere self-commentary, Kuspit found
Fuller guilty of "bifurcation...with its automatic assumption of content
being an objective matter and style a realm of subjective implications".[8]

---

[5] Max Kozloff, "The Critical Reception of Abstract Expressionism", first published in
*Arts* magazine (December 1965); cf. *Abstract Expressionism: A Critical Record*, ed. David
and Cecile Shapiro, (Cambridge: Cambridge University Press, 1990), 150.

[6] Berger, 67.

[7] Peter Fuller, "American Painting Since the Last War", first published in *Art Monthly*
(May–June 1979); cf. Shapiro and Shapiro (hereafter referenced as Shapiros), 172.

[8] Donald Kuspit, 'Abstract Expressionism: The Social Contract', first published in *Arts*
magazine (March 1980); cf. Shapiros, 186.

By thinking according to a "perverse species of false consciousness... Fuller mechanically assumes Pollock's style is necessarily subjective."[9]

A year earlier, Kuspit identified bifurcation in Susan Sontag's *Against Interpretation* (1961). Finding hermeneutics were obstructing our understanding of art with excessive intellectual froth, Sontag had written, "To interpret is to impoverish, to deplete the world—in order to set up a shadow world of 'meanings'."[10] In this she echoed Greenberg's prioritisation of art and literature's physical or sensational properties, prescribing that criticism's role should be "to cut back content... to show *how it is what it is*, even *that it is what it is*, rather than to show *what it means*."[11] Kuspit countered that description alone was "prosaic" and traced Sontag's reductive separation of it from interpretation back to Descartes.[12] A more comprehensive perspective would emerge only by accounting for art's effect on consciousness and the horizons it suggests.

Thus we have before us several instances of opposition that we present at the opening of this essay, laying the base coats of an interpretive accumulation that will treat psalmody like paint. The first is the polarization between Greenberg and Rosenberg's priorities (form/physicality versus content/concept). The second is the theoretical divide between those who think style is subjective and therefore critically insignificant—and those who insist that both style and subjectivity are essential and serious components in humankind's quest for truth. And the third instance of opposition involves the question of whether we should simply say 'what a psalm is', or whether we dare to expand the horizons of criticism by exploring the effects biblical poetry can have on consciousness.

In biblical commentaries, we find parallel records of bifurcation. Today there are those who commit themselves to the text's picture plane—to the texture of the words and their original meanings. Like disciples of Greenberg, they remain faithful to describing the physical layers of history that saturate the two-dimensional printed matter. Many would consider this to be the primary objective approach. Though the historical critic might take exception to the art historian referring to his/her concerns as 'style', the look and flow of cultic poetry are paramount here. Rejecting historical-critical description as prosaic, a wave of Rosenbergs and Steinbergs has risen up to investigate and import a seemingly infinite

---

9 Ibid.

10 Susan Sontag, *Against Interpretation* (New York: Farrar, Straus and Giroux, 1961), 7.

11 Sontag, 14.

12 Donald Kuspit, "To Interpret or Not to Interpret", first published in *Arts* magazine (March 1979), in Shapiros, 386, 389.

spectrum of meanings they find in the ancient textual canvases. While these latter critics are known to sever texts from their historical contexts, treating them in a different way as two-dimensional surfaces that exist purely in the literary present, their work ascribes content by contemplating the structures of stories, the functions of characters, and the effects they have on readers. These interpreters often prioritize the text's social and political significance as if to answer existential questions about the universe of language and our identities as readers.

The analogy blurs if we render the historical critic's focus on 'style' as subjective and the literary critic's concern with content (as it exists in the present) as objective, for many would insist it is the other way around. But here I engage Kuspit's problem with bifurcation itself to ask if both modes of analysis are not simultaneously directed by their own subjective and objective preconceptions. The historical critic subjectively prefers an apparently objective search for an original text, while the literary critic objectively concedes that subjective reflection offers more truth than a solitary concern with past meaning. And there are of course many good theologians (and preachers) who weigh the discoveries of all these scholars either to tease out a *sensus plenior* or to craft integrated interpretations. As someone who creates metaphors for biblical texts by juxtaposing them with unrelated modern images, I naturally defend the importance of style as well as subjectivity. But I do so in the earnest belief that I am highlighting artistic or aesthetic phenomena that exist in the 'original' biblical texts.

A more specific kind of bifurcation occurs in the divide that exists between objective readers of the psalms, by which I mean scholars whose methods are not governed by theology, and those who read them for religious or spiritual reasons. While form-critics, for instance, parse a psalm's constituent parts, faith guides aim to foster an experience of God, selecting verses for daily reflection and making the psalm useful for personal prayer. With the groundwork of form-criticism laid by Gunkel in *Die Psalmen* (1926) and his posthumously published *Introduction to the Psalms* (1928–33), scholarship has classified the psalms according to types (*Gattungen*), as well as other codes, and it has fixated on the cultic poem's *Sitz im Leben*. Its Greenbergian concerns have been each psalm's formal qualities and how it adheres to or strays from the standard hymn or lament, though most fail to follow a typical structure.[13] Within this

---

[13] John Day's introduction to *Psalms* (Sheffield: Sheffield Academic Press, 1992) reiterates how little to expect from a form or type's unity: of the communal event, "there is no

identification system, critics inquire about a psalm's cultic setting, debate about the potential royal identity of a speaker, prove illness is the reason behind a plea, and even propose that the individual lament represents a sacral trial.

In contrast to form-critical pursuits, devotional guides are known to address the personal nature of the individual psalms, helping readers to identify with a speaker whom tradition professes to be David. They illuminate the life-applicable qualities and the human drama, often sanitising unsavoury portions of laments that ask God to blot out the enemy by conceptualising them as signals for Christian forgiveness.[14] But both scholarly and faith-based commentaries make note of the lament's expressive style and emphasise its function as a conduit through which the speaker pours out his soul. Gushing with hope and despair, laments invite the reader to partake in an outbreak of sensation and to take imaginative leaps as the heart channels emotions to a God it conceives of in metaphorical terms.

In the midst of these interlaced ideas about psalms, Abstract Expressionism, and subjective versus objective ways of reading, we encounter Psalm 13. Calvin sees in it a David who is "pinched" with distress and "overwhelmed with long and manifold miseries heaped one upon the other"—a David enveloped by a tortuous terrain of relentlessly layered tribulations. The lashings of despair in these six deceptively short verses unfold in impassioned pleas that spill over the boundaries of what is read and into the realm of uncontained universal grief. Yet relief comes in a final stroke of jubilant colour: "he has dealt bountifully with me" (v. 6).

The parallelisms that give the psalm its textual tautness run like whorls of paint on a canvas, poured deftly across the surface of the hymn. Like Pollock's "surging serpentines", they wind their way through and connect the verses into a "thickly intertwined but transparent"[15] matrix of equivalences and oppositions. In the third of Robert Lowth's *Lectures on the Sacred Poetry of the Hebrews* (1753), he identified an "artifice of composition" he would later call Parallelism. The patterns of Hebrew poetry, he

---

fixed order in what follows"; in the individual lament, "there is no absolute regularity"; and in individual thanksgivings, "Again there is no absolute regularity", 12.

[14] A recording of the pastoral theologian Eugene H. Peterson once played at a seminar for Glasgow's Centre for Literature, Theology and the Arts exhibits the way Christians can make putty of ancient spite. The recording of his sermon on Psalm 108 sought to prove that God's promises to divide up Shechem, make Moab his washbasin, and cast his shoe on Edom (vv. 7–9) constitute the psalmist's plea to be led to Edom so that he can forgive his neighbour.

[15] Anonymous review, 'Jackson Pollock at Art of This Century', in *ARTNews* (Feb. 1947); cf. Shapiros, 364.

found, "treat[ed] one subject in many different ways" and "express[ed] the same thing in different words, or different things in similar forms of words"... making "equals refer to equals, and opposites to opposites". By resorting to this mannerism of style, Lowth's psalmist "seldom fails to produce...an agreeable and measured cadence" that "must have imparted to [the] poetry...an exquisite degree of beauty and grace."[16]

While Lowth's ensuing subdivision of parallelisms into three types somewhat dulls his musings on parallelism's intrinsic beauty, Adele Berlin reminds us that he "was right about the essence of parallelism; it is a *correspondence of one thing with another*. Parallelism promotes the perception of a relationship...of correspondence."[17] Berlin explains how this correspondence is formulated via repetition, substitution, equivalence, opposition and contrast, and she subscribes to a broad definition of parallelism that seeks verbal equivalences beyond the context of the usual two or more consecutive lines. She incorporates Roman Jakobson's "more encompassing definition" and considers phrases and larger segments of text in order to "unify phenomena whose relationships have not been perceived."[18] She takes into account longer streams of text, and the process by which they overlap, to form a more "global view".[19] Reading Ps. 13 as poured paint is not simply a metaphorical exercise, creating resemblances that are not inherently there,[20] but also an act of parallelism that takes a global view of the parallel functions of words and paint. The significance and subtleties of parallelisms can be explained in words, but they can also be conceived in visual terms, even when poetic imagery is not at stake.

---

[16] Robert Lowth, *Lectures on the Sacred Poetry of the Hebrews* (first published, 1753); trans. G. Gregory (London, Thomas Tegg: 1835), 34.

[17] Adele Berlin, *The Dynamics of Biblical Parallelism* (Bloomington: Indiana University Press, 1985), 2.

[18] *Biblical Parallelism*, 3.

[19] *Biblical Parallelism*, 140. Berlin assesses studies by Jakobson to establish this point.

[20] Ricoeur has established that metaphors are not simple substitutions, for "the metaphorical *twist* is at once an event *and* a meaning, an event that means or signifies, an emerging meaning created by language", in Paul Ricoeur, *The Rule of Metaphor*, trans. Robert Czerny (London and Henley: Routledge & Kegan Paul, 1978), 99. I have previously created metaphors for biblical texts by linking them with modern images: 'The Lamentations Project: Biblical Mourning Through Modern Montage', *Journal for the Study of the Old Testament* 28 (2003), 113–127; 'Earth Actions: Disintegration and Diaspora in Isaiah 44 and in Mendieta's *Siluetas*', *The Bible and Critical Theory* 2 (2006); and in 'The Defence of Michal: Pre-Raphaelite Persuasion in 2 Samuel 6' and 'Introduction to a Dandy, Part 2: Qoheleth's Turn, With Duchamp at Monte Carlo', both in forthcoming issues of *Biblical Interpretation*.

A diagrammatic translation illustrates how the parallelisms in Ps. 13 form an interlacing skein, like streams of words poured across a canvas:

How long, **O LORD**? Wilt *thou* forget ~me~ forever?

How long wilt *thou* hide *thy face* from ~me~?

How long must *I* bear pain in *my soul,*

and have **sorrow** in *my heart* all the day?

How long shall *my enemy* be exalted over ~me~?

Consider and answer me, **O LORD** *my God*;

lighten *my eyes*, lest *I* **sleep** the **sleep** of Death.

Lest *my enemy* say, '*I* have prevailed over him',

lest *my foes* rejoice because *I* am shaken.

But *I* have trusted in *thy steadfast love*

*my heart* shall rejoice in *thy salvation*.

*I* will sing to the **LORD**,

because *He* has dealt bountifully with ~me~.

The application of different fonts and sizes highlights the threads that wind their way through the verses like surges of paint across one of Pollock's surfaces. The fourfold repetition of 'How long' creates a bold initial splash, while 'sorrow', 'exalted', and the double appearance of 'rejoice' in 20-point suggests a thematic flow of emotions. The subject 'I' provides another fluid line from v. 2 through to v. 6, while the number of times an italicized 'me' or 'my'-something appears shows how deeply the strands of the self interlace in the psalm. In a plane higher than the subject's own, God's qualities ('thy face', 'thy steadfast love' and 'thy salvation') are superscripted in italics. One can trace the wandering line between the occurrence of any number of oppositions: 'thou' and 'me', 'my soul' and 'my enemy', 'my foes' and 'thy steadfast love', 'my heart' and 'he', and so on. Parallelism thus establishes multiple streams of subjects and contrasts that overlap into a self-inhabited space that commingles with the divine realm.

The arrangement of sentiments in this short but dense psalm is woven from competing and passionate colourful veins. Anger, resentment, hope, desperation, insistence and doubt permeate one another and spill off the page and into the reader's world. Linearly read, the course of invocation, complaint and praise would imply a complete and dramatic transformation at the last stage. Yet the expansive density of this psalm demands that the feelings of the speaker not be subdued by the shift to hope in v. 5 but instead be held expressively in continuous tension with it, as a contiguous totality.

Aside from its overlapping verbal and emotional layers, the psalm shares with Pollock's characteristic work an aversion to distracting detail. John Day's summation of the "vague and general terms" in which individual laments are so commonly couched holds true for Ps. 13: "... many of the individual laments are phrased in such general, stereotyped terms that it is no longer possible to deduce exactly what the complaint is."[21] Like the specifics of the reader's personal situation, detail exists outside the edges of the psalm. The psalm does not put into literal words the particulars of an isolated historic experience and so to a degree disowns verbal, narrative or other fixed forms of imagery.

Pollock and many of his contemporaries avoided explaining their work for reasons not always understood by their detractors. While the founding Director of the Museum of Modern Art Alfred Barr admitted the painters did "nothing to make 'communication' easy",[22] Pollock defended his reticence on the premise that "any attempt to explain it could only destroy it."[23] Similarly the painter Clyfford Still wrote, "to interpose any literary allusion is to establish a serious block to communication";[24] and the sculptor David Smith announced on a 1952 radio program that words were not essential to understanding his work and advocated in place of them a "return to origins, before purities were befouled by words."[25] While we must question Smith's construction of 'pure' pre-verbal origins and his assumption that language corrupts human encounter, several art historians have noted the New York artists' suspicion of French Surrealism's literary roots as well as the ways in which realism came to be equated with the totalitarian propaganda art that had been commissioned by Hitler and Stalin.[26] Shunning words and description was for

---

[21] Day, *Psalms*, 29.

[22] Alfred Barr, introduction to *The New American Painting* exhibition catalogue (New York: Museum of Modern Art, 1958); Shapiros, 196.

[23] As cited in Ann Gibson, "Abstract Expressionism's Evasion of Language", first published in *Art Journal* 47.3 (Fall 1988); Shapiros, 196.

[24] Clyfford Still, letter excerpted in *Tiger's Eye* 7 (March 1949), 60; cf. Gibson, "Evasion", 195.

[25] David Smith in a WNYC radio program broadcast on 30 October 1952, in *David Smith*, ed. Garnett McCoy (New York: Praeger, 1971); Gibson, "Evasion", 195.

[26] Gibson, "Evasion", 197.

them an anti-dictatorial choice. In the case of Ps. 13, vague language may have more to do with making the piece appropriate for public liturgy (it universalises the 'I'), but a correlation can be drawn between the modern artists' elusive aesthetics and the hymn's symbolic words and poetic structures that aim to propel the reader away from material detail toward a realm of sensation.

The short psalm functions in a paradox of scale to Pollock's large drip-painting, *Cathedral* (1947, 181.6 × 88.9cm, Dallas Museum of Art). The vertical configuration of this imposing canvas is unusual for the artist, who more commonly chose the horizontal axis to immerse viewers in his expansive compositions. Its title provides an actual subject (rather than a mere 'Number') and a sanctuary setting, a sacred field of a mesmerising depth and light. Over a bare canvas are splashed black, white, aluminium, and faint skeins of yellow, orange and red—most from household paints rather than artist's oils. "Thus the paint surface becomes a series of labyrinthine patinas—refined and coarse types intermingling".[27] As the colours play off one another, "overarching forms do not emerge ... no compositional architecture subordinates small incidents to bigger ones".[28] Pollock in fact took pride in this 'all-over' effect, remembering in an interview with the *New Yorker* in 1951 how his painting had been criticised for not having "any beginning or end".[29] As a grievance, Ps. 13 also yields the sensation that the pain could be endless. The message of hope poured on in the final verse offers temporary relief, but it is enmeshed in an intermingling labyrinth of emotions that has no definite end.

Aldous Huxley questioned the apparent indeterminacy of Pollock's work, claiming *Cathedral* most aptly suited "a panel for a wallpaper which is repeated indefinitely around the wall."[30] Where others like Huxley saw only chaotic repetition,[31] Greenberg praised its implicit symmetries and Rosenberg found, "it joined painting to dance and to the inward action

---

[27] Parker Tyler, "Jackson Pollock: The Infinite Labyrinth", first published in the *Magazine of Art* (March 1950); Shapiros, 365.

[28] Carter Ratcliff, *The Fate of a Gesture: Jackson Pollock and Postwar American Art* (New York: Farrar, Straus and Giroux, 1996), 65. Many however argue that the repeating patterns formulate underlying structures for the drip paintings, establishing an order out of the chaos.

[29] Ibid.

[30] The painting was likened to a "pleasant design for a necktie" by a Yale professor and to "a most enchanting printed silk" by a curator of the Victoria and Albert Museum; Ellen Landau, *Jackson Pollock* (London: Thames & Hudson, 1989), 179.

[31] See Hilton Kramer, "The Month in Review: Jackson Pollock", first published in *Arts* magazine (February 1957); Shapiros, 368–371.

of prayer".[32] The art historian Robert Rosenblum located the painting's boundlessness in the tradition of the Sublime, evoking as it did the overwhelming beauty of nature.[33] For Parker Tyler, Pollock's paint stream

> ... has the continuity of script but escapes the monotony of calligraphy. It is as though Pollock 'wrote' non-representational imagery... an alphabet of unknown symbols; a cuneiform or impregnable language of image, as well as beautiful and subtle patterns of pure form.[34]

*Cathedral*'s vertiginous gestural matrices bring to life the multiple layers of the psalmist's despair and the sweeping sense of the poem's lack of experiential boundaries.

If the textual surface of the psalm is neither "rough, unfinished, [nor] sloppy",[35] it is surely as adamantly open-ended as Pollock's painting. Willem Prinsloo notes that "... as persuasive texts, these psalms implement hyperbolic and exaggerated terminology and... cannot be interpreted literally",[36] enforcing the reasons for our abstract treatment of Ps. 13. It appears, like Kuspit's description of Pollock's "apocalyptic reality", to assume a "non-hierarchical if unstable unity of exterior and interior realities", a unity which is "essentially that of the profane and sacred."[37] Is the bringing together of the 'I' and 'thou' in oppositional tension not unlike Pollock's visual protest, holding what is sacred accountable at a human level and voicing a complaint against the threats of others? The psalmist's fear that his enemies will triumph over him muddies the mystical mural. He looks up the heights of the vertical canvas and calls to the one entity that can put a stop to his torment, but he remains entangled in a menacing reality of unrighteous foes, be they Philistine, Greek or just plain sinister.[38] And he slings his paint to protest this.

Whether Ps. 13 was first recited as a complaint against death, sickness, or a trauma of a more social nature, it functioned and continues to function within an established liturgical system that allows the sufferer to

---

[32] Harold Rosenberg, "The Mythic Act", first published in Harold Rosenberg, *Artworks and Packages* (Chicago: University of Chicago Press, 1969); Shapiro, 375–381.

[33] Robert Rosenblum, "The Abstract Sublime", *Art News* 59 (February 1961) 38–41, 56–57.

[34] Tyler, "Labyrinth", in Shapiros, 365.

[35] "Introduction", Shapiros, 1.

[36] Willem Prinsloo, "The Psalms", in *Eerdmans Commentary on the Bible*, ed. James Dunn and John Rogerson (Cambridge: Eerdmans, 2003), 370.

[37] Kuspit, "Social Contract", in Shapiros, 193.

[38] This 'private' lament has been dated both to the early monarchy and the post-exilic period.

'pour out' his/her soul to the Lord (cf. 42.4). And just as Pollock's work has lost its shock value by being sanctioned by the art establishment and by becoming popular, so have laments in general drifted somewhat into banality. Stripped of concrete personal details and made suitable for general use, Ps. 13 becomes an echo chamber for endless people's emotions and ideas. Hanging it as a drip painting attempts to revive the potency it has lost at the hands of critics who have typified its painterly features as literary 'components' and of faith guides that have diluted its innate defiance into spiritual watercolour.

*The Style*

In the preface to his *Manual of the Book of Psalms*, Luther praises the "expressive manner" of the "the Psalms of temptations, or of complaints".[39] Delitzsch later summarised Ps. 13 as a hymn that "advances in waves . . . until at last it is only agitated with joy, and becomes calm as the sea when smooth as a mirror."[40] More recent scholarship reads it more plainly, finding no notable thematic complexities or unusual vocabulary in its predictable threefold structure. But when Westermann notes how "the details of suffering are not given", and Craigie adds, "we never learn what was disturbing the supplicant",[41] we realise that without 'realist' images the imagination must abstract what the psalmist's eye has seen. In v. 1 he mentions the face of the LORD but does not describe the lines and contours of it. He speaks of his soul's suffering (v. 2) rather than of wounds or specific historical enemies. He asks that light be given to his eyes (v. 3), a more poetic version of the usual opening of eyes used elsewhere in the Bible. And though he sings to the LORD in the final verse, the parallel that precedes this is his metaphorical rejoicing heart (v. 5).

Beyond the shift from complaint to praise, movement occurs along any number of non-linear avenues. Future hope does not negate the on-going adversity. The total experience of the psalm mixes tenses and sensations. By offering no review of past events and no simple progress from past to present, time is fluid. Suspended "between past experience and future

---

[39] Martin Luther, *Manual of the Book of Psalms* (first published c. 1512–19); trans. Henry Cole (London: Seely and Burnside, 1837), 9.

[40] F. Delitzsch, *Biblical Commentary on the Psalms* I (Edinburgh: T&T Clark, 1880), 252; cf. Peter C. Craigie, *Psalms 1–150* (Dallas: Word Books, 1983), 141.

[41] Claus Westermann, *The Living Psalms* (*Ausgewählte Psalmen* first published in Göttingen, 1984); trans. J. R. Porter (Edinburgh: T&T Clark, 1989), 72; cf. Craigie, *Psalms*, 58.

hope",[42] we experience a less determinate reality than a strict reversal of the speaker's situation. As Berlin explains, parallelisms that oppose God against the speaker, and the sufferer against those who mock him, "provide ambiguity or disambiguation [and] serve a metaphoric function":

> Parallelism does not have meaning; but it structures the meaning of the signs of which it is composed...The result is that the elements in the text, which of necessity occur in a linear sequence (contiguity), are then perceived as equivalent or contrasted (similarity).[43]

In Ps. 13 equivalences and contrasts energise the surface like Pollock's rushes of paint.

In both works, a swiftness of style invites an imaginative encounter. Much in the vein of Erich Auerbach's reflections on Genesis 22 in ' "Odysseus' Scar" (1953), Italo Calvino wrote on literary brevity in his lecture on "Quickness", penned just weeks before he died in 1985. Calvino preferred the laconic quality and repetitions found in folklore to the more detailed legends recounted by Renaissance writers, for in "the bare résumé ... everything is left to the imagination and the speed with which events follow one another conveys a feeling of the ineluctable."[44] He cited the diary of the poet Giacomo Leopardi (1798–1837) to illustrate this point:

> Speed and consciousness of style please us because they present the mind with a rush of ideas that are simultaneous, or that follow each other so quickly they seem simultaneous, and set the mind afloat on such an abundance of thoughts or images or spiritual feelings that either it cannot embrace them all, each one fully, or it has no time to be idle and empty of feelings.[45]

Cathedral's gymnastic swiftness is felt in the psalm's parallelisms and textual brevity. Calvino's observation about the 'secret' to this style's success reads like a visualization of Hebrew poetry's structure: "the events, however long they last, become puncti-form, connected by rectilinear segments, in a zigzag pattern that suggests incessant motion."[46]

---

[42] Craigie, *Psalms*, 143.

[43] Berlin, *Biblical Parallelism*, 138.

[44] Italo Calvino, "Quickness", in *Six Memos for a New Millennium*, The Charles Eliot Norton Lectures, trans. Patrick Creagh (first published by Harvard University Press, 1988; New York: Vintage Books, 1993), 33. Calvino's preference resembles that of Auerbach's own for the style of Genesis 22 over Homer's description of Odysseus' return, in Erich Auerbach, "Odysseus' Scar", in *Mimesis: The Representation of Reality in Western Culture* (first published in Berlin by A. Franke, 1946); trans. Willard R. Trask (Princeton: Princeton University Press, 1953).

[45] "Casual Thoughts" in his diary of 1821; cf. Calvino, "Quickness", 42.

[46] Calvino, "Quickness", 35.

See again the sweeping repetitions:

- "How long?"—"How long?"—"How long?"—"How long?" (vv. 1–4)
- "thou"—"thou" vs. "me"—"me" (v. 1)
- "thy face" (v. 1)—"my soul" (v. 2)
- "my soul", "my heart" (v. 2)—"my enemy" (v. 3)—"my eyes" (v. 3)—"my enemies" and "my foes" (v. 4)—and "thy steadfast love" (v. 5)

The subject 'I' winds in and out of the central verses, bearing pain (v. 2), possibly dying (v. 3), being shaken (v. 4), finally trusting (v. 5) and bursting into song (v. 6). At the middle of this stream of 'I's, the voice of the subject shifts to that of the enemy, who threatens to prevail over the speaker (v. 4). The intertwined 'I' and flood of personal pronouns create a fusion of patterns and feelings that multiply in a self-driven, action-packed painting.

The "physicality of [Pollock's] process" revolutionised the gesture as "a kind of social force" that disrupts the existing order and "debunks the harmonious surface".[47] Commentary that finds Ps. 13 to be 'typical' diminishes its disruptive nature. In a few swift verses, the lament rages and simultaneously insists on the possibility of salvation from sorrow. Like Job, the psalmist demands that his Redeemer lives; his tone presents a challenge rather than a passive pause for contemplation.

Through personally dripped tracery, Pollock's *Cathedral* achieves the sensation of a temple or church, an ethereal field to which the self can surrender itself. The creation of both the painting and the psalm constitute events in which the painter/psalmist pours himself into a performance. Bucking the trend of scholars to read the psalms as private wisdom texts, Susan Niditch studies the oral and performed origins of biblical literature.[48] Other commentaries inquire after the psalms' liturgical notations and suggest a cast of cultic speakers, but little attention is ever given to the nature of the immediate environment in which they were recited. If we are to revive a sense of the psalms as performative texts, it seems important to remember the sensory impact the temple would have had on the people chanting them. Pollock's painting, likened by Huxley to wallpaper, surrounds the performed lament with an enchanted space. Together they create a 'total artwork' (*Gesamtkunstwerk*).[49] So do not the psalms'

---

[47] Kuspit, "Social Contract", in Shapiros, 189.

[48] Susan Niditch, *Oral and Written Word: Ancient Israelite Literature* (London: SPCK, 1996), 117–120.

[49] Richard Wagner coined this term in the essay "The Artwork of the Future" ("Das Kunstwerk der Zukunft" first published in Zurich in 1849) to speak of how several art forms can cohere into a harmonious whole, as in Greek tragedy, grand opera and architecture.

artfully interlaced subjects and themes bear an aesthetic affinity with the
decorated environment in which they were once expressed? The criticism
that downgrades Pollock's work for looking like a pattern begs the question of why something ornamentally appealing should be less legitimate
than other art.[50] The Hebrew Bible yields a different attitude to ornament,
as the elaborate instructions for the building of both the tabernacle and
the temple illustrate. Adornment and pattern were considered vital elements in the Lord's palace.

The descriptions of the tabernacle and temple found in Exodus, Kings,
Ezekiel and Chronicles never articulate the reasons for God's choice in
décor but assume YHWH requires spectacular accommodations; the
house had to convey His holy presence. The architects of the first temple
in Jerusalem worked in the leading Phoenician style of the day, which
was similar to the emerging classical taste of their neighbours to the west.
Windows had "recessed frames" (1 Kgs. 6.4), "side chambers all around"
(v. 5) formed a protective buffer to the inner sanctuaries, and ascending staircases (v. 8) would have added processional grandeur. Every inch
of wall was panelled in cedar (one can imagine the heavenly scent) and
"carved in the form of gourds and open flowers" (vv. 15–18). The floors
were laid in cypress. Different from the common cathedral, "not a stone
was seen" (v. 18). Solomon then gilded the whole inner sanctuary and the
altar to match. Cherubim, palm trees and more open flowers were carved
on other parts of the walls. Columns punctuating the outer walls guided
the eye in the direction of the entrance to the inner sanctuary and caused
the space to appear to expand. Repeated details, such as the 'lily-work' (lit.
'open flowers': פטורי צצים) in the vestibule's capitals, heightened sensation to infinity.

The biblical historian might only have intended to record such details in
order to preserve precisely how the first temple looked, or to contrast the
excesses Solomon committed when building his private palace. Yet these
details of design prove that visual sensation was regarded as critical to
temple worship. Hanging Pollock's *Cathedral* alongside Ps. 13 restores the
lament's dramatic style, as well as the essence of an environment in which

---

[50] Decorative art theory of recent centuries rarely if ever gives ornament legitimate
consideration for its potential to convey God's presence or to facilitate a divine encounter.
Yet many entries in Isabelle Frank's anthology of the subject evidence ornamental design's
inspirational qualities in language that all but utters the divine name. See Isabelle Frank,
*The Theory of Decorative Art: An Anthology of European and American Writings, 1750–1940*
(New Haven and London: Yale University Press, 2000).

God and the individual can and could communicate. The psalm advances in emotionally chaotic but painstakingly structured waves. Action painting and lamenting protest, it fills the space with its objections to personal tragedy, alienation from God, and the presence of others.

## The Self

As an individual's complaint, the psalm asserts that s/he has a right to be heard. Written in the first-person, the psalm situates the reader as the central subject, so that the identities of the original speaker and the reader become momentarily fused. Equally, *Cathedral* is an average human height (5'9") and allows the viewer to identify with Pollock's personal experience as a painter. These are self-important works.

While a number of critics have attempted to situate Pollock's work apart from subjectivity, the artist himself admitted the personal and emotional nature of his practice. He gave credence to Greenberg's notion that art is the embodiment of the painter's self[51] in his widely referenced artist's statement of 1947, "My Painting". Describing how he painted with the canvas stretched on the floor to have greater contact with it, he explained the ritual of walking around the work as a process of immersion:

> When I am *in* my painting, I'm not aware of what I'm doing … I have no fear about making changes, destroying the image, etc., because the painting has a life of its own. … It is only when I lose contact with the painting that the result is a mess. Otherwise there is pure harmony, an easy give and take, and the painting comes out well.[52]

In a later interview he said that he and his contemporaries no longer had to "go to a subject matter outside themselves. Most modern painters work from a different source. They work from within."[53]

Working from within, Pollock revealed the mechanics of his subconscious and his modern self. A brooding alcoholic, he was suspicious of

---

[51] It was Greenberg who insisted that painters "must *find* themselves"; cf. Kozloff, "Critical Reception", in Shapiros, 141.

[52] Jackson Pollock, "My Painting", first published in *Possibilities I* (Winter 1947–1948); cf. Shapiros, 357. Note how Pollock's conception of harmony involves a chaotic and disruptive surface. Here and in other statements he even qualifies the shamanistic aspects of his action-painting.

[53] Jackson Pollock in "An Interview with Jackson Pollock", by William Wright; first published in *Jackson Pollock*, ed. Francis V. O'Connor, (New York: MoMA, 1967); cf. Shapiros, 359.

new faces, and the anguish of his addiction manifests itself in his poured paintings, as if the drops of colour are a record of his tears. If his alcoholism provided the means to wash away an inner loathing, he nevertheless let his friends know that he thought he was the best painter of his time. With a stocky physique and the posture of a cowboy,[54] he partook in brawls but spoke little. De Kooning once remembered how Pollock "would size people up and look at them as if to say 'Fuck off'."[55] As a student under Thomas Hart Benton when he first arrived in New York in 1930, Pollock absorbed his master's appreciation for the sentimental regionalism of American Scene painting. But he eventually abandoned the Depression painter's mission to distinguish a defiant American tradition from European modernisms, and instead he turned inward. Pollock had resisted authority from a young age, attending Communist meetings, opposing totalitarianism and the expectations of others, and retreating into his own subconscious world. Though his style and legacy would succumb to commodification, he was at all costs his 'own man'. *Cathedral* demonstrates his rampant individualism and imparts a fully modern self onto the psalmist's subjective position.

The Victorian essayist Walter Pater located the birth of the modern self in the Renaissance. His collection of lectures on selected artists and philosophers orients their achievements around a common cause—the advancement of the "modern spirit". Having developed an early preoccupation with the "elusive inscrutable mistakeable self",[56] Pater once explained the historical basis for regarding inward response as a legitimate form of perception: "Modern thought is distinguished from ancient by its cultivation of the 'relative' spirit in place of an 'absolute'... To the modern spirit nothing is, or can be rightly known, except relatively and under conditions".[57] Personal impressions formed by the intellect and the imagination were primary to this essentially anthropocentric sensibility. Pater's humanist view, while tinted with equal doses of self-doubt and insouciance, criticised religious orthodoxy as well as the prejudices of scientific thought and other systematic methods of analysis. In *The*

---

[54] Pollock in fact spent most of his younger life near and in Los Angeles but having been born in Cody, Wyoming, fashioned himself as a Buffalo Bill.

[55] James T. Valliere, "De Kooning on Pollock: An Interview", first published in the *Partisan Review* (1967); cf. Shapiros, 373.

[56] Adam Phillips in his introduction to Walter Pater, *The Renaissance* (first published as *Studies in the History of the Renaissance* in 1873); ed. Adam Phillips (Oxford: Oxford University Press, 1986), viii; original reference not cited.

[57] Walter Pater, "Coleridge", *Westminster Review*, N.S. XXIX (January 1866), 260.

*Renaissance* (1873) he rejected traditional structures of historiography and attempted instead to capture the 'spirit' of the age via an entirely subjective treatment of his subjects. The introduction to the 1986 Oxford Classics edition summarises:

> [while Ruskin had stressed] the meticulous education of the eye was the way to a kind of moral authenticity...Pater would elaborate on the artist's internal world of moods and ideas; and by doing so would make vagueness, informed vagueness, intellectually respectable.[58]

In almost every essay, Pater styles the artist or thinker as a subversive Christian whose dalliance with paganism and classical culture informed a faith in the pure hedonistic pleasure of creative vision.

Pater defines Botticelli, for instance, as the type of genius who "usurps the data before [him] as the exponent of [his own] ideas, moods, visions...in this interest [he] plays fast and loose with those data, rejecting some and isolating others, and always combining them anew."[59] Is this not what one can do with an individual lament—take the verses, images and thoughts, project personal experiences onto them, fixate on the familiar, and downplay the not so relevant? The lament's value lies in how it relates to us as individuals. Is Pater's conception of the modern self not implicit in Ps. 13?

In another essay in the collection, Pater fashions Michelangelo as a Platonist, staging him not as a formal believer in immortality but as one concerned with "the consciousness of ignorance—ignorance of man, ignorance of the nature of the mind, its origin and capacities."[60] The speaker in our lament may *hope* for salvation (or, for Catholic critics, immortality), but the number of times he asks "How long?" throws up a veil of unmistakeable vagueness. He is conscious of his ignorance, and his prayer revolts against this fact of life and demands a fairer deal in the universe for his "elusive inscrutable mistakeable self".

The modern and/or ancient reader's use of the psalm validates the individual's experience, chanting the "Me! Me! Me!"[61] heard in Pollock and the Abstract Expressionists. Though one must distinguish between the psalmist's sense of himself and the historically specific "true image of

---

[58] Phillips, introduction to *The Renaissance*, xv.
[59] Pater, *Renaissance*, 35.
[60] Pater, *Renaissance*, 61.
[61] Shapiros, 2.

his identity" towards which the modern artist ventured,[62] the forwarding of his needs to the deity is no less extreme in its assertion of selfhood. The psalm is, as Alfred Barr once wrote of the new American painters, "as uncompromising as ... the religion of Kierkegaard".[63] And where Pollock painted in order to scourge private demons, so does the psalm bring rebellious impulses to the surface to bring justice to his situation. The speaker is dependent upon God but voices his autonomy and visualises a time when he will no longer be the laughing stock of his neighbours. The very existence of laments contends that struggle continues in every generation and that personal dissatisfaction deserves relief. Shifting between Pollock's *Cathedral* and the lament, the splattered self hovers vaguely between author, text, community, history and the unknown.

## The Nations

Conflict with others sends a dramatic streak of paint through Ps. 13 as an abstract cathedral. Pollock's misanthropic splashes translate the psalmist's musings against his adversaries into a pictorial attempt to blot them out. His fate depends on God staving off any real or imagined humiliation and, presumably (as in other laments), bringing him to a place where he may rejoice from the high ground over their eventual fallen state. The parallelisms between the speaker's enemies in verses 4 and 5 ('my enemies': אֹיְבִי; and 'my foes': רִיץ) are overlaid with a heart that rejoices (יָגֵל) in the LORD's salvation.

In *The Identity of the Individual in the Psalms* (1987), Steven Croft outlines criticism on the antagonists in the laments and supports S. N. Rosenbaum's conclusion that "the terms wicked [רשעים] and enemy [איבים] are not synonymous in the Psalms but refer to two different groups ... Israelites who have gone astray and foreign enemies respectively."[64] Croft finds that the wicked are generally not a direct threat to the individual, whereas

---

[62] Rosenberg said the Expressionists were "partaking of the last draughts of an extreme strain of Romanticism"; cf. Shapiros, 2.

[63] Barr, "Introduction", in Shapiros, 96. Barr's reference to Kierkegaard exemplifies how many art historians and artists have lapsed into religious language in order to communicate the power of their subjects. This undermines the greater trend to separate modern art from religion.

[64] Stephen J. L. Croft, *The Identity of the Individual in the Psalms* (Sheffield: Sheffield Academic Press, 1987), 18.

the enemy always is. The lament in Ps. 13 is against the foreign enemy, and this colours the event with a tint of nationalism.

While Craigie dates the psalm to the onset of the Hebrew monarchy,[65] Croft and others locate it in a late post-exilic context, situating the psalm under the threat of Hellenism. Whatever the original and subsequent contexts in which it was read, the mention of foreigners binds personal salvation up with the need for triumph or dignity in the face of the nation's foes. Westermann writes of how the mention of them is a reminder that "living with God cannot be separated from living with others".[66] But he also points out that the confession of sin is as uncommon for the individual as an explicit description of the adversary.

As an American painter, Pollock took advantage of his freedom to make a contrary statement. Having distributed subversive broadsides as a student at Manual Arts High School in Los Angeles and then dodged the draft on the spurious grounds of mental unfitness, he fell momentarily under the spell of Benton and his "evangelical devotion to the idea of an all-American aesthetic".[67] In one of many moments in which Lee Krasner proved herself to be Pollock's personal saviour, his long-suffering lover helped lead him out of Benton's shadow by introducing him to the expatriate abstractionist Hans Hofmann. So instead of the presumed pretensions of European art, Pollock was able to battle a more philosophical enemy.

Max Kozloff records that the villain in both Greenberg and Rosenberg's eyes was not a foreign country but "a Philistine, implacably middle-of-the-road society, without any historical and cultural consciousness."[68] The utilisation of the Philistine as a pejorative harks back to Matthew Arnold and begs the question of who gets to determine who is uncouth and in need of enlightenment, but it is convenient for highlighting an inherent opposition. The expression of "what is *emotionally real*" to the painters,

---

[65] Craigie, *Psalms*, 141.

[66] Westermann, *Living Psalms*, 70.

[67] Ratcliff, *Fate of a* Gesture, 22. Lawrence Alloway has written on how the renunciation of nineteenth-century Europe involves a typology of contrasts—between dedication (America) and exhaustion (Europe), vitality and elegance, honesty and learning; in Lawrence Alloway, "Residual Sign Systems in Abstract Expressionism", first published in *Artforum* (Nov. 1973); cf. Shapiros, 157–168. Alloway adds that the literary critic Benjamin T. Spencer has pointed out, when writing about America, "Emerson resorted to metaphors which implied primal energies rather than mature ideologies"—metaphors such as "a colossal youth" and "a brood of titans", 158; cf. Benjamin T. Spencer, *The Quest for National Identity* (Syracuse: Syracuse University Press, 1957).

[68] Kozloff, "Critical Reception", in Shapiros, 141.

Rosenberg found, provided "the standpoint for a private revolt against the materialist tradition that surround[ed] them."[69] So although a London critic would remark in 1959:

> Abstract Expressionism radiated the world over from Manhattan Island, more specifically from West Fifty-Third Street, where the Museum of Modern Art [stood] as the Parthenon on this particular acropolis[70]

it would be wrong to say that Pollock's abstraction was developed in defence of the American imperialist enterprise. Nevertheless Kuspit directs our attention to the implications of Pollock's "gestural tongues" by arguing that he was speaking as much within a social contract as he was within a personal milieu. With Gottlieb and Rothko opting for a "timeless and tragic art" in order to defy an American society they found "all too concerned with things temporal and banal", Pollock was likewise "desperate ... to escape from American ordinariness, its lure of banality".[71]

Though the manic energy Pollock invested in his abstract *Cathedral* does not target an embodied opponent through figural representation, it protests against an unquestioned life, unleashes a loathing for ordinariness, and at the same time expresses an innate pride in being a free American man. As an exercise in which the speaker rouses himself from the drudgery of others and the otherness of God, the psalm is a place where one can resent one's enemies without regret. Like *Cathedral*, it alludes to experiences beyond the picture plane (beyond borders) and projects its grief onto others.

Pollock's opposition to ordinariness and authority mirrors the situation of the first-person psalmist especially if, as Smend did in 1888, we fashion him as the personification of Israel against the 'philistine' nations.[72] Perhaps such a move is unnecessary given the abundance of communal laments, but as a national representative he politicises the expressive fight against the intrusiveness of other nations. The conclusion of the psalm ("I will sing ... because he has dealt bountifully with me" [v. 6]) thus sends a thin stream of shocking colour (the orange or red in *Cathedral*), from the

---

[69] Harold Rosenberg, 'Introduction to Six American Artists', in *Possibilities* 1 (Winter 1947–48); cf. Kozloff, "Critical Reception", in Shapiros, 141.

[70] Fuller cites a 1959 article in London's *Times Literary Supplement* but does not list the exact date; cf. Fuller, "American Painting", in Shapiros, 179. Note again the religious image of a temple used to express art's significance.

[71] Kuspit, "Social Contract", 191.

[72] See R. Smend, "Über das Ich der Psalmen", in *Zeitschrift für die Alttestamentliche Wissenschaft* 8 (1888), 49–147.

depths of the heavier layers, and puts the power back into God's hands. It is this layer that reminds the sufferer he can fling his anger around all he wants, but it is God who gives order to the chaos.

## The End?

The stream of hope at the close of the psalm eases the pain(t) of the opening verses and allows us temporarily to forget the immediate source of strife. But the question of "How long" the situation will last begs as much attention in today's busy world as it did in temple times. Westermann determines how the repetition of this phrase indicates "time itself [as] a destructive force, wearing down a man's ability to hold out and intensifying the suffering to an inhuman level."[73] Elsewhere he mourns the acceleration of time that occurs at the expense of personal and cultural memory:

> We live in an age whose most distinctive and perhaps most important characteristic is *speed.* The tempo of today's traffic is only one example of the speed with which events of a technical, intellectual, or political nature develop—attracting us and carrying us along as individuals as well as groups. The pace of these developments corresponds proportionately to the *forgetting* that occurs... Because people are limited in their ability to perceive and digest sensory impressions, the only way they can deal with today's constant stream of stimuli is by forgetting most of what they experience.[74]

The cynic might ridicule the apparent nostalgia for the slower pace of decades and centuries past, but Westermann's concern with pace and the process of remembrance is relevant to how we hang the abstract psalm. Time grinds away at the sufferer's endurance, but the six short verses hasten the moment of agony without speeding it along. As contemplative pieces, *Cathedral* and Ps. 13 relive and relieve sorrows and counter the threat of forgetting. The painting and the psalm have the 'quick' qualities Calvino celebrated in folklore, and they encourage repetition, demanding time and memory to counter the forgetting of pain.

At the heart of this abstraction, the "sleep of death" in v. 3 strikes a moribund chord. Craigie treats אישן המות (lit. "I will sleep the death") as a metaphor, but Dahood entrusts that the phrase refers directly to

[73] Westermann, *Living Psalms*, 71.
[74] Claus Westermann, *The Psalms* (*Der Psalter* first published in 1967); trans. Ralph D. Gehrke (Minneapolis: Augsburg, 1980), 6–7.

mortality.[75] Our expression of it capitalises Death to suggest more existential meanings: the loss felt by God's absence and a preoccupation with
an endless sleep. In the psalm's closing verse, the speaker is situated in a
place in which he is "infinitesimally small",[76] for it is God who has the ultimate power to grant all blessings and desires and God who "remembers
that we are dust" (Ps. 103:14).

As much as Pollock's gesture came 'from within', he did have occasion
to envision it as an important moment in the flow of history. In his personal statement for his 1947 application to the John Simon Guggenheim
Foundation, he remarked on the liminal state of his work:

> I intend to paint large movable pictures which will function between the
> easel and mural... I believe the easel picture to be a dying form, and the
> tendency of modern feeling is toward the wall picture or mural... The pic-
> tures I contemplate would constitute a halfway state, and an attempt to
> point out the direction of the future without arriving there completely.[77]

Traditionally mounted and painted on the walls of civic lobbies, chapels
and cathedrals, the mural originates in a public context. Pollock's transition toward it reflects his desire to release painting from the confinement
of the gallery and make it an active force in the world at large. Positioned
at the halfway state between private and public consumption, the short
lament equally exists in a mode of increasing de-privatization. It hangs
before us as a small picture of personal pain and as a moving mural to
be beheld by all. Up on the wall, the psalm's tendrils overlap one another
and meander along endless emotional arcs, like arabesques or lily-work
on an endless decorative panel. Relief from grief comes from following
the intertwining sentiments of despair, resentment and hope. Complaint
is given a beautifully patterned and energetic plexus that expands into
Pollock's dream of limitless space.

Krasner knew that 'misery was capitalism's leading product',[78] and Pollock's *Cathedral* attempts to break beyond the wretchedness of modern
life. His "apocalypse", as Kuspit has called it, ushers in a bountiful display
of colour, form, light, sensation and emotion, and it inclines the viewer

---

[75] Craigie, Psalms, 142; Mitchell Dahood, *Psalms I, 1–50*, Anchor Bible Vol. 16 (Garden
City, NY: Doubleday and Company, 1965), 76.

[76] Westermann *The Psalms*, 9.

[77] As cited in O'Connor, *Pollock*, 39–40; cf. Henry Geldzahler, *New York Painting and
Sculpture: 1940–1970* (London and New York: Pall Mall Press and the Metropolitan Museum,
1969), 22.

[78] The hunger of the Depression was proof of this. Ratcliff, *Pollock*, 29.

away from the material world. Pollock's "gyrating labyrinths" plunge us into "divine fury" and to a place beyond "superhuman turbulence".[79] The trajectory of hope in God's bountiful mercy gestures toward a boundless Sublime. If Pollock's painting gives us "a pictorial equivalent to the American infinite", drawing us into a world of "primal energies",[80] so does the psalm open the door to a chaotic vitality. The silence within the fray, the sound of God's absence, is met by something more challenging than passive plaintiveness.

In the end we have disrupted the critical and pastoral-theological complacency that has treated Ps. 13 as smooth, simple and typical. Stepping back from the image, one observes a concatenation of parallelisms, an energetic but ordered piece of protest in miniature. A literal approach confines interpretation to the four sides of the six verses on the page, but the abstract vision lets the text spill off the page, intersecting with our modern ways of seeing. If *avant-garde* painting since the time of Manet's *Olympia* (1863) and Picasso's *Les Demoiselles d'Avignon* (1907) has been staring back at us and intruding upon our space, then so does the lament capture the reader in its gaze. In the man-made cathedral, the lament asks us to engage with its tortuous interconnection of weariness and anticipation. The abstract reckoning of the psalm's decorative weight integrates art theory with a biblical subject to pour aesthetic meanings over more literal readings. To fail to see beyond the literal—is this not something like the sleep of death?

---

[79] Rosenblum is speaking of *Number 1* (1948), but the description fits the similarly splattered *Cathedral*; Rosenblum, "Abstract Sublime", in Shapiros, 357.

[80] Ratcliff, *Pollock*, 3.

# THE BUIK O JONAH MACAMITY:
## A CONTRIBUTION TO A BIBLE THAT MAY NOT BE ONE

### Hugh Pyper

As my contribution to this volume, I offer a translation of the book of Jonah into Scots.[1] As far as I can ascertain, this is the first Scots translation of this biblical book from the Hebrew ever published. That immediately suggests a few pointed questions. If the world has survived this long without a Scots Jonah, how much need can there be for it? Who would read such a thing and why?

As a partial response to these questions, let me reveal my primary motivation for undertaking this work. It was pedagogical. Teaching the book of Jonah in Hebrew to a variety of students in England over many years, I have found myself at various points saying to them, "It's a pity that you don't read Scots, as there is something going on in the Hebrew here that I can't explain quite so well in Standard English." I have also found that groups who are studying the Bible in English often lack the sense of the strangeness of these texts and have little notion of the ambiguities inherent in the process of translation. Being exposed to a Scots version of the text allows them to experience something sufficiently different to raise issues of translation but without the impenetrable barriers of the Hebrew alphabet and its unknown vocabulary and grammar.

Having said that, there are other motives. One is my enjoyment of Scots and a desire to stretch the sinews of my own knowledge of the language in the process of translating this text into it. Secondly, there is nothing like the exercise of translation to hone one's understanding of the Hebrew and indeed to find the points where translation comes up against the intransigence of the original text and its language. Thirdly, the peculiar status

---

[1] As will be seen below, this is particularly appropriate as a good proportion of those who have been involved in the translation of biblical material in the Scots learned their trade studying the Bible and biblical languages at the University of Glasgow; I count myself fortunate in having followed in their footsteps.

of Scots as a language prompts thoughts as to the nature of the language
we label as 'Biblical Hebrew'. Is Biblical Hebrew a language and, if not,
what is it?

All that being said, a devil's advocate could surely argue that this exercise is a prime example of a waste of time and energy. The usual justification for a new biblical translation, that a population of potential readers
exists who have no access to the Bible in their native tongue, does not
apply in this case. After all, all readers of Scots can read standard English and have available to them the plethora of biblical translations, paraphrases and commentaries that now exist in that language. Any Scots
translation of a biblical book enters this already crowded field of biblical
translations and cannot avoid becoming caught up in the continuing controversy over the nature and status of the Scots language. Is it a language,
a dialect, or a series of dialects? Is it a debased form of English or one
of a large number of 'Englishes' that coexist with the standard written
form, or has it some claim to stand beside, rather than as a subordinate
to, Standard English? The politics of such arguments are still active today,
but may mean that the discussion is carried on by sloganeering rather
than by deeper analysis.

### Tetraglossia, Scotland and the Bible

In trying to articulate my own position on this matter, I have found that
the model of the way that languages work in communities proposed by
Henri Gobard is of help. He builds on the work of Fergusson and Gom-
partz on 'diglossia', the use of two distinct languages or codes in a community, to develop a model of 'tetraglossia'. This distinguishes between
four levels of code, which may or may not represent different languages,
available to any linguistic community:

1. a *vernacular* language, which is the common spoken language of the
   community "less appropriate for communicating than communing",
   which is also considered the mother tongue. It is the language of the
   home, and of the here and now;
2. a *vehicular* language, learned and used regionally, usually the language
   of routine commercial and official writing;
3. a *referential* language, tied to oral and written traditions and which
   refers systematically to classic works of the past;

4. A *mythical* language, which "functions as a ultimate recourse" and "whose incomprehensibility is considered to be irrefutable proof of the sacred".[2]

Gobard's classification was taken up by Deleuze and Guattari in their study of Kafka.[3] They made the characteristic point that particular languages can change position and perform multiple functions within Gobard's scheme, something he had already remarked upon. Where they go further is in asserting that what we have to deal with is, in their words, 'a blur of languages and not at all a system of languages.'[4] What Gobard describes are the poles that map a constant play of tensions as different languages vie for the different positions in a society. Indeed, part of that tension may be which speech communities have their vernacular idiom formally labelled as a 'language.' These tensions drive and are driven by the shifting political and cultural shape of any given society.

In the context of Scotland and the Scots language it is easy to trace this struggle. Put crudely, Scots, or the different varieties of Scots, now exist as vernacular languages in a society where the vehicular and referential languages are Standard English. This means that any access to civic space and to the cultural traditions of the society entails learning and using Standard English. In turn this gives rise to a constant encroachment by Standard English on the realm of the vernacular. Those who wish to defend Scots see it being eroded in the everyday speech of the country. This sense that the vehicular use of English is a threat is something that is shared by many language communities. Indeed, Gobard's work is aimed at elucidating and countering the encroachment of English on the status of French. In Scotland itself the Gaelic-speaking community is subject to similar pressures, exacerbated, of course by the ubiquity and status of English. There is a particular problem for Scots, however, in that it is so close to English linguistically.

In this context, the advocates of Scots in varying ways seek to defend the vernacular language by encouraging its adoption as a vehicular or referential language. The use of Scots in some official documents of the

---

[2] Henri Gobard, *L'Aliénation linguistique: analyse tétraglossique* (Paris: Flammarion, 1976) 37.

[3] Gilles Deleuze and Félix Guattari *Kafka: Toward a Minor Literature*, trans. D. Polan (Minneapolis: University of Minnesota Press, 1986).

[4] Deleuze and Guattari, *Kafka*, 24.

Scottish parliament is an example of the first and the encouragement of
the reading of Scots literature in schools is an example of the second.
Here the appeal to the language of the past represented in such cultural
icons as Burns, Dunbar and the anonymous poets of the Border ballads is
a viable strategy. Where Scots does differ from many other dialects is that
it does have a literature; it was the vehicular and to some extent referential language for a distinct political entity, the court of the Scottish kings.
This means that it has a flexible but recognisable standard literary form
and it has also generated a vibrant lexicographical tradition.

However, for almost all Scots, the specifically Scots references to which
they have access are a subset of their access to the vast referential capacity
of Standard English. Here the lack of a Scots equivalent to the Authorized
Version of the Bible makes itself felt. The Bible is an ineluctable source
of reference in English literature and it is the English of the Authorized
Version that is the referential language in this regard.

One could also argue that there has been drive to enlist Scots as a
mythical language. This is an intriguing category in Gobard's work, especially in his use of incomprehensibility as the index of the sacred. Again,
the situation in contemporary Scottish society is a complex one. Mythical
languages may differ for different communities. Latin and Greek retain
something of their mythical status, as does Hebrew. For speakers of Scots,
however, Gaelic also has the mythical status of a timeless yet incomprehensible language that is somehow the repository of the ancient wisdom
of the culture. For many Scots, moreover, there is an element of incomprehensibility in Scots itself, something that a poet and language reformer
like Hugh MacDiarmid, of whom more later, seeks to heighten by reviv-
ing obsolete and obscure vocabulary and phrases. His 'synthetic Scots', so
called, aspires to the condition of a mythical language. It is not designed
to communicate clearly but to evoke a reverence for the language and its
cultural heritage.

Yet even without MacDiarmid, we have hit upon a dimension that is
not taken into account in Gobard's schema: the way in which the vernacular language can take on the characteristics of the mythical. What is most
familiar can be most strange. Part of this is due to the very separation
between the vernacular and the vehicular. For most Scots, even those who
may live and speak in a distinct vernacular idiom, *reading* written Scots
poses difficulties because the language in which they are taught to read
and write is Standard English. What might seem more comprehensible if
spoken becomes something of a puzzle when read and takes on some of
the cryptic qualities of the mythical. Literary Scots can exacerbate this

disconnection. The ritual recitation of Burns' verse is not always a matter of clear communication but the evocation of something atavistic and inexpressible in Scots identity, although this may tend towards maudlin sentiment and nostalgia.

## Vernacular and Mythical in Biblical Translation

For our purposes, however, the intriguing point is that this seemingly paradoxical fusion of the vernacular and mythical is at the heart of the odd business of biblical translation. One of the paradoxes of the Christian tradition and its heritage of biblical translation, at least as it develops out of the Reformation, is that it has the ambition of articulating the sacred in the language of the people. Indeed, the incarnation itself could be described in linguistic terms as the claim that the mythical is to be seen in the vernacular; "the Word dwelt among us" after all. Rather than preserving the Bible in its mythical language, whether that is Hebrew, Greek or Latin, translators seek to bring the word of God into common speech.

The argument continues, however, as to which of the other linguistic levels, the vernacular or the vehicular, is the appropriate one for any translation, compounded by the fact that the very act of translating the Bible into any particular linguistic system has profound effects on its status. The ideology of the Reformation brings out these paradoxes quite starkly. If Erasmus or Tyndale aspire to a situation where the weaver or the ploughboy has access to the bible in a language they comprehend, does that mean that the bible should be available in every vernacular of the community? How many different translations would be needed to achieve that? In many communities, therefore, the development of the modern vehicular language was profoundly shaped by the translation and printing of the Bible. Whatever dialect of the language was chosen for this purpose almost inevitably becomes the vehicular language of the community, leaving the others to function as vernaculars without a Bible.

In Scotland, notoriously, the reformers opted not to produce a distinctively Scots Bible, for understandable reasons, be it said. Practically speaking, the labour involved and the lack of printers in Scotland ruled out this option, especially as there was an urgent demand for Bibles and a desire to disseminate them as widely as possible. The Geneva Bible was to hand and could be supplied much more easily. In addition, ideologically Knox and his fellow reformers had their eyes set on a Reformed Europe and certainly a Reformed Britain, rather than restricting themselves to

Scotland. For both these reasons, the sensible strategy was to stick to the translation in what was already becoming the vehicular language for the whole of Britain.

Through Knox's zeal for education, the Bible in English became a crucial part in the development of an educational system that was designed to give as many people as possible access to the vehicular and referential language of the society. At the same time, the Bible, even before its translation, is a crucial source of the cultural and linguistic traditions that form the stock of the community's referential language. Yet there is always a tendency for the sacredness of the text to mean that its language becomes imbued with some of the features of mythical language; hence the loyalty to established translations even, or especially, when their language has become sufficiently arcane to acquire a new sort of incomprehensibility. The Bible has, if not a unique, then a prominent role in the linguistic system as the text whose language spans all four of Gobard's strategies but which embodies the constant tension caused by the pressure towards the simultaneous identification and differentiation of the mythical and vernacular levels.

## Muir and MacDiarmid

The famous quarrel between Edwin Muir and Hugh MacDiarmid provoked by the former's book *Scott and Scotland* can be analyzed as a symptom of this tension. Muir's claim is that a Scottish literature of world stature can only now be written in English. Although these are not terms he uses, the essence of his argument appears to be that English is *de facto* the vehicular and referential language of Scotland, whatever the position may have been in the past. To pretend that a literature can be developed out of the diverse vernaculars of Scotland is unrealistic and condemns that literature to parochialism. Indeed, Muir goes further and argues that as the vernacular is the language of childhood and the vehicular that of education, reverting to the vernacular in literature means that its themes become restricted to the passions and feelings of childhood rather than the concerns of the adult world.

MacDiarmid's hope, however, is that Scots can regain its vehicular and referential status. To do this, though again these are not terms he ever uses, he makes an appeal to its mythical status and indeed, through the deliberate resort to dictionaries and reference works, creates a synthetic Scots where individual words are incomprehensible even to Scots readers without retracing his researches. It is not a matter of recovering or preserving the vernacular. A remark of MacDiarmid in an essay on Robert Fergusson bears witness to this; he refers to Fergusson's power of direct statement 'unadorned but passionate and penetrative as Hebrew eloquence.'[5] He goes on to praise the economy of Scots as 'unparalleled in any other European speech, perhaps, since classical Greek.' In such a sentence, it is clear that he is claiming that Scots shares features of the mythical languages of the classical and biblical literature.

In this endeavour, the Bible, as the embodiment of mythical language within European culture, is an inescapable resource. For all his Marxism, MacDiarmid constantly refers to biblical characters and themes and indeed much of his work bears a strong imprint of the volcanic style and vocabulary of biblical prophecy. Muir also constantly appeals to the Bible, but in a way that oddly assimilates it to the classical tradition through his use of myth and archetype. Translating the Bible into any vernacular has the potential to disrupt and rebalance the competing languages of the tetraglossia. In the case of Scots, the argument between Muir and MacDiarmid is precisely about whether such a disruption is possible or desirable.

### The Lorimer New Testament

It is in this climate that a sustained project of translating biblical material into Scots was undertaken when William Laughton Lorimer embarked on his *The New Testament in Scots*.[6] Both a classical scholar and a devoted lexicographer of Scots, Lorimer was uniquely qualified to undertake this task. The introduction to his translation by his son makes it clear that his motives were cultural rather than religious. Rather than seeking to bring the New Testament to a readership which had previously not had access to it, it was the Scots language that he was aiming to promote. He was convinced that any revival of Scots depended on the publication of two works: a good Scots dictionary and a Scottish New Testament. It was

---

[5] Hugh MacDiarmid, 'Robert Fergusson: Direct Poetry and Scottish Genius' in *Selected Essays of Hugh MacDiarmid*, ed. Duncan Glen (Berkeley: University of California, 1969) 129–149, 143.

[6] First published by Southside Publishers in Edinburgh in a limited edition funded by subscription in 1983, some 15 years after his death, Lorimer's translation was an unexpected bestseller and was republished with some minor corrections as a Penguin paperback in 1985 and as a Canongate Classic in 2001. A new revised edition with an introduction by James Robertson was published by Canongate in 2012.

precisely because the New Testament would already be familiar to readers and because nearly every Scottish household would own an English version as a crib that he finally decided to take on the task of supplying this Scots New Testament himself.[7]

Lorimer's project, in Gobard's terms, is to use the disruptive power of the Bible as translated text to aid and encourage the realignment of the system of tetraglossia within Scottish culture by demonstrating the capacity of Scots to act as a vehicular and referential language. Lorimer makes a virtue of the fact that his readership is one that uses English as its vehicular language and where the English Bible is a familiar referential text. He *expects* that his translation will be compared with others and indeed part of the purpose of his Scots translation is to encourage such comparison. Lorimer's aim was to encourage reflection on the richness and variety of Scots, by intriguing the reader by the vividness, unexpectedness and appropriateness of the translation and its success in evoking the original text. Any reading of Lorimer's version is 'shadowed' by the memory of more familiar English translations.

In his appreciative essay on the Lorimer New Testament, David Ogston sums up his experience as a reader as follows: "Reading this 'new' text we experience both recognition and discovery, and the awakening of that most precious faculty—curiosity."[8] This is particularly true for readers such as Ogston who have an intimate familiarity with the text in English, but traces of the same phenomenon hold true for most English-speaking

---

[7] Lorimer's is not the first version of the New Testament in Scots. At some point in the first decades of the sixteenth century, a Lollard disciple of John Wycliffe, Murdoch Nisbet, undertook to rewrite John Purvey's revision of Wycliffe's New Testament in a way that conformed to the spelling and pronunciation of his Scottish compatriots. Nisbet's manuscript was not published until 1903. It was too dangerous to publish in his own lifetime and very soon Nisbet's labour was made redundant by the publication of Tyndale's bible which was translated from Hebrew and Greek rather than the Latin Vulgate which was the basis of Wycliffe's translation.

In 1901, William Wye Smith's *The New Testament in Braid Scots* (Paisley, Alexander Gardner) was published. This was subsequently reprinted and revised, an index of its popularity, with a third definitive revision appearing in 1923, four years after Smith's death. Born in Jedburgh in 1827, Smith emigrated with his parents to the USA in 1830. The family then moved to Canada and it was there that Smith became a minister and spent the rest of his life. His work is addressed as much to the Scottish diaspora as to those in the homeland. Although it has many original turns of phrase, Smith's version is essentially based on the Revised Version of 1881 rather than claiming to be an original translation from the Greek.

[8] David Ogston, 'William Lorimer's *New Testament in Scots*: An Appreciation,' in *The Bible in Scottish Life and Literature*, ed. David F. Wright (Edinburgh: The Saint Andrew Press, 1988) 53–61, 55.

readers. This, Ogston argues, is a great enrichment of the reading experience, leading to new insights as timeworn assumptions are undermined.

Ogston makes a further point that is particularly worthy of note. He emphasizes that Lorimer's first loyalty was to the original Greek text and that his use of Scots was always a means to that end. Indeed, Ogston argues that it is because of this discipline that Lorimer succeeds in demonstrating that Scots could fully meet the demands that the text placed upon it.[9] What should be imitated is Lorimer's commitment to expressing as fully and as economically as possible the capacities of the original text, rather than, say, the more superficial characteristics of his style and vocabulary.

Lorimer's version thus works in two directions. It shows that vernacular Scots has all the subtlety and resonance of New Testament Greek, which is both a referential and mythical language in our culture. At the same time, it reminds us that New Testament Greek has all the vigour and earthiness of the vernacular as it was in its own time. Indeed, the New Testament came under severe criticism from some ancient critics precisely because much of its language did not meet the criteria for the vehicular and referential languages of the educated Hellene, but instead seemed a crude and inappropriate attempt to elevate a debased vernacular.

### A Scots Jonah

The justification for the present translation of Jonah is also based on this assessment of Lorimer. Just as the defamiliarizing strategy of translating into Scots invites the reader to reassess the nature of the language of the New Testament, so this translation aims to intrigue and provoke the reader into a new curiosity about the Hebrew of the Old Testament and to encourage the appreciation of it as a lively and living language of communication in its ancient context. There is no real equivalent of Lorimer's work in the Old Testament and few who would now have the qualifications to emulate his command of both the ancient languages and of Scots. I am only too well aware of how far this new version of Jonah falls short of his standards on both counts. Yet his subversive reanimation of both Scots and Greek seems worth emulating in the hope that it provokes something of the sense of curiosity and enjoyment of the resources of both Hebrew and Scots that his translation does.

---

[9] Ogston, 'Lorimer's *New Testament*', 55.

I also hope that the pedagogical aspect of Lorimer's work is continued
in the current translation. He hoped his translation would awaken the
curiosity of his readers about Scots and spur them on to learn more about
the language. I also share this hope. Quite as important, however, is to
stimulate the curiosity of non-Scots readers over the process of translation
and particularly the frustrations of encapsulating the flavour of Hebrew
in English idioms. It reminds us that biblical Hebrew too embodies
the tension between the vernacular and the mythical, the familiar and the
incomprehensible, but that it has the vigour, or, to use a Scots word, the
'smeddum', of the speech of the home and hearth as well as the mystery
and depth of the mythical. If this translation has any such effect, the effort
is worth it.

Indeed, my hope is that others will see that this effort could be extended
to other books of the Bible with profit and enjoyment. As with Lorimer's
New Testament, it may well be that the moment when a literary Scots
could arise from a biblical translation is long past, given the political
changes and the change in the cultural status of the Bible since the 17th
century, but Scots still lives and the Bible is still read. Both can only ben-
efit, it seems to me, from the possibilities of transformation that all acts
of translation open up.

### *The Buik o Jonah MacAmity as Owerset by Hugh S. Pyper*[10]

I

Noo[11] the wurd o the Lord cam tae Jonah MacAmity:[12] "Up ye get,"
quo he, "and awa tae Nineveh, thon muckle[13] toon, an cry agin it; fur their

---

[10]  The following footnotes are not intended to give a full critical apparatus for the translation or to rehearse all the potential pitfalls and difficulties in reading Jonah. The reader is
referred to the many commentaries on the book. Rather, they are intended to draw attention to some of the ways in which Scots and Hebrew illuminate each other.

[11]  The Hebrew practice of beginning a book with ויהי, usually translated as 'And it came
to pass', has a counterpart in Scots in the use of 'noo' as a marker of the beginning of a
new narrative or a new narrative strand and also conveys the sense that part of an ongoing
story is being related.

[12]  This is an irresistible transposition of the Hebrew patronymic ben-Amittai (son of
Amittai into the familiar Scots form.

[13]  For those not fluent in Scots, the unfamiliarity of the word 'muckle' makes it easier
to register the use in the Hebrew the root גדל as a *leitwort*, a repeated term that provides
a binding element in the narrative.

ill-daeins hae come up in my face."[14] Sae up Jonah gets—tae flee tae Tarshish, oot o the Lord's face.[15] He gaed doon[16] tae Joppa an fun a skiff bund fur Tarshish.[17] He peyed his fee and gaed doon intae her tae gang wi them tae Tarshish, oot o the Lord's face.

But the Lord flung a muckle gowst on the sea an there was a muckle storm on the sea, sae that the skiff was minded tae brak intae shivers.[18] Then the auld sauts[19] were feart and ilkane cried tae his ain goad; they flung the gear oan the skiff intae the sea, forby, tae lichten it fur them.

Noo Jonah hed gaed doon intae the wame o the skiff, lain doon an fa'n intae a dwam.[20] Sae the heid keiler[21] cam and said tae him, "Whit's wi ye,

---

[14] The idiom 'in my face' in Hebrew is often, justifiably, translated as 'in my sight' and also by the more abstract 'in my presence'. However, this may lose the sense of intrusion and provocation that the Hebrew conveys. 'In my face' may go too far, especially if read in a aggressive Glaswegian accent, but reminds us of the offensiveness of Nineveh—and Jonah's—behaviour and of the immediacy in the book of the confrontation between God and the human characters. It also allows for the repetitions of the phrase in the book to be more obvious to the Scots reader.

[15] The regular pattern in Hebrew narrative, probably a device that comes from the techniques of oral storytelling, is that when a character is given a series of actions to do in an instruction—"Get up ... go ... cry out"—the next verse affirms that he carried these out—"So he got up ... went ... cried out." The m-dash here marks the rhetorical effect of the storyteller's pause before he reveals that this time a character refuses to carry an instruction, and a divine one at that.

[16] Jonah 'gaes doon' seven times in the first two chapters of Jonah.

[17] The Hebrew "ship of Tarshish" could mean a ship from Tarshish or a ship that belonged to Tarshish. Either of these translations could make sense, but the point is Jonah's destination, which is proverbially the furthest imaginable city, equivalent to the use of "Timbuctoo" in English or Scots. If there is a need to transpose this to a Scottish reference, we might put Jonah on a boat to St Kilda.

[18] Here the Scots allows a fairly direct transposition of the idiomatic phrase חשבה לשבר where most English translations resort to paraphrase. What is lost is the assonance between the two verbs; however, the coincidence that the Hebrew verb שבר 'to break apart' or 'break into pieces' can be translated by the Scots word 'shiver' is too good to miss, as is the link to the archetypal piratical exclamation "Shiver my timbers!" popularized by Robert Louis Stevenson in *Treasure Island*.

[19] The Hebrew word מלחים, usually translated 'sailors', contains the same letters as the Hebrew word for 'salt' (מלח). Although the etymology is contested, with the argument put forward that it is derived from an Akkadian word for sailor, it is hard to believe that the similarity in sound would not strike a Hebrew speaker's ear in view of the association between sailors and the salt of the sea. The fact that 'saut' in Scots, as with 'salt' in English, is a term for a sailor makes it irresistible to translate the word this way. The expansion to 'auld saut' makes the allusion more comprehensible to the listener.

[20] The Scots word 'dwam' with its connotations of deep and even magically contrived sleep or trance makes the point that the Hebrew verb here is not the usual one for sleep, but one which elsewhere in the Bible denotes a state of unconsciousness that is the prelude to revelation or to death.

[21] 'Keiler' is a rare word that means 'one who coils a rope in the bottom of a ship.' The Hebrew phrase usually translated 'captain' is more literally 'the head of the ropers

ye snoiterer, ye?[22] Up ye get an cry tae yer goad! Mibbe thon goad'll tak tent o us, sae that we dinna dee!"

And they said, ilkane tae his neibour, "Come oan, let's cast caivels sae we can ken wha fur this ill's on us." Sae they cuist the caivels and the caivel fell tae Jonah.[23] They said tae him, "Kindly tell us, fur whit and fur wha hes this ill come upon us? Whit's yer eerant, and whaur are ye frae? Whitna airt dae ye hail frae, and whit's yer fowk?" And he telt them, "It's a Hebrew that I am, and it's the Lord, the goad o the heevans, that I fear, him that makkit sea and dry lan alike." The men were pit in a muckle gast an they spiered at him, "Whit's this ye've dune?" For the men kent that it was frae the face o the Lord he was fleein, for he had telt them.

They said tae him, "Whit should we dae wi ye tae mak the sea lown fur us?" Fur the sea wis stormin an better stormin.[24] He answert, "Fling me intae the sea and the sea will lown fur ye, fur weel I ken that it's aa thro me that this storm's come upon ye." Still an on,[25] the men dug in[26] tae win back tae the land, but they werena able, for the sea wis aye stormin the mair aroon them. Sae *they*[27] cried tae the Lord, "We beg ye, dinna end us fur this man's life, and dinna pit innocent bluid tae oor score! Fur, Lord, juist as ye ettled, ye've dune!" Sae they picked Jonah up and flung him intae the sea and the sea stood still frae its tirriveein. The men were muckle feart at the Lord, and they sacrificed tae the Lord, and vooed their voos.

---

(רש החבל), the second word being a participle formed from a root meaning 'to bind' which gives rise to the noun translated 'rope'. The sailors are thus 'the binders' or 'ropers'; 'keiler' evokes the same association.

[22] In the heid keiler's reply, the Scots allows a use of pronouns that more closely resembles the Hebrew idiom than standard English syntax.

[23] Casting 'caivels' is the idiom Lorimer uses in his translation of John 19:24 where the soldiers cast lots over Jesus's tunic. This is one way in which the referential dimension of Scots can be strengthened by conscious allusion to the language of older Scots versions.

[24] The Hebrew idiom translates more literally as "the sea was going and storming" but conveys the notion of a continuing and intensifying action as the Scots idiom does.

[25] The contrast between Jonah's advice and the sailors' actions merits a stronger connection than the ubiquitous 'and' of Hebrew syntax.

[26] The Hebrew verb literally means 'to dig' but here is used to mean 'rowing'. It may refer to the way that the boat is tunneling through the waves. Here the Scots idiom is a little different, but serves to emphasize the effort and determination of the crew as they seek to avoid the blood-guilt that throwing a paying passenger overboard would entail.

[27] The italics serve to point up the fact that everyone except Jonah cried upon his own god. Although he explains his relationship to God to the crew, he does not address a word to God in this chapter. The sailors take it upon themselves to make good his omission.

## II

Noo the Lord caaed up a muckle fush tae swalla Jonah an there wis Jonah in the fush's wame: three hail days an three hail nichts. An Jonah pit up a wurd tae the Lord his Goad frae the fush's kyte, sayin this:

> I cried oot in ma pine tae the Lord an he answert me;
> Frae the wame o Sheol I besocht ye an ye harkened tae ma voice.
> Ye plowtit me intae the howe, intae the hert o the seas;[28]
> The hurl-come-gush wis roon me; aa yer jaws and swaws were ower me.[29]
> An I said, "Here's me pit awa frae yer sicht; ach, tae see yer hailie hoose aince mair!"
> The watters were aa ower me, up tae ma thrapple;[30] the deip wis aa aboot me. Wrack[31] wis wrappit roon ma heid.
>
> Tae the verra ruits o the bens I gaed doon; the yetts o the yird were ranced agin me.
> But ye liftet ma life up frae the heuch, O Lord ma Goad.
> As ma inmaist bein dwined awa, I minded the Lord and ma prayer won up tae ye, tae yer hailie hoose.
> Them at hauds tae nauchtie whigmaleeries foresak their lealtie.
> But see me; wi a thankful voice will I sacrifice tae ye. Whit I've vooed, I will mak siccar.
> Rescue is the Lord's daein!"

Then the Lord spak tae the fush, an it boaked up Jonah ontae the dry land.

## III

Noo the wurd o the Lord cam tae Jonah a second time: "Up ye get", quo he, "an awa tae Nineveh, thon muckle toon, and cry agin it the cry I'm telling ye." Sae up Jonah got, an hied himsel tae Nineveh, in line wi the

---

[28] It has been suggested that the word מצולה translated 'howe' is a rarer Hebrew term which is explained by a gloss as 'the heart of the seas'. Be that as it may, the same effect is to some extent reproduced in the Scots.

[29] This line is patently 'synthetic Scots', depending on dictionaries and reference works for its unusual vocabulary, but it is offered as an example of the phonetic richness that such Scots can rise to, in homage to the similar sensitivity to sound and rhythm in the original Hebrew. It is a moot point how familiar the Hebrew vocabulary of this chapter would have been to those who listened to its earliest readings.

[30] The Hebrew word נפש, often translated 'soul' is also the word for the front part of the throat. Here I have opted for the more concrete translation that fits well with the extended metaphor of drowning.

[31] 'Wrack' is often to be understood as seaweed, but can mean any floating vegetable matter. For a discussion as to the possible allusion in this verse to the reeds of the Reed Sea and the drowning of Pharaoh's army, see Hugh S. Pyper 'Swallowed by a Song: Jonah and the Jonah Psalm Through the Looking-glass.' In R. Rezetko, T.H. Lim and W.B. Aucker (eds.) Reflection and Refraction: Studies in Biblical History in Honour of A. Graeme Auld (Vetus Testamentum Supplements 113; Leiden: Brill, 2006), 337–358.

Lord's wurd. Noo Nineveh wis a muckle toon richt eneuch and a muckle toon fur goads; three days gangin it wis.[32] Jonah stertit tae gang intae the city a day's walk, and he cried oot, "But forty days, and Nineveh'll be ower-set!" The fowk o Nineveh lippened tae Goad; they caaed a fast an the hail clanjamfrie pit oan sacken duds, frae muckle tae mickle. When the toun's speak cam tae the king o Nineveh, he rose frae his royal seat, rave his plaid, pit oan sacken duds himsel and sat doon i the cinners. Then he hed a proclamation pit oot in Nineveh saying this:

> By the decree o the king an his heid men: Man nor baist, kye nor hirsel, maunna pree naething; they're no tae eat and they're no tae drink watter.[33] Man and baist's tae be cled in sacken duds and they're tae cry lustily tae Goad or the goads,[34] an ilkane's tae turn back frae his ill-deedie ways an frae the gilravagin in his nieve. Fur wha kens? The Goad'll aiblins turn back and tak the rue; he'll turn back frae his stramash and we'll no dee.

When Goad saw their daeins, an that they'd turned back frae their ill-deedie ways, Goad did tak the rue. He turned back frae the ill he'd said he wud dae tae them and didna dae it.

## IV

But whit a muckle ill this seemed tae Jonah! Sae ill did he tak it he wis bleezin.[35] He prayed tae the Lord and said, "Fegs, Lord, is this no juist whit I said when I wis in ma ain land, at gart me flee tae Tarshish? Weel I kent at ye're a guidwillie Goad, slaw in anger, lippen-fou o lealtie and takkin the rue at ill-deeds. Noo, Lord, tak ma life awa frae me, fur better ma daith than ma life!" The Lord said, "Are ye the better fur yer anger?"[36]

Then Jonah skailed frae the toon and sat doon tae the east o the toon; he biggit himsel a bothy there and sat in its scug tae see whit sould come o the toon. Noo the Lord caaed up a kin o bramble they cry a boak-boak

---

[32] This is a rather ambiguous verse in the Hebrew and the translation here reflects some of the rather cryptic syntax.

[33] Unlike Standard English, Scots will allow for the repetition of negatives as an intensification of the king's prohibition.

[34] Here the Scots spells out the (deliberate?) ambiguity of the Hebrew מאלהי; is the king referring to his own gods or to Jonah's God?

[35] This is a rather extravagant translation, to be sure, but it catches both the phonetic echo of the word for evil and the root meaning 'to burn' in the Hebrew word for anger. Heat recurs as a motif in this chapter when Jonah is at the mercy of the sun in the desert.

[36] Catching the meaning and, more importantly, the tone of God's remark is quite challenging. This is one attempt to evoke the enigmatic nature of his enquiry.

plaunt,[37] an he gart it gae up ower Jonah tae be a scug ower his heid an protect him frae ill. Jonah wis unco blyth ower the boak-boak plaunt, wi muckle blythness. Then the Lord caaed up an oobit at the morn's dawin an it struck at the boak-boak plaunt sae it wizened. When the sun cam fu up, the Lord caad up a birslin[38] wind oot o the East, an the sun struck doon on Jonah's heid sae he wis sweltin. He besocht that he micht dee; "Better my daith than my life," quo he.

The Lord said tae Jonah, "Are ye the better fur yer anger ower the boak-boak plaunt?" "Better my anger as far as daith," quo he. Then the Lord said tae him, "Ye're vext fur the boak-boak plaunt, that ye didna trauchle ower and ye nivver hed the growin o: ae day's bairn, an deed in ae nicht. An am I no tae be vext fur Nineveh, thon muckle toon, whaur there's mair nor a hunnert an twenty thousan chiels wha dinna ken their left haund frae their richt—an, forby, a bonnie wheen o baists?"[39]

### Appendix: The Old Testament in Scots

Very little of the Old Testament has ever been published in Scots, as can be seen from the history of Scottish translations or versions of biblical texts definitively set out in Graham Tulloch's *A History of the Scots Bible*.[40] Furthermore, with few exceptions, the works Tulloch lists have been based on existing English translations, not on the original Hebrew. Despite the significant tradition of translation into Scots in the late mediaeval period, no Scots version of the Old Testament was produced.

It is not until 1857 that the earliest Scots version of any Old Testament book was published. In that year a version 'in Lowland Scotch' of the Psalms rendered by Henry Scott Riddell was published, to be followed by his

---

[37] Here the translation is expanded to explain the pun contained in the plant name קיקיון. This echoes the verb קיא 'to vomit' which is used in Jonah 2.11. The standard translations of this plant name depend on the best guess translators can make as to the identity of a plant that can grow up in one night and which deserves a name related to vomiting. In the context, the botanical identity of the plant is not the issue, especially as its growth habit is not a matter of botany but of divine intervention.

[38] The Hebrew word that describes the wind, חרישית, is a *hapax legomenon*. Here we follow the Septuagint in interpreting it as 'scorching' which seems best to fit the context where Jonah is becoming both physically and emotionally heated.

[39] Whether this final sentence is a question continues to be the subject of debate. Both the context and God's habit in this chapter of posing enigmatic questions to Jonah seem to make this a fitting end to this enigmatic book.

[40] Graham Tulloch *A History of the Scots Bible with Selected Texts* (Aberdeen: Aberdeen University Press, 1989).

version of the Song of Solomon in 1858. The impetus for their production
came from a somewhat unlikely source: Prince Louis Lucien Bonaparte
(1813–1891). He devoted considerable time and money to the laudable
project of preserving a record of what he saw as dying languages and dialects across Europe. To this end, he commissioned a large number of versions of biblical texts in these various languages. Those produced in Scots
were explicitly based on the Authorized Version rather than on the Hebrew
as the purpose was to display the distinctive forms of Scots dialect rather
than to provide a new translation of the text. Only two hundred and fifty
copies were printed of Riddell's work so its impact on readers other than
professional philologists was minimal.[41]

Here we see one motivation for the translation of the Bible into Scots;
the preservation of the language. The choice of the Bible as the text is a
cultural rather than a religious one. These are familiar texts where the
reader is likely to be sufficiently aware of the content to be able to con-
centrate on the particular features of grammar and vocabulary that make
Scots distinct. It also immediately raises the question as to whether there
is such a thing as a Scots language, or whether there is a whole family of
dialects none of which can claim authority. After all, Riddell himself only
professes to be using 'Lowland Scotch': are there other varieties that are
not represented? The fact that Prince Louis commissioned further translations in part lies in the recognition of this complex situation.

A rather different motivation underlies the first translations into Scots
directly from Hebrew. These were the work of P. Hately Waddell (1817–91).
The titles of his two major publications in this area proudly proclaim the
fact that these are translations from the original: *The Psalms: Frae Hebrew
intil Scottis* (1871) and *Isaiah: From Hebrew intil Scottis* (1879). Waddell had
strong credentials in both Hebrew and Scots. He was a minister, variously
within the Free Church, as an independent and latterly within the Church
of Scotland, and was well schooled in biblical studies, being a graduate
in divinity from the University of Glasgow. His interest in the Scots language is shown in the fact that as a devotee of Burns he edited his entire
works.

As Graham Tulloch points out, for Waddell the transition from Burns
to the Psalms was a natural one as he thought of Burns as a kindred spirit

---

[41] The Song of Solomon was one of Prince Louis' preferred sample texts and he commissioned three further Scottish versions. These bear a complex relationship to Riddell
and to each other. They reuse felicitous phrases of Riddell's and correct errors in the rendition, but are all, like Riddell's, based on the Authorized Version.

with David, indeed as his equal. Furthermore, Waddell argued, although the Scots language may have fallen out of use in politics or commerce, Burns had honed it as "the language of passion and of sympathy", making it a fit vehicle for the translation of the poetry of the Psalms and Isaiah. This to some extent also provided his answer to the question of what version of Scots he would use. To a large extent, he followed Burns' practice using an eclectic literary language that was based on Ayrshire dialect but drew on vocabulary and syntax from other Scots writers and the ballad traditions. At the same time, Waddell shared the increasingly common view among his contemporaries that the Authorized Version was not only antiquated in its language but also problematic as a translation; he goes so far as to describe it as "often utterly inadequate, and sometimes even erroneous." The time was ripe for new versions that went back to the original texts.

His translation thus meets a rather different goal from the earlier ones. He sees a role for Scottish versions of the biblical texts as a way of achieving a more accurate representation of the Hebrew text for his reader. His versions of the two books contain extensive editorial matter—introductions, marginal notes and footnotes—also in Scots. Waddell's translations antedate the Revised Version but reflect many of the same concerns, although rather than preserving the best of the Authorised Version he seems deliberately to choose alternative readings.

In 1873, Riddell's work came to the attention of an erstwhile near neighbour of his, James Murray, who would later gain fame as the editor of the *Oxford English Dictionary*. He was critical of the fact that Riddell's Scots represented no specific time or place and so embarked on his own translation of the book of Ruth in which he tried to reproduce as accurately as possible the grammar, lexicon and phonetics of the speech of his native area of Upper Teviotdale. This appeared as an appendix to his *The Dialect of the Southern Counties of Scotland* in 1873.[42] In fact, he produced three versions of the first chapter of Ruth in a phonetic alphabet called palaeotype in order to illustrate the differences between the Scots of Teviotdale, Buchan and Ayrshire as well as a full translation of Ruth in the conventional alphabet but with his own phonetic spelling. He does not give details of the way in which his various translations were obtained

---

[42] James A. H. Murray, *The Dialect of the Southern Counties of Scotland: Its Pronunciation, Grammar and Historical Relations; with an Appendix on the Present Limits of the Gaelic and Lowland Scotch, and the Dialectical Divisions of the Lowland Tongue; and a Linguistical Map of Scotland* (London: Asher and Co, for the Philological Society, 1873).

but speaks of them as being dictated by native speakers. Presumably, as Tulloch suggests, he asked his informants to provide an oral reworking of the Authorized Version except for the Teviotdale where he himself felt fully competent to undertake the rendering.[43]

As with the work of those commissioned by Prince Louis Napoleon, with whom he had correspondence, Murray's concern is with the preservation and demonstration of the Scots language, but he differed in having a much clearer and more differentiated view of the variety of dialects that were subsumed under the name of 'Scots'. It is the familiarity of the Bible that makes it suitable as the text to be considered rather than any literary or religious purpose and, again, there is no evidence that he made any use of the Hebrew in deriving his readings.

In 1917, Thomas Whyte Paterson produced a version of the book of Proverbs, in his own words "rendered in Scots" as *The Wyse-sayin's o' Solomon*. This, he says, is based on the Revised Version, but also owes the arrangement of the verses to Richard Moulton's *The Modern Reader's Bible for Schools* (MacMillan & Co, 1922).[44] The rendering is often very free and distinctly colloquial but this freedom has no relation to the Hebrew.

In a similar vein is the rendering of the book of Genesis by Henry Paterson Cameron. Indeed, in his "Prefatory Note" he too acknowledges that his text is founded on the Revised Version and owes its paragraphing to Moulton, but without mentioning Paterson's precedent. Although his *Genesis in Scots* was published in Paisley in 1921, Cameron had emigrated to Australia in the 1890's. The spur for his version is unashamedly the exile's longing for the language of childhood and home. As he memorably puts it in the same "Prefatory Note", "e'en mids the eldritch yowlin o' the dingo, the rowtin o' nowte, the maein o' fe, and the schill crawin o' the 'rooster'" he has heard in his soul "the 'saft, couthie' müsick o' the Doric" and seeks to pass that on to other exiles (70).

After these, a long hiatus ensues, no doubt reflecting the effects of the Second World War but also coinciding with major wrangles in Scottish literary circles over the issue of the use of the Scots language, as was out-

---

[43] Tulloch, *History of the Scots Bible*, 53.

[44] Moulton's work is a triumph of form criticism, in one sense. He explains in the preface that his purpose is to introduce the biblical texts to the widest readership without the daunting apparatus of the traditional commentary, much of which, in his view, is made necessary because of the uniformity of the traditional layout of the biblical page in columns and verses. Instead, he lays the text out as poetry or as prose with headings to explain the function of the various sections. He is also quite unabashed about selecting and reordering the text in order to make it more readable.

lined above. It is not until 1979, the year after his death, that Alex S. Borrowman's *The Buik o Ruth and Ither Wark in Lallans* (Edinburgh: Gordon Wright, 1979) appeared. Borrowman was both a Church of Scotland minister and a poet who had acted as Secretary to the Lallans Society. This offers a version of Ruth together with Psalm 100, a selection of Christmas readings including Genesis 3:8–15, 22:15–18, Isaiah 9: 6–7 and Micah 5:2–4, and a group of his own sermons with embedded passages which included metrical versions of Psalms 8, 23, 84, 121 and Ecclesiastes 3:1–8. Borrowman avows that "the found o the translation is the New English Bible. I hae taken a keek at the Authorised Version, alswell Moffat's translation, in the by-gaun" (10).

That a market for Scots versions of the Bible still exists is shown by the success of a series of paraphrases in Glasgow dialect written by Jamie Stuart. Beginning with *The Scots Gospel*, then more specifically *The Glasgow Gospel*, Stuart presents a conflation of the four gospels into a single narrative. This was followed his *Auld Testament Tales*. In 1997, *A Glasgow Bible* appeared which brought together the previous volumes supplemented with further texts. Interestingly, Jonah is not included. In 2006, Stuart brought out a final volume, *Proverbs in the Patter: Wise Words from the Good Book*. There is no pretention to scholarship in Stuart's work. Instead, he offers a lively retelling of familiar stories in a modern Glaswegian dialect, with the imprimatur of no less a scholar than Robert Davidson, Professor of Old Testament in the University of Glasgow.

There is, however, a more scholarly basis to the translation of the Book of Amos published by Duncan Sneddon in the journal *Theology in Scotland* in 2009.[45] From personal correspondence, it turns out that this was a project to occupy his gap year between school and university, an interesting choice of activity for an eighteen-year-old! It reflects Sneddon's interest in improving his knowledge and facility in Scots as well as the fact that Amos was both one of his favourite biblical books and one that was a manageable size. The *Interlinear Bible* edited by Jay P. Green, Sr, provided the basic text in order to avoid the use of a standard English translation, and he made use of a range of other translations and commentaries. The final text was read and commented upon by a number of readers knowledgeable in Hebrew and in Scots. It was published with the imprimatur of some distinguished Scottish academics.

---

[45] Duncan Sneddon 'The Beuk of Amos' *Theology in Scotland* 16 (2009) 97–110. The article is available online from the journal's site.

2010 saw the publication of two volumes, *Genesis* and *Exodus*, of a *Bible in Plain Scots*, translated by Gavin Falconer and Ross G. Arthur.[46] In the spirit of Lorimer, they make it plain that their aim is to provide an example of a high-register text in Scots for the ordinary reader, not the specialist. This version is based upon the Basic English Bible rather than the Hebrew, with the idea of providing a Basic Scots vocabulary that could form a bedrock for the further literary development of the language. In keeping with a phenomenon we have seen before, these volumes were first published in Canada and are unfortunately not easy to come by at the moment.

It would appear, then, that the version of Jonah presented in this article is one of very few published example of a direct translation from Hebrew to Scots. As such, it is a modest contribution to a Bible that is not yet one: the Old Testament in Scots.[47]

---

[46] Gavin Ferguson and Ross G. Arthur *Genesis: The Bible in Plain Scots* (Cambridge, Ont.: Alektryaina Press, 2010); *The Bible in Plain Scots* (Cambridge, Ont.: Alektryaina Press, 2010). The original aim was eventually to publish the whole Old Testament, but this project is currently in abeyance, I understand. Ferguson has also published a version of the Song of Songs.

[47] At the time of writing, I believe the manuscript of a translation of the Old Testament by the late Rev. James Marshall, whose death prevented him from completing his final revision, remains unpublished in St Andrew's University Library.

# THE BOOK OF DANIEL:
## FROM BIBLICAL ARCHIVE TO POSTHUMAN PROPHECY?

### Hannah M. Strømmen

Could animals be contained in archives? Could our archives be zoo-logical or our animals archival? What might the connection be between the desire to contain, archive and preserve texts and knowledge and the desire to domesticate, tame and restrain? Peter Sloterdijk argues that we have entered an age of archivism, a time in which the knowledge of the past metonymically figures as dusty tomes and obscure scrolls.[1] At the same time there is increased interest in the non-human, putting animals "at the centre of critical inquiry."[2] As Cary Wolfe puts it, the animal is "perhaps the central problematic for contemporary culture and theory, particularly if *theory* is understood as centrally engaging in addressing a social, technological, and cultural context that is now in some inescapable sense posthuman, if not quite posthumanist."[3] Daniel is a text in the biblical archive that troubles the concept of the archivable and the notion of the animal as abyssally other. It conveys the slipperiness of archivisation, witholding the illusion of fully taming or detaining its content. The writing might well be on the wall—*mene, mene, tekel, parsin*—but that does not mean we can fully capture its meaning. The Book of Daniel lends itself to contemporary posthumanist calls to contemplate and confront the elasticity of life forms; the given, usurped, proximate and strategic boundaries of our ontological categories.

### Archive Enclosures

The Greek *arkheion*, Jacques Derrida writes, was

> initially a house, a domicile, an address, the residence of the superior magis-trates, the *archons*, those who commanded. The citizens who thus held and

---

[1] Peter Sloterdijk, 'Rules for the Human Zoo: a response to the *Letter on Humanism*', *Environment and Planning D: Society and Space*, (2009, vol. 27, pp. 12–28) p. 27.

[2] Matthew Calarco, *Zoographies: The Question of the Animal From Heidegger To Derrida*, (New York: Columbia University Press, 2008) p. 2.

[3] Cary Wolfe, *Zoontologies: The Question of the Animal* (Minneapolis/London: University of Minnesota Press, 2003) p. ix.

signified political power were considered to possess the right to make or to represent the law. On account of their publicly recognized authority, it is at their home, in that *place* which is their house (private house, family house, or employee's house), that official documents are filed.[4]

K. L. Noll argues for a similar claim in the case of those handling the Hebrew Scriptures prior to Biblical canonisation as a small number of learned literati, an elite class of literate 'archivers' or collectors of scrolls.[5] We are in a 'home', then, but one that necessarily protects, enshrines, empowers. Moreover, we are already in a *textual* geography. Sloterdijk describes the "close connection between domesticity and theory building," arguing that where "there are houses, there are also decisions about who shall live in them. In fact, and through this fact, it is determined what type of community dwellers will be dominant."[6] Notions of inclusion and exclusion do not relate simply to archival judgements of sacred literature or canonising works of literary and philosophical worth; they are inextricably caught up in theories of ontological distinction and portioning of power (or powerlessness) in societal structures, that rest on *decision* and theorisation rather than natural or arbitrary selection. Architectural splendour is the 'proper' place to hold monarchs, presidents, celebrities; the unemployed and certain animals are homeless; and the mentally ill, criminals and other animals are institutionalised, domesticated, under house-arrest.

Sloterdijk's response to Heidegger's 'Letter on Humanism' describes an aftermath to humanism, a 'post', in which the globalised world—increasingly beyond national literary canons as well as national borders—and its communication technology has displaced what he calls the "quintessential nature and function of humanism: It is telecommunication in the medium of print to underwrite friendship."[7] He writes:

> What is left to us in the place of the wise is their writings, in their glinting brilliance and their increasing obscurity. They still lay in more or less accessible editions; they can still be read, if only one knew why one should bother. It is their fate—to stand in silent bookshelves, like posted letters no longer collected, sent to us by authors, of whom we no longer know whether

---

[4] Jacques Derrida, *Archive Fever: A Freudian Impression*, (Trans. Eric Prenowitz. Chicago/London: University of Chicago Press, 1995) p. 2.

[5] K. L. Noll, 'The Kaleidoscopic Nature of Divine Personality in the Hebrew Bible', *Biblical Interpretation, A Journal of Contemporary Approaches*, vol. IX, No. 1 2001. Leiden/Boston/Köln, Publisher's: Brill, pp. 1–24) pp. 7, 8.

[6] Sloterdijk, 'Rules for the Human Zoo: a response to the *Letter on Humanism*', p. 21.

[7] Sloterdijk, 'Rules for the Human Zoo: a response to the *Letter on Humanism*', p. 12.

or not they could be our friends. Letters that are not mailed cease to be missives for possible friends; they turn into archived things. Thus this—that the important books of the past have more and more ceased to be letters to friends, and that they do not lie any longer on the tables and nightstands of their readers—this has deprived the humanistic movement of its previous power.... Everything suggests that archivists have become the successors of the humanists.[8]

Our 'post' to humanism is somewhat ironic, not only a parting obituary but also a mocking reminder of the epistolary system Sloterdijk alludes to, perceived increasingly as an archaic institution trumped by technologically advanced communication methods of spiralling speed and maximised ease.

In Elizabeth Bowen's novel *The Death of the Heart* one of the central characters describes the way in which she feels 'mummified' at the thought of being written about in a diary.[9] Caught up in the secret writing of a diary-writer, Bowen's character feels herself being eerily wrapped in the layers of subjectivity spun out in a diary, producing an uncomfortable sense of claustrophobia, muteness, immobility. Mummification is the image of perturbed angst and uncontrollable constraint engulfing the subject as she becomes archived as a 'character' in a book (this has a double sense, both in the diary and of course as a reference to the novel as a whole). Writing, in the mummifying sense, is about witness, secrecy and claustrophobia, as if living is made up of crimes committed or uncommitted (or perhaps, witnessed or unwitnessed); writing is judgement. Pages of writing become cells in which one is compartmentalised, captured, caught and quite literally sentenced. Books are thus the very image of the archive as tomb or cell—what is preserved, safeguarded, and oppressively so; airtight, dry, dead space. Like archives, they are first and foremost *containers*, something that enfolds and stores things and people, catching them in its linguistic compartments, plotting them thus on archival shelves by using adjectives, nouns, verbs, like slicing, carving, organising tools.

Language and writing become in this sense a dissecting operation, forcibly ensuring the death and subsequent mummification of the subject. Language itself, in this image, is indeed Heidegger's "house of the truth of

---

8 Sloterdijk, 'Rules for the Human Zoo: a response to the *Letter on Humanism*', p. 27.
9 Elizabeth Bowen, *The Death of the Heart*, ([1938] London: Vintage, 1998) p. 49.

being", [10] but it is a house that is cramped, cell-like, more like a dark tomb than an illustration of architectural splendour—both what we are supposedly wholly *inside* and what we as humans have proudly built. The dryness of pages connote the very ashes of life; the transition from living tree to deadened paper is a testament to writing as death itself, and the marks it thus bears become morbid etchings on the body of a corpse. Like the marks on the risen Christ's hands, these signs must be read with awe, with a sense of the ghostly and strange, the unnatural—the supernatural—the divine. The archive is also then a container of spectres, haunting attempts at preservation against decay. These images are perhaps not far from the symbolic territories of animals archived ontologically as *lesser* lives (or less alive), secondary, subjects under the knife, claustrophobically enclosed in factory farm cells, objectified occupants of dark, dingy, windowless abattoirs, tightly wrapped in super-marked packaging, mummified, silenced, transformed from living beings to price-tagged objects of consumerism and industrial production.

It is perhaps no coincidence that Heidegger displays anxiety at the inflexibility of writing in his uncompromising stance on the abyss that separates humans from animals.[11] In his 'Letter on Humanism', Heidegger writes first of all that it would have been better had his letter taken place in conversation rather than in writing, echoing perhaps this 'mummifying' fear of writing as the straitjacket, the immovable, (human) hands tied. Perhaps, then, having already warned of an inflexibility-to-come in his letter, we might not be surprised at Heidegger's insistence on the absolute distinction drawn between the human and the animal. This is a distinction which, as Matthew Calarco points out, "is meant to be understood in the most fundamental and radical way possible."[12]

With the current concern for the state of the biosphere and the demise of a certain humanism—or the critique of Modernity with its sovereign Man[13]—we are faced with the question of the animal. Within ecologi-

---

[10] Martin Heidegger, 'Letter on Humanism', (Trans. Frank A. Capuzzi, http://archive.org/stream/HeideggerLetterOnhumanism1949/Heidegger-LetterOnhumanism1949#page/no/mode/2up), p. 150.

[11] See for instance, Derrida's *The Beast and the Sovereign volume II* (Trans. Geoffrey Bennington, Chicago/London: University of Chicago Press, 2011) or Matthew Calarco's *Zoographies: The Question of the Animal From Heidegger To Derrida* (New York: Columbia University Press, 2008).

[12] Calarco, *Zoographies*, p. 22.

[13] Luc Ferry argues that what might be termed the posthumanist "renaissance of feelings of compassion for natural beings is always accompanied by a critique of modernity—designated, dependent on the frame of reference, as 'capitalist,' 'Western,' 'technological,'

cal debates, the animal has come to represent something of a question and a symbol. To pose this question is to invoke numerous issues, ethical, political, philosophical, commercial, legal, etc. but in its most contracted form it stands in as a call for responsibility and humility. It confronts the "limits of the human" and what such a recognition *opens* up, rather than claustrophobically and teleologically closes.[14] In other words a gaze that looks beyond the human ego towards a wider frame of inter-dependence and co-habitation in a less human-centric world. It is a prizing open of the moral prism that desires to distance and reduce the other; to confront what Christine Korsgaard calls the "complex centres of subjectivity, conscious beings" that are nonhumans, recognizing affinity without diminishing difference.[15]

## The Biblical Archive

*Arkhe*, Derrida writes, denotes both commencement and commandment;[16] in other words, notions of beginning (and therefore past, history) authority and decision. The Bible is a pivotal example of the archive, an archetypal archive.[17] It is both commencement and commandment, poetics, prophecy, history and apocalypse. It is arguably archival desire incarnate, stories from origin to end—creation to eschaton—the world itself archived, past, present and future. Also a cultural archive, the Bible stands accused of elevating the human as central, sacred and selected as sovereign creature, thus mummifying subjectivity or subjecthood as determinedly *human*.[18]

---

or, more generally, 'consumerist.'" (pp. xxiv, xxv) Luc Ferry, *The New Ecological Order*. trans. Carol Volk, Chicago/London, The University of Chicago Press, 1995 [1992] p. xxviii.

[14] Calarco, *Zoographies*, p. 6.

[15] Christine M. Korsgaard, 'Facing the Animal You See in the Mirror', in *The Harvard Review of Philosophy*, vol. XVI 2009.

[16] Derrida, *Archive Fever, A Freudian Impression*, p. 1.

[17] Of course, the Bible is not (and never can be) a pure, closed and singular archive. As K. L. Noll points out in what he calls "a long and probably very chaotic history of writing and rewriting for each of the biblical scrolls", the time of the final canonised form of the Bible is under debate, especially since research done on the Dead Sea Scrolls and the Qumran Archive, revealing the ways in which other documentation—lost and found—might inform what we know of the biblical, and in turn, what we know of external sources and its histories. ('The Kaleidoscopic Nature of Divine Personality in the Hebrew Bible', pp. 4–5) This is not exclusive to the Biblical archive; as Noll contends, where "there are intellectuals, there will be rewriting, expansion, contraction and exegetical glossing of literature" (Ibid., p. 6).

[18] See for instance, Atterton & Calarco 2004 (p. xvii), Cavalieri 2009 (pp. 2, 5–6), Fellenz 2007 (pp. 2, 31).

There is a sense that to fully enter the biblical archive one must have entered the realms of elite literacy—the super-scholarly—mastering *at least* ancient Hebrew, ancient Greek, Aramaic, perhaps also Ugaritic, Latin and German; be acutely aware of the historical minutiae of the various texts, places and periods, spanning centuries, as well as its formation, reception history, source theory, archaeology, theology, etc. At the same time, it is also a best-seller, read by lay-people all over the world, quoted by politicians, held up as slogan for both peace and war, adopted in literary and everyday language, assumed into our moral codes and a major influence in the constitution of Western culture. One could begin to mention examples, but this is a dizzying operation, partly because there are so many to draw from[19] but also because of the opaque nature of this relationship between 'world' and 'Bible.' Derrida asks: "where does the outside commence? *This question is the question of the archive.*"[20] It is difficult to tell what is strictly 'biblical' and what is not, what belongs and what does not; where what came from and who or what came first; such matters remain to some extent confusion and conundrum. The archive is about memorialization and preservation, canonization, selection and collection. "Archive will never be memory as spontaneous and internal", Derrida writes. Rather it "takes place at the place of originary and structural breakdown of the said memory."[21] "There is no archive without a place of consignation, without a technique of repetition, and without a certain exteriority. No archive without outside."[22]

Certainly for Western culture, the Bible is an ancient archive that lumbers and lingers. In numerous ways it has embodied the *ahuman* or *supernatural*, haunting with its divinely authorial signature, its 'God-breathed' pages—*theopneustos*—while being at the same time supremely historicized. The Bible stands as that mummified corpus that signifies something extra and irreducible. This symbolism is reinforced by its most prominent home in church buildings, caricatured as over-sized vaults for the living dead, ritually poring over the flesh and blood of the crucified Christ, with a taste for the morbid, the cannibalistic and vampiric. The Bible is lifted reverently (tenderly) and kissed, like a zombie-bride, leather-lipped, dry as death. The archive is that which reaches into Time, that which traces

---

[19]  See for instance Timothy Beal's *Biblical Literacy* (2009), or Maggie Dawn's *The Writing on the Wall: High Art, Popular Culture and the Bible* (2010).

[20]  Derrida, *Archive Fever, A Freudian Impression*, [my italics] p. 8.

[21]  Ibid., p. 11.

[22]  Ibid.

and collects traces. Or, if it fails to do so its vast vault-like secrets continue to echo in the cavities of history, what we *do not know*, what we have forgotten or lost, intangible but tantalizingly 'present'.

## Humiliating Descents

In its representations of the human/the animal/the divine, crinkles and creases appear in the biblical archive. How can such a collection of books be a divine composition? Is it fully 'human'? What is it to be a religious animal? Subjected to non-human power? To be a biblical creature-character? Is the God of the Bible schizophrenic? Animal, monstrous, or divine? Or are we ourselves mad, or under the spell of zooanthropy?[23] Daniel references the biblical archive in both his commitment to Mosaic Law,[24] mentioning Moses in chapter 9, v. 11–13, and referring to his reading "the word of the Lord to the prophet Jeremiah" (9:2).[25] Hugh Pyper points out that this "is the first explicit evidence of canonical texts being read as scripture—and the upshot is failure and incomprehension."[26] It might not be the biblical archive as we know it now, but this explicit 'inside' reference to the 'outsideness' of Daniel as writer and prophet, anxiously leafing through old 'biblical' scrolls and papyri, is a sign of the self-consciousness of the biblical writer-figure inserting himself into an archival tradition.[27]

Daniel is a book about impossible interpretations made-possible as well as haunting secrecy; about exegesis as dream, and writing as a breaking through into the future, a tearing, splitting movement that rips pieces of the past out of its catalogued space and inserts them into an anachronistic future. Daniel presents the shiftiness of our categories of being,

---

[23] Steve Baker argues that Heidegger's assessment of the animal in contrast to the human with his 'hand' leaves the animal, 'gazing across the abyss not only at all that is human, but also at all that is associated with thought, generosity, and creativity.' ('Sloughing the Human', *Zoontologies, The Question of the Animal*, Minneapolis/London: University of Minnesota Press, 2003, p. 152).

[24] Hartman and Di Lella, *The New Jerome Biblical Commentary*, Eds. Raymond E. Brown, S. S. Joseph A. Fitzmeyer, S. J. Roland E. Murphy, O. Carm. (New Jersey: Prentice Hall, 1968) p. 409.

[25] All quotations from the Bible are taken from the NSRV anglicised edition, Oxford University Press, 1995.

[26] Hugh Pyper, 'Reading in the Dark: Zechariah, Daniel and the Difficulty of Scripture', *The Journal for the Study of the Old Testament*, 29.4 (2005) (pp. 485–504), p. 492.

[27] Lester L. Grabbe calls Daniel a "biblical exegete, trying to make sense of earlier Scripture as he knew it, such as Jeremiah's 70-years prophecy which he reinterpreted as 70 weeks of years". (in, *The Book of Daniel, Composition and Reception*. (Eds. John J. Collins and Peter W. Flint, Volume I. Leiden/Boston/Köln: Brill, 2001) 'A Dan(iel) for all seasons: For Whom was Daniel Important?' pp. 231, 232.

experimenting with what subjectivity might mean in varying politico-religious guises.

Are we already animals that must be tamed, civilised, made-human, as Sloterdijk proposes has been the "hidden thesis" of humanist thought, the "constant battle for humanity that reveals itself as a contest between bestializing and taming tendencies"?[28] Can genius, power and psychosis be human, or must it necessarily be other, sliding into the realm of the animal and the divine, the monstrous or the religious? Nebuchadnezzar's awe at Daniel's skilful interpretive insight translates to a deifying of Daniel (2:46); the King's lesson in humility transforms him into an animal (4:33); Daniel's visions hold mutant beings that are beast-like and divine-like, symbolically representing Kings and Angels, but neither are wholly identifiable as such (chs. 7 and 8). Likeness is parasitical and opaque, life forms are proximate and mutable. Who speaks when I speak? Who am I possessed by? What (or who) is it to be inspired or to dream, to be religious, filled with the spirit? To be prophet or sovereign, author/authored? Derrida asks this question of the writer's work and its language: "but who exactly possesses it? And whom does it possess?"[29] King Nebuchadnezzar's dreams and King Belshazzar's writing on the wall carry meanings held by Daniel, an Other, an outsider, ultimately to be preserved *by* this other in his own textual inscription as a biblical creature. It is perhaps as Judith Butler argues about politics and religious multiplicity: "We are, to be sure, already in the hands of the other before we make any decision about with whom we choose to live."[30] Bound to the stranger before choice or contract. She argues that "concrete political norms and ethical prescriptions emerge from the unchosen character of these modes of cohabitation."[31] This is perhaps what we glean in Daniel as a story of Jewish exile. Its norms and prescriptions arise from the proximity to animal life as that which is frequently and systematically enchained, tamed, caged, killed, sacrificed or eaten, but which is at the same time empowered and enlightened by a non-human power that is uncontrollable, unpredictable, impossible, divine.

---

[28] Sloterdijk, 'Rules for the Human Zoo: a response to the *Letter on Humanism*', p. 15.

[29] Jacques Derrida, 'Monolingualism of the Other', in *Monolingualism of the Other, Or, the Prosthesis of Origin*, (Stanford, California, Stanford University Press, 1998) p. 17.

[30] Judith Butler, 'Is Judaism Zionism?', in *The Power of Religion in the Public Sphere: Judith Butler, Jürgen Habermas, Charles Taylor, Cornel West*. p. 88.

[31] Judith Butler, 'Is Judaism Zionism?' p. 84.

The bilingualism of Daniel, split between Hebrew and Aramaic,[32] is not only structural, it is arguably also thematic. The text is as if torn and stuck back together, like an archaeological artefact, a pottery relic, an archival treasure, a textual mutation: a creature with two tongues, the text itself resembling Daniel's mutant dream-creatures. It thematizes assemblage, corporeal parts collected and archived, with Daniel as the Jewish exile drawn into the Babylonian king's court and domesticated through his new education, language and name (1:4–7). Experimenting with characterisations that play out rifts of difference and surprising sameness—*being* divine-like and animal-like—the text (anachronistically) echoes Agamben's view that life is what "gets articulated and divided time and again through a series of caesura and oppositions that invest it with a decisive strategic function".[33] Everything happens, Agamben writes, "as if, in our culture, life were *what cannot be defined, yet, precisely for this reason, must be ceaselessly articulated and divided.*"[34] With the biblical corpus in hand, we encounter Daniel—the Jew, the near-martyr, the interpreter, the divinely inspired, the vegetarian, the visionary—up against the figure of Sovereignty—as usurper, invader, pagan, prideful, greedy, violent, all-powerful 'beast' or psychotic.[35] Hubris and humility circumscribe a spectrum of *being* that is never sovereignly human. The text of Daniel plays out the likeness between life forms under subjection to power, as tamed, domesticated and incarcerated bodies, like Daniel's dwelling with the lions in their pit in chapter 6. Daniel is seen to be kneeling in prayer—un-erect like an animal—an act that is both a submission to the divine sovereign rather than the human king and an act of resistance, breaking the law.[36] We might then confront the possibility both that political man is indeed

---

[32] With sections 1:1–2:4a, 8:1–12:13 in Hebrew, and 2:4b-7:28 in Aramaic.

[33] Giorgio Agamben, *The Open: Man and Animal* (Trans. Kevin Attell, Stanford California: Stanford University Press, 2004 [2002]) p. 13.

[34] Agamben, *The Open*, p. 13.

[35] Foreign sovereign rulers are equated to mutant beasts, as depicted in the visions in chapter 7, symbolizing kings and kingdoms to come. Sovereign hubris as psychosis is aptly summed up in the pun on second-century ruler Antiochus IV Epiphanes, who called himself '*God made manifest*', and whose "peculiar behaviour led some of his contemporaries to refer to him instead as Antiochus Epimanes, '*mad man.*' (Martha Himmelfarb, *The Apocalypse, A Brief History* (Chichester, Wiley-Blackwell, 2012. p. 34).

[36] Louis F. Hartman and Alexander A. Di Lella, 'Daniel', in *The New Jerome Biblical Commentary* (Eds. Raymond E. Brown, S. S. Joseph A. Fitzmeyer, S. J. Roland E. Murphy, O. Carm. New Jersey, Prentice Hall, 1968) p. 415. Hartman and Di Lella explain that although "the Jews ordinarily stood at public prayer, in the postexilic period they began the custom of kneeling during private prayer" (1 Chr 6:13; Ezra 9:5; Luke 22:41; Acts 9:40, 20:36) (p. 415).

animal and "that the animal is already political":[37] politics is inextricably tied up in notions of strategic subjection and violence as human-bestial, societal structures and assimilation as taming, restraining and domesticating motions. Daniel is the figure of the domesticated, tamed subject under human-sovereign rule, who nonetheless simultaneously and tantalizingly occupies a space outside the law as a religious animal. But embodiments of divinity and animality are both internally split, opening up for the possibility of mismatching: of dying for a false god, or shackling oneself to a tree, hair "growing long as eagles feathers, nails like birds' claws" (4:33) as psychosis rather than redemption. Aaron Hebbard writes: "Identity in Daniel is ultimately displayed by the functionary role of interpretation."[38] It is a matter of performance, embodiment and recognition—epistemological uncertainty requires an interpretive corollary. Daniel demands this critical interpretive stance, and in the end denies fixed formulas. The answers are not archived, not to be found in the back of this book we call 'Bible'. If continuous interpretative exploration or repeated re-readings are thus an inherent part of the promise of the archive (and archive-activity) we might indeed want to leave behind the fixity of the human-centric gaze as a method of taxonomizing and capturing meaning, as well as the carnivorous structures of power as a hunting-down, and adopt instead a Danielic animal stance of humility and curiosity in our explorations.

The setting of Daniel, life in Babylonia during the reign of the last kings of the Neo-Babylonian Empire and their first successors, the early kings of Medes and the Persians during most of the sixth century BCE,[39] has figured as a puzzle for biblical scholars, although consensus on its composition date has been reached for probably shortly before the death of Antiochus IV Epiphanes in 164 BCE. So despite being written as if at the given time of its setting, evidence points to a period long after the Babylonian exile, rather written in the Hellenistic Age.[40] Calling Daniel "fanciful, unhistorical, and unreal,"[41] one canonical commentary debunks its prophetic truth-content in one fell swoop, pointing out that its falsity

---

[37] Jacques Derrida, *The Beast and the Sovereign Volume I*, (Trans. G. Bennington, Chicago/London: University of Chicago Press, 2009,) p. 35.

[38] Aaron B. Hebbard, *Reading Daniel as a Text in Theological Hermeneutics* (Eugene, Oregon, Pickwick Publications, 2009) p. 14.

[39] Louis F. Hartman, Alexander A. Di Lella, *The New Jerome Biblical Commentary*, (New Jersey: Prentice Hall, 1968) p. 406.

[40] Hartman, Di Lella, *The New Jerome Biblical Commentary*, p. 408.

[41] Charles F. Pfeiffer, Everett F. Harrison (Eds.) *The Wycliffe Bible Commentary* (London/Edinburgh: Oliphants, 1963) p. 770.

was contended as early as 233–304 CE by the Neo-Platonist philosopher Porphyry.[42] Porphyry denied that the book was written as claimed and asserted that it was written in Palestine by a Jew living in the time of Antiochus.[43] Caught out, our writer-figure and protagonist-'prophet' Daniel, is re-labelled and slotted into a different archival space as fiction or forgery.

The political landscape of Daniel's author is elastically extended backward to gather in its grasp a previous time of similar oppression, historicizing the present by introducing the past into its remit and showing how the present might be assembled as a repeat-performance, a political pattern.[44] The text's thematic interest in conversions, metamorphoses and hybrid creatures spills into its structural properties, experimenting with the idea of categorical classifications, causing borders to tremble. Structurally, then, folding sixth century Jewish history into a second century setting reinforces the imagery of assemblage-animal figures of the future political orders in the latter part of Daniel (ch. 7:3–9, 19; 8:4–15); these are hybrid creatures just as 'history' and the 'contemporary' are hybrid, made up of each other and assembled conceptually, textually, and crucially, politically. Similarly, the presence of Hebrew *and* Aramaic in the text reinforces this sense of assortment, amalgam, fragmented fusion and awkward synthesis, a tongue-tied double-speak or lingering bilingualism that splits the textual identity. It is perhaps as Derrida testifies: "I have only one language and it is not mine; my 'own' language is, for me, a language that cannot be assimilated. My language, the only one I hear myself speak and agree to speak, is the language of the other."[45] Daniel too must learn and speak the language of the other as a Jew in non-Jewish context.

---

[42] John J. Collins sums up the issue for scholarship on Daniel in the following way: "The problem with any attempt to reconstruct the social setting is that the book of Daniel is pseudepigraphic, and so the explicit setting in the Babylonian exile is known to be fictional. Scholars then have to infer information about the actual settings in which it was composed, from literature that attempts to hide those very settings." (*The Book of Daniel, Reception and Composition*, Eds. John J. Collins and Peter W. Flint, Volume I. Leiden/Boston/Köln: Brill, 200) p. 9.

[43] Charles F. Pfeiffer, Everett F. Harrison (Eds.) *The Wycliffe Bible Commentary*, p. 769.

[44] Daniel L. Smith-Christopher argues persuasively for the organic nature of this doubling motion of past and present, that folds these (hi)stories into each other. 'Prayers and Dreams: Power and Diaspora Identities in the Social Setting of the Daniel Tales', in *The Book of Daniel, Composition and Reception*. Eds. John J. Collins and Peter W. Flint, Volume 1. (Leiden/Boston/Koln: Brill, 2001) p. 280.

[45] Jacques Derrida, 'Monolingualism of the Other', in *Monolingualism of the Other, Or, the Prosthesis of Origin*, (Stanford, California, Stanford University Press, 1998) p. 25.

Daniel's play at being scripture, pseudoepigraphically *embodying* and trying on the 'biblical', (the prophetic, the legendary, literary) conveys the mortal desire to auto-archive, situating one's body within a larger corpus. This archive desire is Daniel's version of sovereign power. The sovereign human in Daniel is calcified in the recurrent greeting to the king figured to "live forever" (Dan, 2:4, 3:9, 6:7), an effort to ensure preservation beyond mortality. But while this is an effort to divinize human power, Daniel's auto-archiving writing *as scripture*, as prophecy, is an immortalising gesture that remains anonymous, humbly incorporating secrecy and incomprehension into its corpus and pointing to a *non-human* presence.[46] And so Daniel is always already divisible, slippery and untameable.[47]

Ecological thought, Timothy Morton writes, is a "humiliating descent", arguably something akin to King Nebuchadnezzar's descent from sovereign ruler to shackled animal. Morton writes that ecology "is the latest in a series of great humiliations of the human, humiliations that might even constitute the human as such".[48] Like Bowen's haunting sense of writing, there is a touch of morbidity in the eco-prophetic proclamation in our collective future doom.[49] We are tied to the natural world in a way that resists detachment or disinterest. We are strapped to it like a patient awaiting diagnosis and fearing death. The end of the world is proclaimed by eco-warriors and evangelical environmentalists; these are purportedly today's 'prophets'. Like Ecclesiastes they proclaim the world to be full of vanity, but refuse the supplementary lament that generations come and generations go "but the earth remains for ever" (Ecc. 1:4). Generations do indeed come and go and the more they do the more they appear to spoil the riches of the world, leaving havoc and destruction in their wake: the earth might not remain for ever. There might be little, or nothing, "new under the sun", we might merely be "chasing wind", but we ought at least to try to save the wind and sun, if nothing else (Ecc. 1:9, 14). Archives become in this apocalyptic scene the emblem of inaction, passivity, past and stagnation,

---

[46] As Hugh Pyper notes, Daniel is a "constant reminder of communication in abeyance". 'Reading in the Dark: Zechariah, Daniel and the Difficulty of Scripture', p. 500.

[47] The text is arguably taxonomically tantalizing, in its refusal to *be* one thing or another. P. R. Davies calls Daniel a 'curious' book, as if examining a textual body that is two-headed, bilingual, and perhaps even authorially schizophrenic. *Daniel* (JSOT Press, Sheffield, 1985) p. 11.

[48] Timothy Morton, 'Thinking Ecology: The Mesh, the Strange Stranger and the Beautiful Soul', *Collapse* 6 (2010: 265–293), p. 265.

[49] For a rigorous examination of the implications of ecological thought, see Luc Ferry's *The New Ecological Order* (trans. Carol Volk, Chicago/London, The University of Chicago Press, 1995 [1992]).

the very opposite of a progressive posthumanism that seeks redemption for the planet if not for its people (it is perhaps already too late for us).

But contrary to the concept of the archive as stasis, Paul Strohm argues, "the archive does not arrest time, but rather exists as an unstable amalgam of unexhausted past and unaccomplished future."[50] It is open toward the future, a repository of meanings that awaits discovery. As Virginia Burrus argues, it is interpretive activity that determines the status of text and of writing, of the 'thing' it 'is'; "Scripture does not preexist its interpretation but emerges as an effect of interpretation."[51]

### The Dark Animal-Divine Unconscious

The biblical character Daniel is sealed in secret words and meanings of a future history he confesses to not understand, (12:8–10) the "dark and enigmatic sayings" that are according to Edward J. Young the very nature of prophecy.[52] The words he hears are to "remain secret and sealed till the end of time" (12:9), and Daniel will be the "keeper" of this secret (12:4). How to keep a secret as prophet and protagonist? How does one preserve secrets, archive them, without spilling their substance? Apocryphal literature was originally thought of as "hidden or secret writings destined to be read only by those initiated into a given (Christian) sect, but it came to designate books similar (in content, form, or title) to scriptural books but not accepted into the canon."[53] Secrets in other words are somewhat suspect; the archive ought to be public, transparent and accessible. But this is perhaps the very tension of the archive, because in another sense it is precisely inside-information, private documents, esoteric knowledge, specialised, singular and secret papers that become the stuff of archives, namely that which is stowed away, placed and preserved within the realms of the institutional and the academic, so-called supplements to the origin, the real.

---

[50] Paul Strohm, *Theory and the Premodern Text*, (Minneapolis: University of Minnesota Press, 2000) p. 80.

[51] Virginia Burrus, 'Creatio Ex Libidine', *Derrida and Religion: Other Testaments*, (Eds. Yvonne Sherwood and Kevin Hart, New York/London: Routledge, 2005) p. 144.

[52] Edward J. Young, *The Prophecy of Daniel, A Commentary*, (Michigan/Grand Rapids: WM. B. Eerdmans Publishing Co. 1949) p. 21.

[53] Raymond E. Brown and Raymond F. Collins, 'Canonicity', *The New Jerome Biblical Commentary*, p. 1036.

In Daniel, dreams and visions are publically interpreted, meticulously recorded and highly politicised; they are the very content of the archive, and yet are perhaps what is most unarchivable. They perform their own slippage, signalling what is most elusive, unruly and detached from the daily, the routine and the systematic. Could dreams be filed in an archive, as history, or indeed, political prophecy? Are they archivable material? Can they be textual without remainder, without slipping away from the pen or keyboard, just as we try to pin them down, evaporating into a memory bank we cannot access? For Daniel, his insight abides in his understanding the dreams of another—his foreign superior, King Nebuchadnezzar. It is the role of the psychoanalyst gone a step further, to uncanny knowability. Of course Daniel is quick to assert it is *not him* who knows, but God (2:28); Daniel's humility places divinity at the centre of his interpretive insight, making of his human mind a slate upon which divine power inscribes impossible, mind-reading, supernatural knowledge. When he embodies this state he is no longer Daniel, or human, but Divine, or divine-like, replacing his humanity with humility *and* simultaneously evoking the intimate presence of divinity as proximate and possessive. This humility takes the shape of animality in Daniel, as King Nebuchadnezzar experiences in his brief conversion and metamorphosis to shackled animal.

Derrida discusses Freud's legacy on dreams and the archivable. He reflects over the ways private turns to public when Freud's private home is turned into a museum, and in which Freud's private correspondence is merged into the psychoanalytic corpus. "What is this new science of which the institutional and theoretical archive ought by rights to comprise the most private documents, sometimes secret?" he asks, beginning "with those of its presumed founder, its arch-father, its patriarch Freud?"[54] One might ask a similar question regarding what happens to the biblical archive when it is turned, and keeps turning, from numerous, variant and varying scrolls, to public Scripture—from secret vision, revelation and archived reverie to public property, published and canonised Book in the singular. J. Paterson Smyth aims to elucidate the story of the "making of the Bible simply and frankly" in the light of modern scholarship and the "disturbance" it has caused in threatening the perception of the Bible as "divinely inspired".[55] Smyth asserts there is nothing theologically "disquieting"

---

54  Derrida, *Archive Fever. A Freudian Impression*, p. 20.
55  J. Paterson Smyth, *The Bible in the Making, In the Light of Modern Research*, (Harper and Brothers, London/New York, 1914) p. 10.

about the methods of construction and composition of the biblical corpus. Rather, he argues that once understood properly, the Bible should appear "a more living throbbing human presentation of God."[56] But this image of a 'throbbing' book and more 'human' God is perhaps more disquieting than any break-through revelation in modern scholarship concerning origins, dates and extra-biblical material. Smyth writes:

> Old classic legends tell of the young sculptor who carved his statue of surpassing beauty and then, as he gazed at it on its pedestal, fell in love with the work of his own hands. He prayed to the Gods to give life to his creation and lo! As he prayed came stirring breath and colour, and at length it came down into his arms, a living throbbing woman to be his joy and companion and comfort in his daily life. If the fuller light which has fallen on the story of the Bible should tend in any degree to bring it down from the conventional pedestal on which verbal inspiration and such like theories have placed it, may it not be to bring it closer to our hearts, and make us feel more truly behind it the real, living, throbbing spirit of God who inspired it? [57]

This recurrent image of the 'throbbing' bible, as a breathless, sexual companion to be embraced and carried off into the sunrise merely re-enforces the alarming images of sexual repression, or what we sometimes call animal instinct, lurking in the pages of the biblical body. Removing the biblical corpus from its dusty grave opens a new chasm of secrecy: the unconscious, the murky waters of the human mind. In the biblical archive, then, the repressed leaps up as the question of human/divine mutation, its composition and inspiration potentially sullied by the unconscious. The unconscious figures in some ways as the animal 'inside' the human, necessarily tied down, captured, shackled, to avoid its instinctual presence seeping into the writing or interpretation of biblical texts. This can also be equated to unruly, incalculable divine inspiration as another emptying of 'human-ness'.[58] The Freudian signature stamps itself thus firmly onto the biblical corpus, scarring the scrolls with potent, secretive extra-material traces. But perhaps there were always already unknown, unidentified animals lurking inside these textual vaults.

---

[56] Ibid., p. 10.

[57] Ibid., p. 10.

[58] P. R. Davies discusses this in relation to Daniel, explaining that with the crisis of biblical authority in nineteenth-century England, associated with Darwin's *On the Origin of Species*, Daniel was at the forefront of this issue. Daniel was held up as the textual divide: either divinely inspired *or* damningly fraudulent. (*Daniel*, Sheffield: JSOT Press, 1985, p. 17).

*Anachronistic Dream Interpretations*

King Nebuchadnezzar's dreamscapes 'contain' what we might characterise as two major symbols for contemporary crisis. In the first of the dreams there is a great tree at the centre of the earth with beautiful foliage, its abundant fruit providing food for all: "The animals of the field found shade under it, the birds of the air nested in its branches, and from it all living beings were fed." (Dan. 4:12) This eco-fantasy quickly morphs into a scene of destruction, with cutting, chopping, stripping, scattering movements, leaving only a stump with roots. In King Nebuchadnezzar's second dream, we stand before a huge statue, both brilliant and frightening, of gold, silver, bronze, iron and clay (Dan. 2:31–36). The great statue is struck by a stone, breaking apart, its pieces dissolving in the wind. The first dream could be read as a vision of fantasy-turned-apocalypse proclaimed by many contemporary eco-prophets as the future of humanity on earth, the second, for human technological and material constructions, akin to the Tower of Babel narrative in which the desire to build manmade structures that reach to heaven symbolise both the exuberant ambition as well as the more overblown hubris of the human ego, echoed in the skyscrapers of modern civilisation, and exemplified most gruesomely in the imagery of the twin towers of 9/11.

Both the image of the tree of life reduced to a sad old stump, and the symbol of a towering man-made structure destroyed, shattered and scattered by the wind, loom hauntingly in contemporary debates, minds and media. They are powerful reminders of the vulnerability of human life, and the uncontrollable powers 'out there' (force of nature and force of human violence). It is about *being* what we perceive of as more or less 'human'/'humane', more or less civilized, rationalized, or natural/supernatural: edible, killable, irrational, instinctual, sanctified or sinful. We face a crisis as to how to *preserve* our natural resources, how to archive animal species in a way that ensures future life, how to read scriptural archives in ways that eschew fanaticism and violence, how to repress or restrain the human as violent beast and how in turn to protect animals from the violence of humans; industrial, systematic, private, consumerist and sacrificial. It is both a question as to *how to read* and how to *inhabit* the world by means of protection, preservation and sustainable cohabitation. It is a desire to conserve what (and whom) we love, just as the desire for preservation of knowledge is perhaps at heart, as Derrida argues, "a compulsive, repetitive, and nostalgic desire for the archive, an irrepressible desire to return to the origin, a homesickness, a nostalgia for the return to the most archaic place of absolute commencement."[59]

Both the themes of 'animal' and 'archive' are associated with questions of enclosure, in fields, pens, factory farms, cages, paddocks, or canons, books, vaults, libraries, cellars. Arguably a sense of morbidity, mourning and claustrophobia haunts this posthumanist era of conceptualising the 'human' and its place in the world. We might want to think about dropping the mournful 'post' altogether, as well as 'humanism', allying ourselves simultaneously with Derrida's stance on the inanity of the term 'animal' to encompass such a richly diverse set of species and thus perhaps a new conception of the subject, or of being altogether in the wake of humancentric dominance.[60] But what then are we left with? Wordless silence? The end? As Derrida points out, our position is perhaps inevitable; "every reading is not only anachronistic, but consists in bringing out anachrony, non-self-contemporaneity, dislocation in the taking-place of the text."[61] Recognising this dislocation and non-self-contemporaneity is perhaps the first tentative step towards entering the archive as alive and enlivening, as futuristic and always already unfolding.

### Flexibility of Life: Anti-Abyssal Likenesses

Perhaps in the same way that dreams and visions in Daniel are that which cannot be wholly contained within writing, the animal too is that which is irrepressible, unruly, shifting. Like a badly kept secret, it spills over in its vastness, diversity and complexity as that which has escaped the archive.[62] Daniel presents the anti-abyssal, radical *proximity* between human/animal/divine and the politics of this proximity. On one hand, Daniel is god-like, filled with the spirit, a human-divine visionary and interpreter extraordinaire for the human sovereign (with the "spirit of the gods" in

---

[59] Derrida, *Archive Fever, A Freudian Impression*, p. 91.

[60] See Derrida's 'The Animal That Therefore I am' in *The Animal That Therefore I am*. (Ed. Marie-Louise Mallet. Trans. David Wills. New York: Fordham University Press, 2008).

[61] Jacques Derrida, *The Beast and the Sovereign, Volume II*, (trans. Geoffrey Bennington, Chicago/London: University of Chicago Press, 2011) p. 87.

[62] Cary Wolfe notes that "the pressing relevance of the question of the animal has been generated in contemporary culture more outside the humanities than within." (p. x) He argues that the humanities are "now struggling to catch up with a radical revaluation of the status of nonhuman animals." (p. xi) Cary Wolfe, ed., *Zoontologies: The Question of the Animal* (Minneapolis/London: University of Minnesota Press, 2003).

him and "wisdom like the wisdom of the gods", Dan 4:8, 5:14, 5:11). On the other, he embodies the humility that King Nebuchadnezzar has to learn by becoming-animal, as if Daniel himself is already reconciled to his animality. Proximity in Daniel is a presence of divine, human, animal in a shared world, what Timothy Morton would call a "mesh", recognising an interdependence of life forms that is "like being caught in your own shadow".[63] Daniel's refusal to eat the royal food in the King's court (1:8) is mirrored by the lions abstaining from devouring Daniel later in the narrative (ch. 6). In his subjection to foreign kingship, Daniel's subjecthood is made animal-like, he is made consumable and tameable, just like Hananiah, Azariah and Mishael who are thrown into the fiery furnace to be roasted alive. Such decisions of status and 'killability' are a "question of limits, and knowing whether a limit is divisible or indivisible,"[64] a "trade without contract", "which consists, precisely, in a strange and equivocal economy, a strange and equivocal ecology that consists in expropriating the other, appropriating the other by depriving the other of what is supposed to be proper to him or her, the other's proper place, proper habitat, oikos."[65] Being is inextricably caught up in relations of power. Daniel inverts this power-dynamic by implicitly asserting that under God all are mortal and none have *reason* for hubris; sovereign becomes animal, the minority Jew becomes politically powerful, the lions become saviours. Daniel plays out textual and bodily assemblages as created and composite. All bodies—animate/inanimate—are composed and decomposable, edible and inedible. Not only animals are edible, and not all prophecies become biblical or sacred. Daniel conveys how being "able to suffer is no longer a power; it is a possibility without power."[66] Derrida writes that morality "resides there, as the most radical means of thinking the finitude that we share with animals, the mortality that belongs to the very finitude of life, to the experience of compassion, to the possibility of sharing the possibility of this nonpower, the possibility of this impossibility, the anguish of this vulnerability, and the vulnerability of this anguish."[67]

---

[63] Morton, 'Thinking Ecology: The Mesh, the Strange Stranger and the Beautiful Soul', pp. 292, 293.

[64] Derrida, *The Beast and the Sovereign, Volume 1*, p. 298.

[65] Ibid., p. 299.

[66] Jacques Derrida, *The Animal That Therefore I Am*, (Ed. Marie-Louise Mallet; Trans. David Wills. New York: Fordham University Press, 2008) p. 28.

[67] Ibid.

## (Im)Possible Conclusive Remarks

Peter Sloterdijk writes that up until the dawn of modern nation-states the power to read was reserved for a secret elite.[68] "The person who could read would be thought easily capable of other impossibilities."[69] If the reader is thought capable of impossibilities, the writer is perhaps the powerful prophet-figure of making-possible the impossible, of conjuring up possessions and opening possibilities as well as stratifying or straitjacketing the possible. One might be accused of "distorting" things, of setting "traps" and of saying "unspeakable" things,[70] reminding us of Derrida's characterisation of literature as the institution "which in principle allows one to say everything."[71] The institutional element—archivisation or canonisation—might indeed feel somewhat akin to mummification, but the promise that lurks in such archival structures lies in the impossibility of taming its own material as whole and indivisible, making room for inevitable ruptures in reading that reveal what is beyond current comprehension, taxonomy and ontological understanding. Neither human bodies nor textual bodies are wholly self-contained, or fully under our own control. In other words, our readings are perhaps always impossible and uncanny: animal and divine, potentially monstrous, politicized and powerful. Like Daniel's textual mutation of past, present and future, our interpretations break into pasts and futures, criminally perhaps, anachronistically, perhaps prophetically, glimpsing more than is possible, always affirming that we are both more and less than we think.

Paul Strohm argues that even "when we try to stop time, to freeze a moment for synchronous investigation as a part of a literary cross-section, that moment nevertheless turns out to bear within itself intimations of past and future that amount to a form of implicit diachrony."[72] According to Strohm this is "an unruly diachrony, referring in the most surprising and unpredictable ways to what has been and what is not yet, to the residual and the emergent."[73] Our archive Bible-zoo is not static, stable

---

[68] Sloterdijk, 'Rules for the Human Zoo: a response to the *Letter on Humanism*', p. 13.

[69] Ibid.

[70] Elizabeth Bowen, *The Death of the Heart*, p. 250, 282. André Lacocque describes the 'message' of Daniel as "presented in a form full of traps and snares for the reader" (*The Book of Daniel*. trans. David Pellauer. London: SPCK, 1979) p. 1.

[71] Jacques Derrida, '"This Strange Institution Called Literature": An Interview with Jacques Derrida', *Acts of Literature*, (Ed. Derek Attridge. London: Routledge, 1992) p. 36.

[72] Strohm, *Theory and the Premodern Text*, p. 93.

[73] Ibid.

and strapped in, but potently preserving texts for scenes of reading that themselves unleash, make-possible and open up in ways that are anything but passive, dead or mummified. The "unknowable weight" of the concept archive, Derrida writes, is ultimately about everything "that ties knowledge and memory to the promise."[74] This promise is perhaps fulfilled in a future always still to come, that is in the end (and has always been) partly ancient, partly vision or dream. Our archived past is always still to come; still awaiting what it will have been and what it will come to be.

---

[74] Derrida, *Archive Fever, A Freudian Impression*, p. 30.

# EXODUS AND LITURGY: A PROPOSAL TO READ EXODUS AS A LECTION FOR THE SACRED YEAR IN POST-EXILIC JUDEA

Alastair Hunter

## On Methodology

The genesis of this essay lies in an instinct, based on years of teaching of the Book of the Covenant (Ex. 19–24), that Exodus has a liturgical purpose in its final[1] form that is more important than its usefulness as a source of history or tradition. Such a claim neatly side steps the need for valorisation of its supposed history; for just as the liturgies of Easter, the Eucharist, and the birth of Jesus in Christianity have long since floated free of their prosaic origins in time and place, so do the festivals of Israel continue undisturbed by scholarly debates about the number of Israelites who may or may not have travelled from Egypt via Sinai under the leadership of Moses.

A second prompt comes from the work of Michael Goulder who produced a series of studies of the Psalms in which he defended their liturgical importance—albeit arguing for an antiquity and historicity which I would be reluctant to endorse—and a study of Matthew as a liturgical midrash.[2] Goulder's work was always provocative and to some extent marginalised, though his early endorsement of the questionable nature of Q and his arguments against it have surely been vindicated.[3] He was one

---

[1] I will have more to say later in the article on the subject of the final form; for now, it will suffice to make the naïve assumption that the final form of Exodus is more or less the unvocalised Hebrew version implied by the traditional Tanakh text found in BHS and other scholarly editions.

[2] Michael D. Goulder, *Midrash and Lection in Matthew* (London: SPCK, 1974); *The Psalms of the Sons of Korah* (Sheffield: JSOT Press, 1982); *The Prayers of David* (Sheffield: JSOT Press, 1990); *The Psalms of Asaph* (Sheffield: Sheffield Academic Press, 1996); *The Psalms of the Return* (Sheffield: Sheffield Academic Press, 1998).

[3] An opinion which might seem hubristic coming from an Old Testament scholar—but if ever there were a clear candidate for Occam's razor, it is the burgeoning foliage of Q and its myriad outgrowths, including that ultimate exercise of the imagination, the critical edition of Q. James McConkey Robinson, Paul Hoffmann and John S. Kloppenborg (eds.), *The Critical Edition of Q: Synopsis Including the Gospels of Matthew and Luke, Mark and Thomas with English, German, and French Translations of Q & Historical Commentary on the Bible* (Hermeneia Supplements. Minneapolis: Fortress Press, 2000). See also Goulder's own summing up, at the end of his life, of the Q controversy and his work on Psalms and Lection in his autobiographical *Five Stones and a Sling* (Sheffield: Phoenix Press, 2009), 134–6.

of the few Biblical scholars of modern times who was equally at home in both 'testaments', and was closely involved in the (notorious?) *Myth of God Incarnate* volume, edited by John Hick, which was (in Goulder's words) a 'succès de scandale' in 1977.[4] Michael was always very supportive of younger scholars, something from which I myself benefited; it is a pleasure therefore to acknowledge him, albeit posthumously, as an inspiration for this latter-day imitation.

Behind this tentative thesis lies a question, one which perhaps should be put more often than it is: 'What is this book/text[5] for?' Particularly in the era of publish or be damned—be that the damnation of failure of tenure, or of REF disgrace—we ought to be more persistent in raising the awkward issue of purpose (fit for, or not). While much of the academic work of the post-WWII era is no doubt best suited to landfill, or recycling as more useful forms of paper, the question 'why?' remains as an intriguing and tantalising interrogation of what lies before us in the form of a text within the Old Testament/Tanakh. It is intriguing because, as empathetic human beings, we can hardly avoid the wish to enter into the mind and experience of those whom we meet only in the shape of the text. It is tantalising because this desire is, of course, another form of the 'intention' question which has been so despised by postmodernism. Its persistence is testimony to human curiosity, and the natural belief that what someone once intended to convey in words merits consideration— not least because to deny this is seemingly to render all our speech vain: a fate worse than death to academics above all, who fancy themselves masters and mistresses of the noble arts of reading, interpreting, and communicating. Thus finding out 'why' remains an elusive but alluring object, something we believe in despite ourselves—a kind of literary holy grail the quest for which is the ultimate challenge of the knights of the Biblical Round Table.

There are many, of course, who need little persuading of the validity of the Quest. A significant range of biblical scholarship continues, and

---

[4] And a considerable financial success for its publisher, SCM Press, selling 40,000 copies! (*Five Stones*, 79).

[5] In the light of Derrida and his followers it is impossible to write the word 'text' without its attendant trail of qualifiers and disclaimers. Undoubtedly the 'Exodus' most of us are likely to encounter is a pretty traditional *text* made up of words, punctuation marks, and diacriticals impressed in ink on paper (or their simulacra on a screen). I am content, nevertheless, for readers to adopt as wide an understanding of 'text' as they wish, even if this expression might be thought to be an improper attempt by the author to defy his (*sic*) death.

has always continued, to work its methodological wonders of tracing Ur-texts and original intentions with sublime indifference to the suspicions of the Saussureans and the dithering of Derrideans (with both of which I align myself). I am not persuaded by reconstructions of 'original' texts of biblical books, and sceptical even that there *were* in some cases 'originals' susceptible of reconstruction. But I am compelled to confess a heresy in the form of a lingering attachment to some form of 'authorial intention', though not in that strong form which has traditionally identified *the intention of the author* as *the* meaning of the text. I remain sceptical about the chances of recovering the mind of the author, and open to the rich variety of reading which is the best legacy of the 'theory' movement of the late twentieth century; but something in me clings stubbornly to the idea of *purpose*, a word which I think encapsulates something less prescriptive than intention, but more graspable than the shifting sands of deconstruction. And it is that concept of 'purpose' which I want to apply in this essay to the book of Exodus.

It might be helpful first to define my chosen term more exactly, since at first sight it may seem to be a simple synonym for 'intention'. No doubt some of the ways in which the word functions are tied to the idea of an individual having a purpose (or intention); where they differ is in the possibility that a non-animate system can be said to have a purpose, but not an intention; consider for example the phrase 'purpose-built' which is regularly applied to machines and structures. Purpose also implies a use of some kind which has at least a degree of independence from the designer/ originator, whereas intention belongs more to the realm of ideas and meanings and arguably evaporates when the 'intender' can no longer be identified or interrogated. Attempts to resolve the latter conundrum have been made using the device of various forms of real or supposed 'reader'[6] (original, implied or ideal, narratee, or actual, to itemise just a few), in the hope that intention can be recovered in tandem with an analysis of the supposed reader.[7] Not surprisingly this can lead to deeply circular

---

[6] For more on readers, see Wolfgang Iser (*The Implied Reader*, 1972, and *The Act of Reading*, 1976) and his followers in New Testament Studies—e.g. Alan Culpepper (*Anatomy of the Fourth* Gospel, 1983); John Darr (*On Character-Building: The Reader and the Rhetoric of Characterization in Luke-Acts*, 1992); Robert M. Fowler (*Let the Reader Understand: Reader-response Criticism and the Gospel of Mark*, 1991); and W. Carter & J. P. Heil (*Matthew's Parables. Audience-Oriented Perspectives*, 1998).

[7] The discussion thus far relates to written materials. In an oral context we might also want to suppose 'listeners' or 'an audience' and where there is a strong presumption in favour of an oral tradition and/or oral performance this might be pertinent. However,

argumentation, with assumptions about intention serving to define intended readers who, once defined, are used to clarify intention. Thus the project of reading with the 'reader' becomes both fraught and complex, raising new problems even as it elucidates existing ones.

My advocacy of *purpose* as a potential technical term is intended to sidestep the difficulties of intentionality without entirely emptying the bath. I propose the following defining characteristics:

1  Purpose, while part of the design of the text in question, is separable from authorial intention.
2  Purpose has more to do with functionality than ideology, ethics, theology or philosophy.
3  There are likely to be objective features of the text which can be aligned with its purpose, and which do not require mind-reading.
4  From the perspective of purpose, readers are less interactively involved. The text is there to be used—for example, as instruction manuals (much of Mishnah or the biblical accounts of Passover), as set items of worship (the Aaronic blessing, many of the Psalms), or as lists for information (thus the forbidden and permitted creatures in Leviticus)—rather than to be engaged with. My proposal to read Exodus as a lection belongs to this category.
5  Even where purpose is present in oral presentation, the relative passivity of the audience is assumed.
6  Purpose may be implicit, especially in pre-modern texts where labels which define the work generically are very rare. We cannot, in short, avoid entirely the guessing game which is so damaging to intention.

With this tentative definition in place, let me turn now to my proposal regarding the purpose of the book of Exodus.

---

unless these oral hearers are in a position to affect the continuing tradition, their relevance to interpretation is hard to evaluate. The arguments I will propose in relation to Exodus are not strictly speaking that of oral performance, since I shall argue for a liturgical use; and liturgical performance does not engage the audience in the same way as, for example, an epic poem: the engagement is much more passive, and less likely to be open to informal emendation.

## On Putting the Question

The importance of asking the right question, arguably attributable to
Socrates through Plato, and revitalised in Collingwood's undervalued
masterpiece, *The Idea of History*,[8] is central to the approach taken in this
essay. I have long been convinced that attempts to find early sources or
historical traditions in Exodus fail because the questions they presuppose
are inappropriate,[9] regardless of the frustrating knowledge that there *were*
sources and histories; and the reason for this failure is that (to put my conclusion ahead of my argument) the purpose of the book does not include
any (modern) historical agenda.

The assumption that there was some purpose to Exodus is, admittedly,
unprovable. What I hope to show is that it nevertheless produces interesting results which in turn suggest that the question is an appropriate one.
What questions are appropriate is certainly difficult to define with any
rigour, though there are some pointers which seem natural. The book is
embedded in the literary traditions of a religious community whose beliefs
and practices—both cultural and cultic—are well attested from the classical Roman period. Thus questions about theology, ethics and liturgical
practice are strongly indicated, on the assumption that the written texts
are *in at least some sense* relevant to these matters and were collected,
preserved, and honoured for that reason. To return to 'purpose', which in
my definition embraces all of these specific concerns, I assume that this
operates at a rather more functional level than these others: that is, it
entails a structuring element evident to its readers/users, which affected
the use of the text, and which leaves objective traces visible to modern
scholarship.[10] It is these traces which provide a control on the (large)

---

[8] The most recent edition is that edited by Jan van Dussen, published by OUP in 1994.

[9] That these questions are *interesting* remains certain, and it is no part of my agenda
to suggest that the cross-examination of books like Exodus to find traces of history or of
the undoubtedly complex process which brought them into being should be abandoned.
The point I am making is that asking these questions will tend to lead to answers which
are not vital to the heart of the book 'as we have it' (I discuss this challenging phrase later,
in considering what the 'final form' of the book might be).

[10] Liturgical or religious practice is of course not the only kind of purpose which can
be identified. Evidently religious texts can have meaning—and literary structure—which
do not relate to religious practice. Thus, for example, Job: a highly structured work whose
purpose (in my sense) seems to relate to the process of questioning and faith within the
community in relation to real ethical and philosophical challenges to belief. See for example my essay, 'Could not the universe have come into existence 200 yards to the left? A

element of subjectivity which is unavoidable; whether I shall entirely escape from circularity into a more productive hermeneutical spiral will be for others to judge.

There are a number of questions I want to put to the book of Exodus, relating to my primary concern to identify, if possible, what might be (one of) its purpose(s). Purpose, of course, assumes a historical context and an individual or group whose agenda is in the driving seat, and so it will be necessary to look briefly at matters of authorship and date. There is, however, an even more pressing question: namely, what do we mean by the book of Exodus? In truth, no-one living has ever seen the object of my investigation, which is quite simply the Hebrew text of what we might anachronistically call 'Exodus' or (slightly less improperly) *Shemot*, inscribed on a scroll stored, I surmise, in the Jerusalem Temple of the 4th century BCE.[11] That text would almost certainly have been similar to that which we now have in Tanakh, though not identical, and would not have had any apparatus of vowel signs. Whether it might have had cantillation marks of some kind is less clear, though I imagine not; there is some agreement that musical directions in ancient times were by hand gestures, and in any case if they existed at all it would most likely be in the Psalms. I further assume that, textual variants aside, the content of the narrative was much as we now have it. In short, I assume a phantom but not improbable scroll text kept in a safe place in the temple as it was shortly after the time of Ezra and Nehemiah.

I turn now to the matter of source and context (or, to put it more traditionally, authorship and date). Over the two hundred years or so of critical study a wide range of candidates have been proposed as having had a hand in the creation of Exodus, including the famous four—J, E, D and P (not necessarily in chronological order). The pre-critical tradition assigned authorship to Moses, and the most recent 'Persian-Hellenistic Period' school looks to groups of theologically and politically motivated persons in 5th or 4th century Jerusalem, or even later. Dozeman's recent commentary[12] sets out the various options, both traditional and recent,

---

thematic study of Job' in *Text as Pretext*, ed. Robert P. Carroll (Sheffield: Sheffield Academic Press, 1992), 40–159.

[11] A dating inspired by the work of Davies and others in the school of thought that attributes most of the materials in Tanakh effectively to the Persian and Hellenistic periods in Judah. The key studies here are P. R. Davies, *In Search of 'Ancient Israel': A Study in Biblical Origins* (JSOTSup 148. Sheffield: JSOT Press, 1992) and *Whose Bible Is It Anyway* (JSOTSup 204. Sheffield: Sheffield Academic Press, 1995).

[12] Thomas B. Dozeman, *Exodus* (Eerdmans Critical Commentary. Grand Rapids, Michigan: Eerdmans, 2009), 31–43, 48–51.

adding for good measure a contribution designated 'the non-P history'; but he clearly concurs with the post-exilic dating for the final edition. The sheer complexity of the form as we now have it, at least from the perspective of any attempt to disentangle sources, is evident, for example, in close reading of the so-called 'Book of the Covenant'. Traces of all four members of the documentary quartet can be found, ironically enough representing D in precisely those passages (19:3–8 and 24:3–8) which give rise to the quintessentially Exodus soubriquet 'Book of the Covenant'. Chapter 19 is a complete nightmare, defying all attempts to distil sources,[13] and the famous scene on the top of Mount Sinai in 24:9–11 could be a very ancient Ugaritic theophany, or a very late proto-apocalyptic vision, depending on whom you consult. Thus Dozeman mentions the Ugaritic parallel, but notes also that Ezekiel uses similar language for the throne of God (1:26; 10:1); he also draws attention to the feast on the mountain in Isa. 25:6–8.[14] Both of these sources are surely post-exilic, and it may not be unimportant that both Ezekiel and Exodus conjure temples which are not yet in existence, and may never have been. The symbolism of the temple as the earthly manifestation of the heavenly dwelling place of God is key to the placing of this vision as the last episode before the retreat of Moses to the mountaintop to receive his detailed briefing from God.

Obviously Exodus has a complex history of development, and we can for the most part only offer hypothetical illustrations of what that might be: oral traditions about Passover, for example, or a core litany of commandments, and legends about origins in Egypt involving a heroic water-ordeal; perhaps also some expert knowledge of the customary legal materials of Mesopotamia. Even the drawing up of this very limited list begs more questions than it answers: who among our putative authors knew the law? Were the Passover materials drawn from some Priestly

---

[13] See Brevard S. Childs, *Exodus* (Old Testament Library. London: SCM Press, 1974), 49. He observes that there are fundamental problems in applying the traditional criteria to the project of identifying sources in Ex 19, and suggests that it is no longer possible to identify with any accuracy what might have constituted earlier sources. John I. Durham, *Exodus* (Word Biblical Commentary, vol. 3. Waco, Texas: Word Books, 1987), 59 agrees. Discussing the compromise of the final form in the context of Chapter 19 he notes: "However disruptive that form may be ... it is in fact the one sequence we know without speculation. Though it is an obvious compilation, it is a compilation based on a coherent theological intention. ... A still further complicating factor is posed by the nature of the narratives themselves: they too are obvious compilations, in some cases so often expanded and contracted that they can no longer be unravelled into the separate strands that made them up. Nowhere in Exodus is this more clearly the case than in the Sinai narrative sequence." For an attempt to disentangle the sources, see Martin Noth, *Exodus* (Old Testament Library. London: SCM Press, 1962), 153–68, *passim*.

[14] *Exodus*, 567f.

stock of instructions? Do the accounts in chapters fourteen and fifteen inspire or presuppose the diverse Exodus-type materials in Nehemiah, Psalms and Jonah?[15] We might try, as others have done, to associate different types of source material with P or D or J as appropriate, but that only pushes the problem a bit further into touch. Was D in Babylon? Did P really serve in the Temple? Are we to imagine J as a kind of mediaeval wandering troubadour entertaining the people round the campfire on auspicious occasions? In general, there is an increasing consensus that D is, at the very earliest, from the period of Josiah;[16] P is of course post-exilic; E is elusive, and has been dismissed by many as a phantom source—certainly Dozeman discounts it in respect of Exodus;[17] and even John Van Seters' thesis is an exilic tradition. At the very least there is a growing agreement that JE (or 'non-P' to use Dozeman's preferred terminology) is closely related to the D traditions.[18] There is little reason, therefore, to look for some pre-exilic Exodus which preserves a structured account of matters historical or liturgical.

The question of context (or date) is of course dependent on (a) the identity of the various authors, and (b) their historical context, if that can at all be determined. It further depends on an assessment of what we might reasonably describe as a 'first edition' of Exodus, by which I mean an identifiable earlier form which constitutes a viable proto-Exodus.[19] There are some books for which this is a plausible exercise: Deuteronomy, for instance, or Job without Elihu, or Genesis before the first eleven chapters were added, or the eighth century book of Isaiah, or the prototype of the Greek version of Jeremiah. It is far from clear, however, what sort of beast an earlier Exodus might be—and this is a clue, I think, to the decision we are driven towards: that it is realistically only the

---

[15] See further my essay 'Jonah from the Whale: Exodus motifs in Jonah 2' in *The Elusive Prophet: The Prophet as a Historical Person, Literary Character & Anonymous Artist*, ed. Johannes C de Moor (Leiden: Brill, 2001), 142–58.

[16] This requires two assumptions: that there some kind of historicity to the legend in 2 Kgs 22–23, and that the 'lost' book which was recovered was indeed a prototype of Deuteronomy.

[17] *Exodus*, 6. Dozeman uses the adjective 'elusive' to describe the supposed author of E.

[18] Dozeman, *Exodus*, 37–41.

[19] It might be argued that the Golden Calf material in Ex. 32–34 represents a separate source. There is a briefer version of it in Dt. 9–10, and there may be a relationship to the account of Jeroboam's inauguration of the rituals of the Northern kingdom in 1 Kgs 12:25–33. But attempts to remove it to produce an earlier version of Exodus leave more questions unanswered: why, for example, is there apparently repeated material about the furnishing of the tabernacle and the priestly vestments within chapters 35–39? On balance, I prefer to remain with the 'final form' approach.

final form that is available for our scrutiny. Exodus is not history, nor, in my estimation, does it preserve even a core of history. In the final account, what happened in Egypt, if anything and the miraculous events surrounding the Exodus and the sojourn in the wilderness are firmly in the territory of legend. What the 5th or 4th century final form of the *book* of Exodus made of them is, however, quite another matter. And it is to that question I now turn: the question, quite simply, what is the purpose of the book of Exodus?

## On Giving a Purpose to Exodus

In the brief account of *purpose* which I provided in the first section I noted specifically the requirement to look for 'objective' features of the text which can be offered in support of a particular purpose.[20] In the present case the clear signs of liturgical purpose[21] provide the prompt for a closer examination of the book to see whether this turns out to be a more important feature of Exodus than has generally been recognised.

The structure of Exodus encourages us to see three grand expositions, two of which are widely accepted as fitting into a clear festival structure, and all of which reveal an imaginative and innovative liturgical and theological mind at work.

## A   (*Ex. 1:1–15:21*): *The Story of Yahweh Who Redeems*

Hebrew has two principal verbs for 'to redeem': גאל (*ga'al*) and פדה (*padah*). While there is semantic overlap between them, there are important differences in practice which are noteworthy:

- A striking absence of their use in parallel. Given the fondness of Hebrew for parallelism it is highly significant that there is only one verse in the entire Psalter (69:19) where these verbs occur together, despite the fact

---

[20] While readers will of course be aware of the relative nature of 'objective' evidence, it is perhaps best to be open on this topic. I do not here argue that what I will put forward is unassailable. My case is simply that the evidence is visible and that it does not need knowledge of intention. Obviously the *interpretation* I then proceed to offer is at a different level of probability.

[21] The highly detailed prescriptions for Pesaḥ, for example, and the inclusion of two specific datings (12:2 and 19:1). See also the ceremonial carried out on the first day of the first month (40:11–33).

that the relevant roots occur respectively eleven and sixteen times. Other pairings occur in Lev. 27:27–29; Isa. 35:9–10; 51:10–11; Jer. 31:11; and Hos. 13:14–a negligible total given the respective overall totals (in round figures) of 100 for *ga'al* and 60 for *padah*.

- A clear semantic distinction at certain points. Thus only *ga'al* is used in the phrase 'the blood avenger'[22] and to refer to the 'next of kin'.[23] By contrast, only *padah* is used for situations where the payment of a ransom is entailed.[24]
- Even where they cover approximately the same meaning, their distribution is almost wholly divergent. Thus both roots are used with reference to God's redemptive activity (though there is, as we shall see, a distinction to be made); but while *ga'al* has a major locus in Isaiah, that of *padah* is Deuteronomy. Both are used in Psalms, but there are, as we have seen, very few overlaps.[25] Also, their use as legal terms (for the redemption of land and people, for example) is also similarly distinct, with *ga'al* largely confined to Leviticus and *padah* found mainly in Exodus and Numbers.

I conclude that the use in Ex. 6:6 and 15:13 of *go'el* for redeemer is significant. Elsewhere in Tanakh it is found predominantly in the postexilic parts of Isaiah,[26] and in a number of Psalms mostly from books three and four.[27] This exilic and post-exilic emphasis coheres nicely with the likely dating of Exodus; in particular the theme of the redeemer in Ps. 74:2; 77:16; 78:35 and 106:10 is closely tied to the legends of Egypt and the wilderness.

The placement of *go'el* is important: once at the point where Moses and Aaron are just about to embark on their 'mission impossible' to Pharaoh ('Say therefore to the Israelites, "I am the Lord, and I will free you from the burdens of the Egyptians and deliver you from slavery to them. I will redeem you with an outstretched arm and with mighty acts of judgement", 6:6), and once at the point of freedom, in the psalm sung by Moses

---

[22] Num. 35:12, 19, 21, 24, 25, 27; Dt. 19:6, 12; Joshua 20:3, 5, 9; 2 Sam. 14:11; Job 19:25.

[23] Num. 5:8; 1 Kgs. 16:11; Ez. 11:15; Ruth 2:20; 3:9, 12, 13; 4:1, 3, 4, 6, 7, 8, 14.

[24] Ex. 21:8, 30; Lev. 19:20, 20; 27:7, 29; Num. 3:46, 48, 49, 51; 1 Sam. 14:45; Ps. 49:8, 9, 16; 55:19; 71:23; 119:134.

[25] *Ga'al* in Isa. 41:14; 43:1, 14; 44:6, 22–24; 47:4; 48:17, 20; 49:7, 26; 52:, 9; 54:5, 8; 59:20; 60:16; 63:9, 16; Jer. *31:11*; 50:34; Hos. *13:14*; Mi. 4:10; Ps. 19:15; *69:19*; 72:14; 74:2; 77:16; 78:35; 103:4; 106:10; 119:154; Lam. 3:58; and *padah* in Dt. 7:8; 9:26; 13:6; 15:15; 21:8; 24:18; 2 Sam. 4:9; 7:23; 1 Kgs. 1:29; Isa. 50:2; Jer. 15:21; 31:11; Hos. 7:13; 13:14; Mi. 6:4; Zec. 10:8; Neh. 1:10; 1 Chr. 17:21, 21; Job 5:20; 6:23; 33:28; Ps. 31:6; 34:23; 69:19; 78:42; 111:9; 130:7, 8. Parallels are indicated in italics.

[26] Isa. 41:14; 43:1, 14; 44:6, 22–24; 47:4; 48:17, 20; 49:26; 52:3, 9; 54:5, 8; 60:16; 63:9, 16.

[27] Ps. 19:15; 69:19; 72:14; 74; 77:16; 78:35; 103:4; 106:10; 107:2; 119:154.

and the Israelites on their escape from Egypt ("In your steadfast love you led the people whom you redeemed; you guided them by your strength to your holy abode", 15:13). Apart from one instance in Israel's dying blessing (Gen. 48:16: "the angel who redeemed me") these are the only cases of its use to describe God as redeemer anywhere Torah.

The FESTIVAL OF REDEMPTION is, of course, *pesach*, and the creator of Exodus is at pains to give this festival a very precise dating. The Hebrew of Ex. 12:2, where the month in which Passover is instituted is described, is unique: הַחֹדֶשׁ הַזֶּה לָכֶם רֹאשׁ חֳדָשִׁים: רִאשׁוֹן הוּא לָכֶם לְחָדְשֵׁי הַשָּׁנָה.

The NRSV translation, "This month shall mark for you the beginning of months; it shall be the first month of the year for you", does not quite convey its force, particularly in the second part, which I read as "it shall be the foremost of months of the year for you"; accordingly I would propose in the first part not 'beginning' but 'most important'.[28] What this verse conveys, in short, is an affirmation of the supreme importance of Pesach, not a note about its date. For, contrary to the usual interpretation, it is my assertion that the dating in Exodus should not be linked to the much later Babylonian calendar adopted by Rabbinic Judaism; rather its hinge is the 'turn of the year' festival of ingathering. Passover's *importance* is undeniable, but it is not in the first month.

The other important aspect of Passover in Exodus is that we are provided with a full story and all the necessary background information to enable the celebration of a *family* event. This is arguably the only place in Tanakh where this happens: the formal notes in Leviticus, Numbers and Deuteronomy are of central, communal events, where Unleavened Bread has equal importance; and the actual Passovers described in various places are either royal initiatives or large communal events.[29] It is not until the emergence of Pharisaic and Rabbinic practice in the 2nd century BCE and later that the celebration we know from Mishnah becomes the norm. It is possible that Josiah's instructions in 2 Kgs. 23:21–23 might reflect an attempt (probably post-exilic) to follow through the

---

[28] Durham (*Exodus*, 53) translates 12:2 as 'This month is to be for you the lead month' and comments: "On the one hand, the statement may be connected with an annual calendar, but on the other hand, it is surely an affirmation of the theological importance of Yahweh's Passover."

[29] See Hezekiah's 'great Passover' in 2 Chr. 30 and Josiah's in 2 Chr. 35:1–19. On this reading, The Passover recorded in Ez. 6:19–22 also seems to be a public communal event. The difficulties for my thesis presented by these passages are chronological: if, as is commonly held, Chronicles is a 4th century production, it might seem that the Exodus programme was ignored. Perhaps so, or perhaps the main concern of the Chronicler is to emphasise the Davidic dynasty's authority, regardless of whatever popular trends were emerging.

example set by Exodus, though Langton[30] reports a consensus that this in fact represents a reform of an older private domestic ritual in the direction of a public one. While the biblical evidence is far from clear, I believe that it can sustain the following very broad reconstruction:

i)   A tradition, of uncertain antiquity, of a public celebration of Pesach (see Dt. 16:1–8; Lev. 23:4–8; and Num. 28:16–25);

ii)  Explicit narratives of grandiose royal celebrations of Passover (2 Chr. 30 and 35);

iii) A revision proposed in 2 Kgs. 23, perhaps in the direction of a private celebration, though this is not the scholarly consensus; more probably a relocation of various communal celebrations to the single temple locus in Jerusalem;

iv)  An exilic 'invention', originating in Ex. 12–13, which realigns the festival as a primarily private one;[31]

v)   The popular adoption of this change under the influence of the Pharisaic movement (evidence for this is found in the New Testament) though note the possibility that all that is indicated in the Gospel narratives is a communal meal eaten by 'associates' (haverim);[32]

---

[30] Scott M. Langton, *Exodus Through the Centuries* (Blackwell Bible Commentaries. Oxford: Blackwell, 2006), 106–7: "[A]spects of Passover observance apparently changed with time and circumstances. Whereas the instructions in Exodus indicate that each household is to individually slaughter the Passover lamb, the account in Ez. 6 reflects the Levites performing this deed": On Josiah's Passover in 2 Kgs. 23, he notes that most "scholars ... believe that the Josianic observance reflected a reform of the festival from a private domestic ritual to a public one administered by a central government in accord with the regulations given in Dt. 16." This implies, however, that the Chronicler's account of Hezekiah's Passover (2 Chr. 30) is anachronistic; "Sara Japhet, though, has raised questions regarding this judgment and concludes that the Chronicler's story 'quite likely' was based on authentic tradition."

[31] In a recent study—*The Development and Symbolism of Passover until 70 CE* (London: T & T Clark International, 2004)—Tamara Prosic has cast considerable doubt on the traditional scholarly view that Exodus represents an ancient family ritual subsequently centralised. She argues that the Passover rituals in Exodus "are just the author's interpretation of how the Passover must have been observed in the absence of a temple. In other words, their nature is functional rather than structural" (47). "The peculiar features of Passover sacrifice are ruled by the circumstances of the situation in which the author places the Israelites. They are the result of the author's envisioning of how the ritual on the first day of the festival should be performed without a temple while still pertaining to the requirements of its performance in reality" (50).

[32] Prosic, *Symbolism of* Passover, 51: "[A]s Josephus testifies, the groups performing the eating [of the flesh of the sacrificial Passover animal] were not families ... but associations of not less than ten people." Cf. Josephus, *Antiquities* III, 248 and *The Jewish War* VI, 423.

vi) Preliminary codification of the re-defined festival in Mishnah (publication ca. 200 CE, but referring to usage and teaching from at least the previous two centuries).

### B　(*Ex 15:22–24:8*): *The Story of Yahweh Who Covenants*

The topic of God's covenant is present in Exodus in 2:24; 6:4–5; 19:5; 24:7–8; 34:10, 27–28. There are signs of progression in the way that these are presented. The first (2:24) is a simple, backward-facing reminder: "God remembered his covenant with Abraham, Isaac, and Jacob." The second (6:4–5) is also reminiscent, but in a context where the 'new' name of the deity is introduced: "I [God] also established my covenant with them [i.e., Abraham, Isaac, and Jacob]...and I have remembered my covenant." In the next verse the deity goes on: "Say therefore to the Israelites, 'I am the Lord'." In 19:5 it is Yahweh who speaks, and this time there is a reminder of the older covenant and an announcement of the new one; it is anticipatory of the events of 20–24: "Now therefore, if you obey my voice and keep my covenant, you shall be my treasured possession out of all the peoples."

What makes this section significantly a covenant affair, however, is the well-known passage in 24:3–8 in which the Israelites gathered at the foot of Mount Sinai perform a dramatic ritual (which may possibly relate to Gen. 15)[33] and enter into a covenant with Yahweh *for the future*; the key verses are 7–8:

> Then he [Moses] took the book of the covenant, and read it in the hearing of the people; and they said, "All that the LORD has spoken we will do, and we will be obedient." Moses took the blood and dashed it on the people, and said, "See the blood of the covenant that the LORD has made with you in accordance with all these words."

The remaining references (34:10, 27–8) are part of the reiteration of the law-giving event at Sinai which takes place in the aftermath of the Golden Calf episode, and do not alter the centrality of the covenant event to the present section.

The FESTIVAL OF THE COVENANT is, it seems, *shevu'ot*—though this identification is by no means as clear as in the previous instance. There are, nevertheless, strong grounds for the association. The precision of the dating to the beginning of the third month, together with the events at

---

[33] E.g. Childs, *Exodus*, 506.

the foot of the mountain (see, famously, Cassuto),[34] brings us satisfyingly
to an appropriate timing for the festival. That said, it should be recognised that there is surprisingly scant biblical evidence for this dating for
*shevu'ot*.[35] While it is clear that there was a festival at this point in the
year, it seems to have been much less well defined than either Passover
or Sukkot. Perhaps Exodus is taking over a rather generalised early harvest
festival in the interest of its second major liturgical turning point. Ronald S.
Hendel makes it clear that by the 2nd century BCE the link was well
established:

> In the Priestly chronological framework of the Exodus it is clear that the
> ceremony in Ex 24:3–8 occurs during the spring festival of Shabuot (Ex. 19:1).
> Later Jewish tradition follows this date for the celebration of the covenant
> and the giving of Torah. For example, Jubilees 6:17 relates the command
> to "observe the Feast of Shabuot in this month, once per year, in order to
> renew the covenant in all (respects), year by year." Similarly the Qumran
> community commemorated their new covenant during Shabuot.[36]

A very similar ceremony, including sacrifices[37] and a covenant renewal, is
found in 2 Chr. 15:10–15 (though not in the 1 Kgs. 15 parallel).[38] The explicit
reference to the 'third month' as a religiously significant date is only found

---

[34] U. Cassuto, *A Commentary on the Book of Exodus* (Jerusalem: The Magnes Press, The
Hebrew University, 1967) 224–30 *passim*.

[35] Only Ex. 19:1 and 2 Chr. 15:10 refer to the third month—but not explicitly to 'weeks'.
Weeks, identified with 'first fruits', is specified in Ex. 34:22 and Num. 28:26–31. Weeks is
found alone in Dt. 16:9–12, 16 and 2 Chr. 8:13, and possibly in Jer. 5:24. First fruits is found
in isolation from weeks in Ex. 23:16. Finally, Lev. 23:9–14 refers to an offering of a sheaf of
the first fruits, followed (v. 15) by a period of seven weeks (literally 'sabbaths'), after which
there is to be an offering of new grain. This does not match with any normal timing for
Shevuot, since it seems to imply a date closer to Sukkot (on the assumption that first fruits
would be in May or June). This is similar to the dating implied in Dt. 16:9.

[36] 'Sacrifice as a cultural system: the ritual symbolism of Exodus 24:3–8', *ZAW* 101, 1989,
366–90 (373)

[37] The element of sacrifice at weeks/first fruits is confirmed in Num. 28:26–27 and 2
Chr. 8:12–13; the relevant parallel in Exodus is 24:3–8.

[38] Admittedly, the connections between Exodus and 2 Chr. 15:10–15 require the recognition of elements from Ex. 19 and 24:3–8 which are echoed in Chronicles. Not everyone
agrees that there is a link—Dozeman ignores it completely—but I believe it to be real.
J. Philip Hyatt, in his *Commentary on Exodus* (New Century Bible. London: Oliphants, 1971),
200, thinks there may be a relationship, and notes the probability "that this material concerning Sinai, or a part of it, was used in the cult", (195) citing von Rad's interpretation of
Ex. 19–24 as a festival legend for covenant renewal at Sukkot (*The Problem of the Hexateuch
and Other Essays*, 1966, pp. 21ff). Sejin Park, *Pentecost and Sinai: The Festival of Weeks As a
Celebration of the Sinai Event* (New York & London: T & T Clark, 2008), 52, notes that both
Ex. 19:1 and 2 Chr. 15:10–15 are commonly cited in support of the link between the Sinai
event and the Festival of Weeks, and a further proposal that Weeks forms the background
to Dan. 10–12 (pp. 52, 55, 60f).

in these two places: another example, perhaps of the deliberate use of unique dating forms. The absence of this ceremony from 1 Kings could argue for the Chronicler's adaptation for narrative purposes of precisely the liturgical dimension I am proposing for Exodus. Again, as with Passover, we have here a story (the journey to Sinai, its dramatic events, and a vivid ceremonial) which provides the midrash for a potentially very significant ceremony. There is no real parallel in Tanakh, though the Chronicler may have used it to enhance the story of King Asa. I noted above that some commentators have suggested an echo of Gen. 15 in the division of the blood of the sacrifice into two parts; but this is very limited and I am agnostic as to its appropriateness.

Before leaving this second strand, let me make a couple of further observations. The section begins as the journey through the wilderness commences, and begins *theologically* with an anticipation of its major theme. I refer to 15:25b–26:

> There the LORD made for them a statute and an ordinance and there he put them to the test. He said, "If you will listen carefully to the voice of the LORD your God, and do what is right in his sight, and *give heed to his commandments and keep all his statutes*, I will not bring upon you any of the diseases that I brought upon the Egyptians; for I am the LORD who heals you." (Emphasis added)

I have defined the end of the section, perhaps arbitrarily, at 24:8; however, there is much to be said for treating 24:12–15 as a bridging passage which concludes part two and introduces part three. The remaining visionary piece—24:9–11—then constitutes *either* a heavenly parallel to the covenant meal (if that is what it is) in 24:3–8 *or* an anticipatory vision of the mysterious dwelling of Yahweh on earth which is the dominant thought in the third section.

### C (*Ex 24:9–40:38*): *The Story of Yahweh Who Dwells*

The verb 'to dwell' *shakan* when used with Yahweh as subject is an important theological marker, associated with the related noun *mishkan*—the 'tabernacle', God's dwelling place amongst the Israelites—which is cited no fewer than fifty-eight times in Ex. 26–40, with no references elsewhere in the book. Yahweh 'dwells' on four occasions:

> The glory of the LORD settled [*shakan*] on Mount Sinai, and the cloud covered it for six days; on the seventh day he called to Moses out of the cloud. (24:16)

And have them make me a sanctuary, so that I [the LORD] may dwell among them. (25:8)

I will dwell among the Israelites, and I will be their God. And they shall know that I am the LORD their God, who brought them out of the land of Egypt that I might dwell among them; I am the LORD their God. (29:45–46)

Moses was not able to enter the tent of meeting because the cloud settled [*shakan*] upon it, and the glory of the LORD filled the tabernacle. (40:35)

The first and last of these four passages form an *inclusio*, with the section as a whole beginning and ending with the dramatic account of Yahweh's glory (*kavod*) descending on the place of greatest sanctity. There is a wider pattern which I cannot discuss in detail here, which shows how on either side of the Golden Calf episode the various aspects of the physical cult and its priesthood which are introduced in 25–31 are enacted in 35–39; to a limited extent, this structuring can be seen in the parallels set out in Figure 1, below.

| Making the covenant (*berit*) 24:3–8 | Renewing the covenant (*berit*) 34:10–28 | The Ark of the Covenant (*'edut*)* 40:3–5, 20–21 |
| --- | --- | --- |
| Mystical mountain top encounter 24:9–11 | Mystical tent of meeting encounter 34:29–35 | Moses excluded from the tent 40:35 |
| Moses and others 'behold God' 24:11 | Moses unveiled 'before Yahweh' 34:34 | |
| Tablets of stone carved 24:12–14 | Tablets of stone renewed 34:1–9 | |
| Yahweh's glory in a cloud on the mountain 24:15–18 | Yahweh in a cloud on the mountain The Merciful Lord (vv. 6–7)† 34:5–9 | Yahweh's glory in a cloud over the tent of meeting 40:34–38 |

Figure 1[39]

[39] * The use of the term העדות ('testimony, witness') is another striking feature of Exodus, and in particular of section three. The formula 'the ark of the testimony' (ארון העדות) is found twelve times in this part of Exodus and only three times elsewhere. Of these, two in Numbers (4:5 and 7:8–9) appear to be direct echoes of Exodus; only Joshua 4:16 remains as an unexplained variant. Outside Exodus by far the commonest qualifications of the ark are either 'the ark of the covenant (הברות) or 'the ark of Yahweh/God' The importance of this practically unique formulation is that it emphasises the central location of God's presence (the ark) as a locus also of the people's witness or testimony—something which relates very precisely to the overall pattern of lection and liturgy.

Throughout section three, the importance of *dwelling* is emphasised: Yahweh's dwelling in the midst of the people; the ark as the special place of God; and the tabernacle (literally *mishkan*, the dwelling place) as the shared space where God and the people—or God and Moses, as the people's representative—can meet. What we have, then, in this third stage of our journey through the festivals of Judah, is an affirmation that the God who redeemed, and who made a covenant with Israel, is the same God who is present in her midst. But present, of course, in a special way and in a special place; and here another aspect of the tragedy of the Golden Calf becomes apparent. It dramatizes a response to the sense of abandonment and the fear of absence: when the beloved disappears, a substitute will be found to fill the gap.

A number of scholars have pointed out the similarity between the building of Yahweh's Temple and Mesopotamian and Ugaritic traditions about the building of a palace for the deity following a notable victory. Thus Kearney:

> Temple-building consequent upon the divine act of creation is a motif known in the literature of Egypt and Babylon. This study has proposed that the P editor adapted this ancient theme in a remarkable new way, fashioning a unity of Ex. 25–40 by way of the sequence: creation (ch. 25–31), fall (ch. 32–33) and restoration (ch. 34–40).[40]

Timmer also refers to this pattern, though he observes that "the victory or enthronement of the god concerned" is not the primary motive in Exodus, despite the fact that Exodus "certainly celebrates Yahweh as warrior". He offers the alternative proposal, in line with his broader thesis, that

---

† The presence in 34:6–7 of the magnificent affirmation of Yahweh's merciful nature is surely of the greatest importance. These familiar words, repeated in one form or another throughout Tanakh, constitute a high point in the expression of the Israelite experience of their God; the fact that they are deployed at the culminating drama of the renewal of the covenant after the Golden Calf incident is a further sign that this episode is not a redactional addition to a prior form of Exodus, but an integral part of the whole festival lection. It constitutes, as it were, a testing of the covenant to destruction. This bears comparison with the many stories in Genesis which dramatise the threat to God's promise to Abraham and his descendants first made in Gen. 12:2–3 (barrenness, for example; the multiple stories of the wife/sister of Abraham and Isaac at risk from foreign rulers; rivalry between brothers; and the ultimate threat of the putative sacrifice of Isaac). The result is that a certain tension is built up between the plans for the tabernacle and their realisation, a tension which reflects the trauma of Moses' and Aaron's dealings with Pharaoh in section one, and the complaint motif and the challenges to mere survival in section two.

[40] Peter J. Kearney, 'Creation Liturgy: The P Redaction of Ex 25–40', *ZAW* 89 (1977) 375–87 (384). He cites ANET 417 (Merikare) and ANET 67–69 (Tablets 4–6 of the creation epic) as examples.

Ex. 39–40 echoes the conclusion of the Genesis creation narrative:[41] "The creator God has finished the construction of his domain... and is in a sublime rest even as he rules."[42] Propp also spells out "the manifold ways in which the Tabernacle pericope in Exodus 15–31, 35–40 echoes P's creation account in Genesis 1:1–2:3", and makes the interesting observation that "because we read the Bible forward, first Genesis and then Exodus, we naturally perceive the Tabernacle as recapitulating Creation. The reverse is equally true: Creation anticipates the Tabernacle." He cites various rabbinic sources for this observation.[43]

I think that it is arguable that the outcome of the Golden Calf episode represents a victory for Yahweh, following which the actual construction of the Tabernacle fits the ANE parallels. Again, Propp's instincts here are sound when he adduces the following as a parallel:

> The Ugaritic poem called 'Of Ba'lu'... describes the storm god's ascent to power. As the story begins, tent-dwelling 'Ilu is the source of divine authority. But in the end, the younger, more dynamic Ba'lu triumphs over his foes and, having built a palace atop mount Zaphon, is acclaimed king of gods and men; an old order yields to a new.[44]

In line with this triumph of the named god Ba'al over 'Ilu, I note that while the Golden Calf is dedicated to *'elohim*,[45] after his destruction the named god Yahweh triumphs and the Tabernacle is built.

The 'tabernacle' is of course a model for the Temple; but it is also, in Exodus, the place of God's protection. There are examples elsewhere of the identification of this concept of the place of protection with the term *sukkah*. Thus Isa. 4:2–6:

> On that day the branch of the LORD shall be beautiful and glorious, and the fruit of the land shall be the pride and glory of the survivors of Israel.³ Whoever is left in Zion and remains in Jerusalem will be called holy, everyone who has been recorded for life in Jerusalem,⁴ once the Lord has washed away the filth of the daughters of Zion and cleansed the bloodstains of Jeru-

---

[41] Note also Mark S. Smith, 'Like Deities, Like Temples, Like People' in *Temple and Worship in Biblical Israel*, ed. John Day (London: T & T Clark, 2007), 3–27. He observes that the root *eden* (to fructify) is a significant element in the building of Baal's house (4f).

[42] Daniel C. Timmer, *Creation, Tabernacle and Sabbath: The Sabbath Frame of Ex 31:12–17; 35:1–3 in Exegetical and Theological Perspective* (Forschungen zur Religion und Literatur des Alten und Neuen Testaments, Band 227. Göttingen: Vandenhoeck and Ruprecht, 2009), 144.

[43] William H. C. Propp, *Exodus 19–40* (Anchor Bible, 2A. NY: Doubleday, 2006), 675f.

[44] Ibid., 707.

[45] Note also that *'Ilu* and *'elohim* have related roots.

salem from its midst by a spirit of judgement and by a spirit of burning. [5]Then the LORD will create over the whole site of Mount Zion and over its places of assembly a cloud by day and smoke and the shining of a flaming fire by night. Indeed, over all the glory (*kavod*) there will be a canopy (*chuppah*). [6]It will serve as a pavilion (*sukkah*), a shade by day from the heat, and a refuge and a shelter from the storm and rain.[46]

The language of v. 5 is a clear reminiscence of the glory, the cloud and the fire which guided the Israelites in Exodus, and which was over the tabernacle (34:34–38); it follows that the terms 'canopy' and 'pavilion' are signifiers for the tabernacle/temple. A similar and suggestive prophetic usage is found in Amos 9:11:

> On that day I will raise up
> the booth (*sukkah*) of David that is fallen,
> and repair its breaches,
> and raise up its ruins,
> and rebuild it as in the days of old;

There can be no doubting the identification of *sukkah* here with the temple, whose reconstruction is envisaged; it seems accordingly that Isa. 4:5–6 and Amos 9:11 share the same vision.

Another Davidic expression of a similar kind is to be found in Ps. 18:11–12 (= 2 Sam. 22:12–13). The context is to be found in verse six, "From his temple he heard my voice, and my cry to him reached his ears":

> He made darkness his covering around him,
> his canopy (*sukkah*) thick clouds dark with water.
> [12]Out of the brightness before him
> there broke through his clouds
> hailstones and coals of fire.

This is, of course, a Psalm of deliverance—in which respect it is similar to Isa. 4—in which the combination of clouds, fire and the *sukkah* is signally present. Here, of course, the temple is God's heavenly abode, of which the tabernacle in Exodus is a mere shadowy replica; nevertheless the link between *sukkah* and temple remains evident.

Finally there is the curious apocalyptic account of the importance of Sukkot in Zech. 14:16–19, where the punishment that awaits the nations who do not observe it is a plague. It cannot be coincidence that the only nation specifically named is Egypt—a sign, perhaps, that Zechariah was

---

[46] Note the parallel between v. 6 and Jon 4:6–8; of course, Jon. 4:2 is one of the notable occurrences of the affirmation from Ex. 34:6–7.

aware of the emphasis that Exodus tacitly places on this culminating festival of the year.[47] Admittedly Exodus does not use the noun *sukkah*, though the related verb appears in two contexts, both relating to the ark. In 25:20 and 37:9 the cherubim are portrayed as '*overshadowing* the mercy seat', and 40:3, 21 refer to the curtain *screening* the ark.

It is clear that the FESTIVAL OF YAHWEH'S PRESENCE AND THE TEMPLE is *sukkot*. The indications listed above are readily supported by the fact (agreed by both 1 Kgs. 8:2–66 and 2 Chr. 5:2–7:11) that it was at this time that the Temple was dedicated. Surely, therefore, the final piece of the Exodus jigsaw is the celebration of this festival. The final act of Exodus is the setting up and the consecration and dedication of the *mishkan* (40:2 cf. Num. 7:1), and this is said to be held 'on the first day of the first month' (*bᵉyom-hachodesh hari'shon*). The modern numbering of the Hebrew months begins with Nisan, the month in which Passover is held; on this convention new year (Rosh Hashanah) takes place in the seventh month. I want to suggest that, as I argued earlier in this essay, for the writer(s) of Exodus Nisan (if they even knew that name)[48] was not the first month in calendrical terms, but the 'most important' month. Sukkot (the inauguration and dedication of the Temple) then occurs at the end of the year, and completes the liturgical cycle in Exodus. Whether this signal event marks the conclusion of the year or its beginning is perhaps a moot point.[49] New Year is, after all, a time for facing in two directions—like the two-faced Roman deity Janus after whom the Julian calendar's first month is named.

The cycle is thus complete, with its attendant narratives (lections): dedication of the presence at the end of the year equals the beginning of the year; family Passover soon thereafter; covenant renewal in the middle of the year. Given that these three seasons continue to provide a defining structure for the Jewish year, one might argue that what Exodus proposed was in the end a resounding success.

---

[47] Note that, though Lev. 23:34 dates Sukkot to the seventh month, Ex. 23:16 and 34:22 place it at the end or the turn of the year.

[48] It is possible that the Babylonian names for the months which were later adopted by Judaism were unknown to, or at least not used by, the Biblical writers.

[49] William H. C. Propp, *Exodus 1–18* (Anchor Bible, 2. NY: Doubleday, 1998), 384–87, provides a balanced and informative discussion of the calendar problems raised by 12:2 and other dating references in Exodus. Of particular interest is the concept of a six-month cultic year (Spring–Autumn) which might resolved the apparent paradox I have addressed here. See M. E. Cohen, *The Cultic Calendars of the ANE*, Bethesday, MD: CDL, 1993.

# CRACKING THE CANON: JOHN TOLAND, 'LOST' GOSPELS AND THE CHALLENGE TO RELIGIOUS HEGEMONY

## Jonathan C. P. Birch

> This essay falls into the almost legendary category of analysis of analyses of the Bible in which not a single text is examined, not a single exegesis undertaken (Hans Frei).[1]

This essay intersects with the theme of religious pluralism (among other questions of socio-cultural diversity), and some of the critical methods employed by biblical scholars and historians of ancient Christianity. More specifically, it offers a sketch of personalities and controversies in the history of modern scholarship, focussing on debates about the authenticity of ancient religious texts, and the legitimacy and limits of religious diversity within a modern context. The essay will conclude with an appreciative assessment of historical scholarship in this area, before offering some sceptical, though not hostile, remarks on the modern tendency to appeal to non-canonical sources in attempts to unsettle the religious certitude of those who espouse religiously and socially discriminatory views.

It is appropriate that the protagonist in the second half of this essay, which enquires into the religio-political possibilities of biblical scholarship in the Augustan Age of literature, is a former student of the University of Glasgow: the radical Irish writer John Toland (1670–1722). One of the many controversial characteristics of Toland's work on the Bible and Church history is his flirtation with non-canonical sources in his reconstruction of Christian origins, and the role of canonicity as a theme in his rhetorical skirmishes with defenders of the English Church-State establishment: for such establishments, textual authenticity and religio-political authority were often closely connected. Whether in the end we judge Toland to have been a disingenuous mischief maker, or a highly moral writer who got carried away with the irenic possibilities of the Christian apocrypha, he ought to be seen as a trailblazing figure among modern biblical scholars who have sought to utilise antiquarian learning for religious, social and political ends; in particular, the end of combatting totalising theological

---

[1] Hans W. Frei, *The Eclipse of Biblical Narrative: A Study in Eighteenth and Nineteenth Century Hermeneutics* (New Haven / London: Yale University Press, 1974), vii.

dogma and religious exclusivism. But for whom did Toland blaze a trail? Before examining the work of Toland himself, it is worth reflecting on the power of the apocrypha in more recent times—for while the legitimacy of Western governments may no longer depend on biblical texts, the legitimacy of particular religious institutions and worldviews certainly do, and challenges to those worldviews are sometimes furnished by appeal to non-canonical sources: the Nag Hammadi library, the Dead Sea Scrolls and a 'lost' Gospel of Mark are all exemplary in this regard.

### The Apocrypha and Christian Origins since the Enlightenment: Letting Many Flowers Bloom

The modern project of reconstructing the historical figure of Jesus and Christian origins began to establish itself as a major intellectual concern during the European Enlightenment,[2] and it became a staple of the theological curriculum (especially in German universities) in the nineteenth century.[3] During that time, the vast majority of scholars focused their attention on the texts of the New Testament and the Church fathers. Fragments of ancient non-canonical Christian writings were unearthed in the nineteenth century,[4] but it was two major twentieth-century discoveries that really helped to expand the textual horizons for scholars wishing to understand the context for the birth of the Christian religion: the Nag Hammadi Library in Egypt, and the Dead Sea Scrolls.[5] Few developments in any historiographical tradition are as exciting as the discovery of new literary sources, and when those sources concern the origins of one of the world's major religions, the stakes are higher, the interest wider, and the potential for scandal so much greater. After all, different versions of

---

[2] The catalyst for this tradition of enquiry is usually said to be the posthumous publications of Hermann Samuel Reimarus's *Vom dem Zwecke Jesu und seiner Jünger* (1778), collected in *Reimarus: Fragments*, ed. Charles H. Talbert, trans. Ralph S. Fraser (London: S. C. M. Press, 1971). I have joined the ranks of those who argue for earlier beginnings: see Birch, 'The Road to Reimarus: Origins of the Quest for the Historical Jesus', in *Holy Land as Homeland? Models for Constructing the Historic Landscapes of Jesus*, ed. Keith Whitelam (Sheffield: Phoenix Press, 2011), 19–47.

[3] This, along with other trends within modern New Testament studies, is superbly documented in William Baird, *History of New Testament Research*, 3 vols. (Minneapolis: Fortress Press, 1992–2013).

[4] Notably the Gospel of Peter; see Bart D. Ehrman, *Lost Christianities: The Battles for Scripture and the Faiths We Never Knew* (Oxford: Oxford University Press, 2003), 16.

[5] Perhaps no scholar has done more than Geza Vermes to make the secrets of the caves of Qumran available to an English speaking audience: see Vermes (ed. & trans.), with Nigel Andrews, *The Complete Dead Sea Scrolls in English* (London: Allen Lane, 1997).

religious history function to legitimise different forms of religion and different religious authorities. Of these two discoveries, only the texts found at Nag Hammadi actually contained Christian writings, and they will be my focus below, although it should be noted that the Dead Sea Scrolls probably generated the most extravagant claims about the revolutionary implications of new sources for our understanding of Christian origins.[6]

As the project of producing English translations of the Nag Hammadi library came to completion during the 1970s, their contents began to be examined by scholars interested in the reconstruction of Christian origins. Much of the focus centred on the so-called 'Gnostic Gospels' contained within the library, and especially the Coptic sayings Gospel of Thomas, 'arguably the single most important Christian archaeological discovery of the twentieth century'.[7] By the end of the 1970s and throughout the following decade, historians were digesting the significance of the documents and communicating their findings to the wider reading public. From our vantage point today, Elaine Pagels's *The Gnostic Gospels*[8] and John Dominic Crossan's *Four Other Gospels*[9] can be seen as indicative of the increasing importance that at least some late twentieth-century scholars were according non-canonical sources in their historical analyses of early Christianity, and, indeed, of Jesus himself.[10] In the present century, Bart Ehrman has taken up the theme of non-canonical Christian literature for a wider audience, not because he is persuaded of their importance for understanding the historical Jesus, but because of the light they shine on

---

[6] In the vacuum created by the constant delays in publication and official announcements, a myriad of conspiracy theories were born, with the credibility of the Christian religion itself said by some to be hanging by a thread (or a fragment), and only the nefarious intervention of the Catholic Church keeping 'the truth' from the world (the Vatican was said to have been alerted to the dangerous secrets of the scrolls by the significant Catholic contingent of scholars working on them). The germ of this argument can be traced back to one of the earliest scrolls scholars, John M. Allegro. Sensationalist interpretations of the scrolls and their significance are discussed and rejected in a number of scholarly publications, including Joseph A. Fitzmeyer, *The Dead Sea Scrolls and Christian Origins* (Grand Rapids, Mich.: W. B. Eerdmans, 2000). Allegro's academic reputation went into decline in the years since he completed work on the scrolls, reaching its nadir with his notorious *The Sacred Mushroom and the Cross* (London: Hodder and Stoughton, 1970).

[7] Ehrman, *Lost Christianities*, 14. Whether Thomas actually is a Gnostic document is a matter of dispute.

[8] See Elaine Pagels, *The Gnostic Gospels* (New York: Vintage Books, 1979).

[9] See Crossan, *Four Other Gospels: Shadows on the Contours of Canon* (Minneapolis: Winston Press, 1985).

[10] Crossan would later emerge as a major historical Jesus scholar, with sayings from Thomas featuring among the earliest authentic material according to his analysis: see his 'Appendix', *The Historical Jesus: The Life of a Mediterranean Jewish Peasant* (Edinburgh: T&T Clark, 1991), 427–428.

the diversity of the Christian communities who once took such texts as theologically authoritative.[11] All three of these scholars are, in their own way, religious controversialists: opponents of dogmatic, exclusive claims to religious truth.[12] This marriage of scholarship on the Christian apocrypha and a pluralistic (or sceptical) religious stance is something we will find when we consider the work of Toland below. But there are other features of Toland's work which also find recent parallels, not least claims by a scholar to have discovered a historically revelatory document concerning Christian origins, and the subsequent accusation of skulduggery by their critics.

*Jesus, Sex and Magic: The 'Lost' Gospel of Mark*

By any estimation, Morton Smith was a remarkably learned historian, with an exceptional range of expertise within the often highly specialised modern academy: his critical skills ranged over classical Greek and Roman literature, pagan religions, second-temple Judaism, Rabbinics, the New Testament, and Patristics.[13] He is perhaps best known today, however,

---

[11]  See Ehrman, *Lost Christianities*.

[12]  What may be a subtext in scholarly work becomes explicit in more popular writings: see Pagels, 'No More Creeds: How the Gnostic Gospels are Transforming Christianity— The Discovery of Ancient Texts Challenges the Idea that Christianity Always Had a Single, Authorized Set of Beliefs', *Beliefnet: Inspiration, Spirituality, Faith* (on-line), undated, accessed 13 Sep. 2012: http://www.beliefnet.com/Faiths/Christianity/2003/06/No-More-Creeds-How-The-Gnostic-Gospels-Are-Transforming-Christianity.aspx?p=1; and Crossan, 'Exclusivity or Particularly', in Rita M. Gross and Terry C. Much (eds.) *Buddhists Talk About Jesus, Christians Talk About the Buddha* (New York: Continuum, 2000), 83–86. The implication that injustices have been done to minority Christian movements at the hands of the orthodox, and the idea that this has impacted on both the books included in the canon and the content of those books has been a running theme in Ehrman's publications, including *Lost Christianities* and the earlier *The Orthodox Corruption of Scripture: The Effect of Early Christological Controversies on the Text of the New Testament* (New York: Oxford University Press, 1993). Ehrman has explicitly renounced his Christian identity, and has engaged in public debates with noted Christian apologists, taking a sceptical position. More recently, Pagels's 'brilliant work' is cited by Hal Taussig as having made possible the publication of *A New New Testament Testament: A Bible for the 21st Century Combining Traditional and Newly Discovered Texts*, ed. Hal Taussig (Boston: Houghton Mifflin Harcourt, 2013), 535, while Crossan contributed the foreword (xi–xv).

[13]  Smith's straddling of Old and New Testaments, and of Jewish and Greco-Roman history, made him a guru for some of the most notable twentieth-century scholars trying to understand the historical context of Hellenistic Judaism and Christian origins: see Jacob Neusner (ed.), *Christianity, Judaism and Other Greco-Roman Cults: Studies for Morton Smith at Sixty* (Leiden: Brill, 1975); and E. P. Sanders, *Jesus and Judaism* (London: SCM Press, 1985), especially 5–10, 162–170.

for something which has its roots in his fledgling scholarly career. While a graduate student in Jerusalem, early in 1942, Smith spent time at Mar Saba, an Orthodox Greek monastery in the Judean Desert, established in the fifth century CE, South East of Jerusalem. World War II was a rather inauspicious time for a young scholar to be roving around Palestine examining obscure texts, but it was during this period that Smith first encountered the monastery's collection of rare books in the tower library. Long after the end of the war, Smith returned to Mar Saba, this time as a professional scholar, and once again set to work in the library which had fired his imagination as a student. And it was there, in 1958, that Smith claimed to have discovered part of a hitherto unknown letter by the early Christian writer Clement of Alexandria, addressed to a certain Theodore.[14] An addition to Patristic literature would have been a massive find in itself, but the contents of the letter promised much more than this. The letter referred to and quoted from a Gospel attributed to 'Mark', which was reputed to have been circulating among early Christians, but which differed considerably from canonical Mark.[15] In fact, the letter implies the existence of three versions of the Gospel: 1) the Gospel that became canonical, based on selected recollections by Jesus' disciple Simon Peter, who met the author in Rome; 2) a longer and more esoteric version, written in Alexandria, for the more experienced or spiritually developed Christian, based on stories about Jesus and his teachings not included in the first Gospel; and 3) a corrupted version of this longer Gospel which purported to sanction the unidentified abominations of an early Gnostic sect known as the Carpocratians, named after their second-century founder Carpocrates of Alexandria, who is alleged to have adopted the esoteric Gospel of Mark and supplemented it with materials designed to give a theological underpinning to his reputedly depraved philosophy.

The Carpocratians named in Clement's letter were already well known to historians of early Christianity, serving as a target for polemical treatment by the Church fathers, who condemned them for their theological

---

[14] Smith's translation of the text of the letter is collected in his *Clement of Alexandria and a Secret Gospel of Mark* (Cambridge: Harvard University Press, 1973), 446–447; for the 'Transcription of the Text', see 448, 450, 452).

[15] There are many accounts of the background to the discovery (see Ehrman, *Lost Christianities*, 70–74). Smith's own account is best told in *The Secret Gospel: The Discovery and Interpretation of the Secret Gospel According to Mark*, (New York: Harper and Row, 1973). His most detailed scholarly analysis, however, appears in *Clement of Alexandria*.

doctrines,[16] their practise of 'magical arts and incantations',[17] their taste for 'love-potions' and their generally debauched behaviour.[18] According to that pioneering heresy-hunter Irenaeus of Lyons, the Carpocratians held that the emancipation of the soul required the experience of all possible lifestyles and behaviours, including 'things which we dare not either speak or hear of'.[19] That the Carpocratians were sexually licentious was implicit though not clearly defined in Irenaeus's discussion. Smith's discovery would put male flesh on the bare bones of the Carpocratians' reputedly erotic religious practises.

What tended to shock readers of the hitherto unknown letter of Clement was references to the secret Gospel's depiction of an episode of spiritual pedagogy νύκτα ('at night') between Jesus and a νεανίσκος ('young man').[20] According to the secret Gospel used by the Carpocratians, referred to by Clement, the man in question had been raised from the dead by Jesus, following an appeal by the boy's grieving sister in Bethany.[21] Six days after this 'resurrection', and acting on the instruction of Jesus, the young man presented himself wearing a σινδόνα ('linen cloth') over his otherwise γυμνός ('naked') body.[22] Reference is made to a youthful follower of Jesus, 'wearing nothing but a linen cloth' in canonical Mark (14:51), although he is not directly connected to Jesus' ministry in Bethany. Also absent from canonical Mark is any mention of the night that Jesus spent with the youth, teaching him the μυστήριον τῆς βασιλείας τοῦ θεοῦ ('mystery of the Kingdom of God'),[23] nor is there any reference to men who were γυμνός γυμνῷ ('naked together').[24] In one of his more popular works, Smith speculated that this episode may lay behind an early homosexual initiation rite for Christian men, who were received into the Church in the

---

[16] See Irenaeus, *Against Heresies* I xxv, trans. Alexander Roberts and William Rambaut, *Ante-Nicene Fathers: Vol. 1*, ed. Roberts et al. (Buffalo, NY: Christian Literature Publishing Co., 1885). The doctrines held by their founder, Carpocrates, are reputed to have included the idea that the creation of the world was not an act of God, but, rather, the work of lesser (though angelic) beings, hence the world's less than perfect nature; in terms of Christology, Carpocrates seems to have subscribed to some form of adoptionism.

[17] *Against Heresies* I xxv.3.

[18] *Against Heresies* I xxv.

[19] *Against Heresies* I xxv.4.

[20] 'Transcription of the Text', 452.

[21] Ibid.

[22] Ibid.

[23] Ibid.

[24] Ibid.

manner modelled by Jesus himself.[25] Even without such titillation, when one considers that a scholarly consensus had long been established that Mark's Gospel constitutes the oldest existing source for the life of Jesus,[26] the historical implications of finding other versions was potentially very significant, and, at one level, entirely credible.[27] The points of contention revolved, and continue to revolve, around the manner in which the letter was discovered and publicised, and the fact that it has never been examined by independent experts.[28]

Smith took photographs of the letter, and these images have been subjected to considerable scrutiny, but the material text itself has never been investigated, and is feared lost.[29] The letter, authentic or not, was a modern transcription. It had been copied into the back pages of a 1646 edition of the letters of another notable Christian writer, St. Ignatius of Antioch.[30] The letter was written in Greek in what some experts have judged to be a convincing eighteenth-century handwriting style,[31] which would locate the scribe in close historical proximity to the publication of the book it was written it; other authorities have judged the letter to be the work of a much later writer, merely imitating the style of eighteenth-century

---

[25] In Jesus' ministry, 'Freedom from the law may have resulted in completion of the spiritual union by physical union' (Smith, *Secret Gospel*, 114).

[26] Two seminal texts arguing for Markan priority were published in the same year by a pair of German scholars working independently: Christian Gottlob Wilke, *Der Urevangelist* (Dresden and Leipzig: G. Fleischer, 1838); and Christian Hermann Weisse, *Die evangelische Geschichte kritisch und philosophisch bearbeitet*, 2 vols. (Leipzig: Breitkopf and Härtel, 1838).

[27] That there are slightly different versions of all four Gospels in the ancient world is a scholarly given, and one of the most famous examples has always concerned Mark's Gospel: some of the earliest manuscript evidence shows that the Gospel once circulated without the post-Resurrection appearances of Jesus (Mark 16:9–20).

[28] Some have gone further claiming that Smith was the only man to ever see the text, but this has been disputed (see Ehrman, *Lost Christianities*, 83–84). Frances Watson, one of the more prominent New Testament scholars to take up the question in recent years, is more confident than others that the question of authenticity can be established by examining the internal evidence provided by the letter: see Watson, 'Beyond Suspicion: On the Authorship of the Mar Saba Letter and the Secret Gospel of Mark', *Journal of Theological Studies* 61 (2010), 128–170.

[29] See Ehrman, *Lost Christianities*, 84. Photographs of the letter are collected in Smith, *Clement of Alexandria*, 449, 451, 453.

[30] The letters are collected in *Epistolae Genuinae S. Ignatii Martyris*, ed. Isaac Vossius (Amsterdam: Apud Ioannem Blaeu, 1646).

[31] See the 39 page report by the forensic handwriting analyst Venetia Anastasopoulou commissioned by the *Biblical Archaeological Review* and published on-line, 14 Oct. 2009: http://dbcfaa79b34c8f5dfffa-7d3a62c63519b1618047ef2108473a39.r81.cf2.rackcdn.com/wp-content/uploads/secret-mark-analysis.pdf, p. 4.

Greek.[32] Outside the forensic study of handwriting, some scholars in the field of patristics, including experts on Clement himself, have accepted that the content and style of the letter is consistent with the preoccupations and literary manners of this Church father in question.[33] Without the original document, however, which would facilitate chemical testing of the ink, the most probable date at which the letter was written into the book cannot be verified with any degree of certainly, and the possibility that it is a clever fake produced at a later date cannot be discounted. Moreover, some interdisciplinary researchers, patristic scholars and statisticians, have wondering if the composition was written in the style of Clement almost to the point of parody.[34] Is it plausible that a relatively short text (less than three pages) should be so crammed full of the kind of vocabulary and stylistic habits which scholars identified as characteristic of Clement when considering his *whole* corpus of work? Some critics have not found this plausible, and judged that whoever wrote the text was trying rather too hard to sound like Clement.[35]

It is certainly true that academic resources on Clement existed in the twentieth century which would make the forging of such a document easier than it might otherwise have been.[36] While some critics have always been open in their judgement that the letter was most probably a fake,[37] they were initially less forthcoming when it came to pointing the figure at a likely forger, but the suggestion that the letter may be a *twentieth century* creation obviously narrowed the field of suspects. For those who suppose fakery, accusing fingers have all tended to point towards the same man. The earliest reference to this letter by any known writer in history came from the pen of the man who claimed to have discovered it, the man who enhanced his academic fame on this basis of that find, and the man who

---

[32] See the findings of palaeographer Agamemnon Tselikas, also commissioned by the *Biblical Archaeological Review* and released on-line in 'Agamemnon Tselikas' Handwriting Analysis Report'. 14. Oct. 2009: http://www.biblicalarchaeology.org/uncategorized/agamemnon-tselikas-handwriting-analysis-report/.

[33] See Ehrman, *Lost Christianities*, 77–78.

[34] See A. H. Criddle, 'On the Mar Saba Letter Attributed to Clement of Alexandria', *Journal of Early Christian Studies* 3/2 (1995), 215–220; and Andrew R. Solow and Woollcott K. Smith, 'A Statistical Problem Concerning the Mar Saba Letter', *The American Statistician* 63 (2009), 254–257.

[35] See Erhman, *Lost Christianities*, 85–86.

[36] Foremost among them was the monumental work by Otto Stählin, whose multivolume study includes indexes to all Clement's vocabulary, *Clemens Alexandrinus*, 4 vols. (Leipzig: J. C. Hinrichs, 1905–36).

[37] Among the earliest and most distinguished doubters was the historian of Christianity and pagan religion Arthur Darby Nock (see Erhman, *Lost Christianities*, 82).

devoted a significant proportion of his career to defending its authenticity and developing a new and controversial picture of early Christianity on the basis of it. For commentators trying to solve the mystery through the application of the *Cui bono* principle, it was perfectly clear who benefited most from this discovery: Morton Smith.[38]

Amidst the conspiracy theories, pop psychology and innuendo, some critics have tried to offer positive evidence that Smith had contrived the whole episode,[39] and, having found a receptive audience, persisted with the scam until it took on a life of its own and became an established scholarly curiosity. Palaeographers, specialists on the Gospel of Mark and patristic scholars remain divided on the authenticity of Smith's discovery, and I do not intend to assume the position of judge here. It does strike me as seems prima-facie implausible that a man as talented as Smith would devoted quite so much time and energy on a practical joke, or a piece of wish fulfilment which got out of hand,[40] but personal incredulity is scarcely a decisive argument for the defence.

Smith's prize-winning book *Jesus the Magician* was shaped,[41] in part, by the view that magical (if not sexual) practises were features of early Christianity. This view derived in part from Smith's reading of the so called 'secret' Gospel of Mark, with its references to rituals which are said to have their roots in the ministry of Jesus himself. A noteworthy dimension of the alternative forms of Christian life in the ancient work, suggested by Smith's discovery, is how the plurality of religious values unveiled by 'new' documents could be used to challenge some influential attitudes within modern socio-political contexts. Smith's version of Christian beginnings presented a sex-positive Jesus and sex-positive early Christian communities,[42] which could be juxtaposed with the sexless Jesus of

---

[38] Even some critics originally drawn into the controversy because of their technical expertise have not been able to resist this line of argument: see Tselikas's 'Handwriting Analysis Report'. See also Jacob Neusner, 'Foreword', Birger Gerhardsson, *Memory and Manuscript: Oral Tradition and Written Transmission in Rabbinic Judaism and Early Christianity* (Grand Rapids, Mich.: Eerdmans, and Livonia, Mich.: Dove 1994), xxvi.

[39] For instance, some have compared samples of Smith's handwritten Greek with the Greek used in the letter: see Stephen C. Carlson, *The Gospel Hoax: Morton Smith's Invention of Secret Mark* (Waco, Texas: Baylor University Press, 2005), 23–47.

[40] My reluctance to join the ranks of Smith's accusers is in no way an indication that I am persuaded of the authenticity of Clement's letter, which is another matter entirely.

[41] First published in 1978, Smith's *Jesus the Magician* (New York: Harper and Row) won Columbia University's Lionel Trilling Award for that year.

[42] See Smith, *Secret Gospel*, 114, where a 'physical union' is speculatively linked with 'freedom from the law'.

orthodox Christian theology and mainstream Church history, and the negative attitude to sex in general and to homosexuality in particular which
is associated with some major figures in early Christian thought, most
notably Paul.[43] Smith had a long-standing interest in these issues. He was
ordained as an Episcopal priest in 1946,[44] and defended the traditional
Christian position on homosexuality,[45] before abandoning active ministry
in the 1950s.[46] The socio-political resonance of these issues during Smith's
time needs no introduction: the Church's attitudes to sex in general, and
homosexuality in particular, were among the longest and hardest fought
battles in the American culture wars of the twentieth century. That war
continues, and not only in the US: in the UK the Mar Saba document has
been cited (with commendable caution) in a discussion of sexuality and
the Church by the most famous gay rights activist of the late twentieth
century.[47]

The idea that a particular mode of Christian life was 'suppressed' by
orthodox parties committed to shaping the Church in their own (narrow)
image was explicit in Smith's own writings,[48] and it is a persistent theme
in writings which are keen either to champion the historical or religious
authority of non-canonical sources (Pagels), or as a deflationary stance
against the certitude of Christians who try to locate their orthodox theology in the 'secure' foundations of the New Testament (Ehrman). In the
case of Smith's claim to have discovered a historically revelatory document, and the subsequent claims of fraud which have been levelled at
the finding, there are a number of interesting co-incidences and historical
parallels with much earlier controversies involving John Toland.

### Contested Documents and Alternative Christianities:
### Back to the Enlightenment

As noted already, the book in which the 'lost' letter of Clement was written down was actually a collection of epistles by Ignatius of Antioch,

---

[43] I am thinking of Romans 1:18–32 and 1 Corinthians: 6:9–11.

[44] Peter Jeffery, *The Secret Gospel of Mark Unveiled: Imagined Rituals of Sex, Death, and Madness in a Biblical Forgery* (New Haven, Conn.: Yale University Press, 2007), 150.

[45] See Smith, 'Psychiatric Practise and Christian Dogma', *Journal of Pastoral Care* 3 (1949), 12–20.

[46] See Jeffery, *Secret Gospel*, 150–151.

[47] Peter Tatchell, 'Was Jesus Gay? The Sexuality of Jesus is Queried', *Peter Tatchell* (online), 18 Mar. 1996, accessed 25 Mar. 2013: http://www.petertatchell.net/religion/jesus .htm.

[48] Smith, *Jesus the Magician*, chap. 1.

which had been published by the Dutch humanist scholar Isaac Vossius. The letters of Ignatius were themselves the subject of controversy during this time. In the medieval period there were a dozen or more letters attributed to Ignatius in circulation,[49] but their provenance and authority acquired new theological and political significance following the Reformation, largely due to the opinions offered in some of the letters on the subject of Christian leadership, indicating as they did a hierarchical Church centred on the bishopric. In this early modern context, the form that Christian organisation should take was fiercely contested, and Anglicans who defended the Episcopal structure, as a continuation of the Apostolic Church, would appeal to sources such as the letters of Ignatius as historical evidence for the ancient credentials of their position. One radical critic of a hierarchical Church, the poet and polemicist John Milton, challenged the theological authority of these sources, questioning whether a corpus of letters he claimed to be anachronistic, and lacking stylistic consistency, could ever be attributed to Ignatius with any degree of certainty.[50] The collection published by Vossius is an early critical edition, and represents a seminal attempt to isolate the authentic letters of Ignatius from the pseudonymous,[51] while identifying supposed interpolations into the otherwise authentic texts. Later scholarship has broadly vindicated Vossius's position over against Milton's more general skepticism.[52] As we will see, Milton was a serial forgery hunter in an age when religio-political establishments appealed to authoritative texts, sacred or otherwise, to legitimise their power. And it was in a sympathetic biography of John Milton that another republican writer would announce his entry into the potentially dangerous world of the Christian apocrypha.

## John Toland and the Question of Canon

Reputed to be the son of an Irish Catholic priest, Toland arrived at the University of Glasgow from County Donegal as a precocious sixteen year old,

---

[49] B. A. Zuiddam, 'Other Letters of a Martyr? The Vossian Recession of Ignatius Reconsidered', *Ekklesiastikos Pharos* 92, N.S. 21, (2010), 181–193: 181–182.

[50] John Milton, *Of Prelatical Episcopacy* (London: Underhill, 1641).

[51] Vossius judged that six of the letters are genuine: his letter to St. Polycarp, and to congregations in Ephesus, Magnesia, Tralles, Philadelphia and Smyrna.

[52] Although Zuiddam, in 'Other Letters of a Martyr?', makes a case for an 'all or nothing' approach to the question of Ignatius' authorship, whereby a textual unit of eleven letters, used by some notable scholars prior to the work of Vossius, is either accepted or rejected *en bloc*.

having already rejected the Catholicism of his youth.[53] After spells studying at the universities of Edinburgh, Oxford, Leiden and Utrecht, Toland
emerged with the linguistic competence and historical-critical skills to
facilitate his career as a hired literary gun in the European Republic of Letters: a writer who survived through the patronage of those who required
dedicated researchers and talented wordsmiths to produce works which
were sympathetic to their religio-political causes. Some of Toland's own
persistent preoccupations are beyond doubt, however, including his commitment to religious and civil liberties.

Toland became notorious following the publication of *Christianity Not
Mysterious*,[54] a work of radical biblical scholarship and rational theology, which sought to purge Christianity of any elements which might be
considered mysterious and thereby open the door to the kind of priestly
mediations that Toland had developed a keen distaste for. This was
Toland apparently writing as a radical Christian,[55] arguing for the transparency of the gospel, as revealed in the New Testament, and expressing his allegiance to a *Solus Christus* theology.[56] But as Toland's career as
a public writer unfolded,[57] it became clear that a critical affirmation of
reformed Christian belief would not suffice in his battle with the English
establishment. As an opponent of religio-political prejudice in the public
sphere, Toland would have to confront a range of texts which functioned
to authorise the kind of social attitudes and political policies he rejected:
deference to priestly authority, religious coercion and censorship.

---

[53] I have taken the biographical details concerning Toland from Stephen H. Daniel,
'Toland, John (1670–1722)', in *Oxford Dictionary of National Biography*, Oxford University
Press, Jan. 2008, http://www.oxforddnb.com/view/article/27497, accessed 17 Oct 2012. I
have also consulted Justin Champion, *Republican Learning: John Toland and the Crisis of
Christian Culture* (Manchester: Manchester University Press, 2003).

[54] John Toland, *Christianity Not Mysterious* (London, 1696).

[55] Whether Toland was still a faithful Protestant is contested, but I think it is reasonable
to locate Toland within the margins of radical Protestantism during this period, although
he may have already been on an intellectual trajectory away from Christianity.

[56] *Christianity Not Mysterious*, xxvi.

[57] I am inclined to accept Champion's characterisation of Toland as a 'public writer',
who deployed different rhetorical strategies, and exhibited different religious sensibilities,
depending on the nature of his commission and audience, rather than someone who was
strictly concerned with articulating a settled (or evolving) religio-political stance. This is
Toland as the creator of 'authorial *personae*', so as to 'engage as many types of reader as
possible' (*Republican Learning*, 51).

*Eikon Basilike* was one of the most controversial documents to appear in seventeenth-century England.[58] Reputed to be the spiritual confessions of Charles I, written in the twilight of his life, it paints a sympathetic picture of the monarch as the central character in a royal passion narrative. It constitutes a firm but humble defence of monarchy from a pious man who asked for God's forgiveness for those who refused his peaceful overtures.[59] The text was a gift for royalists and a thorn in the side of republicans. In his biography of Milton, Toland drew dangerous parallels between the credulity of those who failed to recognise *Eikon Basilike* for the forged piece of royalist propaganda Milton had judged it to be, and the credulity of those from the ancient world who had embraced fraudulent texts attributed to Jesus and the Apostles.[60] Toland's silence on the question of canonical warrants raised the question of the writer's motives: some critics took him to be undermining the biblical canon, if only indirectly, and with it the whole theological edifice upon which the Church of England and its monarchical ruler depended.[61] Instead of qualifying his reference to the apocrypha, however, or explaining it away as a 'mere' rhetorical device to draw people's attention to the idiocy of subscribing to the authenticity of *Eikon Basilike*, Toland added to the offence in his next publication, under the provocation of a notable and well-connected preacher.

In a sermon to the House of Commons on 13 January 1699, the royal chaplain and future Bishop of Exeter, Ofspring Blackall denounced the 'Infidel' Toland for his 'shameless' act of "declaring his Doubt, that several Pieces under the Name of Christ and his Apostles…are supposititious."[62] In *Amyntor*, Toland defended himself against Blackall's charges, but in such a way that the potentially explosive issue of the authority of the

---

[58] For an on-line edition at *Project Canterbury*, see Edward Almack (ed.), *Eikon Basilike, Or The King's Book* (London: A. Morning, 1904), accessed 05 December 2012: http://anglicanhistory.org/charles/eikon/.

[59] *Eikon Basilike*, chap. 18, where the author is referring to lasting treaties, which the king looked upon as a transition 'from fighting like Beasts, to arguing like men'. The specific focus during this lament is the failed Treaty of Uxbridge (1645).

[60] See Toland, *The Life of John Milton* (London: John Darby, 1699), 91–92. The general context for Toland's ruminations was provided by his review of the Milton corpus. In direct response to *Eikon Basilike*, Milton penned a piece of counter propaganda for the republican cause, which defended the execution of Charles I and rejected all monarchical government: *Eikonoklastes in Answer to a Book intitl'd Eikon Basilike* (London: Matthew Simmons, 1649).

[61] See Ofspring Blackall, *Sermon Preached Before the House of Commons, January 30th 1698* (London: J. Leake, for W. Kettilby, 1699).

[62] Blackall, quoted by Toland, *Amyntor, Or a Defense of Milton's Life* (London, 1699), 12.

New Testament canon shifted from being little more than a provocative aside in Toland's original biography of Milton, and took centre stage in his defence of the book. The characteristic ambiguity in Toland's writing allowed him to claim that he was not referring to the writings of the New Testament in his remarks about dubious texts, for among "Supposititious Pieces in the Name of Christ…there is none ascrib'd to him in the whole Bible."[63] This is true, thought it would not automatically account for those of "the Apostles, and other Great names" who Toland queried,[64] when he entertained the possibility that "the spuriousness of several more such books is yet undiscover'd."[65] Which books might these be? Toland does provide an answer, but not before enlightening the supposed ignorance of Blackall, by providing an impressive catalogue of apocryphal works, whose authority was presumed by at least some Christian communities, and which he had compiled from full manuscripts, fragments, and references by the Church fathers. They include non-Canonical works reputed to be written by or about Jesus, Mary, Peter, Andrew, James, John, Philip, Bartholomew, Thomas, Matthew, Paul, Judas, and Dionysius the Areopagite;[66] most incredibly of all, there are references to works of the patriarch Abraham and the first woman, Eve![67] Texts which are not attributed to any one author, but are associated with some ancient and authoritative community include the *Gospel of the Hebrews*, the *Gospel of the Egyptians*, and the *Apostolic Constitutions*.[68] Finally, there are works purported to be by 'Heathens' in defence of Christianity,[69] including the *Sibyllin Oracles* and the *Letter of Pontius Pilate to Tiberius*, with a speech by the latter to the Roman senate.[70] Toland's cataloguing of 'spurious' sources for the life of Jesus, and the theology of the early Church, finds a counterpart in the work of a contemporary scholar such as Ehrman:[71] written in accessible form, and aimed at popularising the fact of ancient Christian diversity, while problematizing the whole question of scriptural authority.

On the question of his impiety towards the canon, Toland may, with some plausibility, have been able to deny any direct reference to the New

---

[63] *Amyntor*, 16–17.
[64] *Amyntor*, 15.
[65] *Amyntor*, 15.
[66] *Amyntor*, 20–39.
[67] *Amyntor*, 33.
[68] *Amyntor*, 35–38.
[69] *Amyntor*, 40.
[70] *Amyntor*, 41.
[71] See, for example, Ehrman's *Lost Christianities*, which opens with a systematic summary of 'Major Christian Apocrypha' (xi–xv).

Testament in his original remarks on the ease with which persons could be duped by fraudulent texts in ancient times; after all, he judged this to be an age when the world was "entirely overspread by the Darkness of Superstition."[72] But the lack of any specified historical mode of authentication from Toland, and the implicit charge that, at least at the edges, a commitment to the New Testament canon to the exclusion of other early witnesses was arbitrary from an evidential point of view, would do little to convince Toland's critics that his enquiry into the question canonicity was a theologically innocent rhetorical strategy. The Irish scribe was not finished with his foray into the apocrypha.

### Christianity, Judaism, Islam and the 'Lost' Gospel of Barnabas

Rather than being a major historical scholar in his own right, Toland was a creative disseminator of Christian historiography and biblical scholarship, which furnished his religious and political ends as a public writer.[73] He was fortunate, therefore, to be writing at a time when pioneering work was being carried out on the historical origins of the books of the Bible, and on the Jewish and Christian apocrypha.[74] At the summit of the former discipline was the French Oratorian priest, Richard Simon;[75] at the pinnacle of the latter, the German classicist and bibliographer, Johan Albrecht Fabricius.[76] Toland borrowed liberally from both, not least in his research for a book which was to prove among his most controversial.[77]

---

[72] *Amyntor*, 15.

[73] Champion, *Republican Learning*, 51.

[74] The growth of patristic scholarship, for both antiquarian and theological reasons, is also immensely important for understanding the intellectual context for Toland and his work on the apocrypha: see Champion, 'Editorial Introduction', John Toland, *Nazarenus* (Oxford: Voltaire Foundation, University of Oxford, 1991), 1–106, especially 39–53.

[75] Simon was censored, under the influence of by Jacques-Bénigne Bossuet, during the absolutist reign of Louis XIV: Patrick J. Lambe, "Biblical Criticism and Censorship in Ancien Régime France: The Case of Richard Simon," *Harvard Theological Review* 78 (1985), 149–177. The book that made Simon famous (or infamous) was his *Histoire critique du Vieux Testament* (Paris, 1678), which he followed up with major studies of the New Testament canon.

[76] Fabricius was the father-in-law of H. S. Reimarus, though their pedagogical relationship preceded this familial tie. Both men were associated with Hamburg's famed educational institutions, the *Gelehrtenschule des Johanneums* and *Akademisches Gymnasium*; see Almut Spalding, *Elise Reimarus (1735–1805), the Muse of Hamburg: A Woman of the German Enlightenment* (Königshausen & Neumann: Würzburg, 2005), 36–39.

[77] For evidence of Simon's influence on Toland in *Nazarenus*, see Champion, 'Introduction', 8, 11, 37, 87–88; for Fabricius, see 'Appendix 2', 296–300.

In an originally clandestine work, circulating in French under the title
*Christianisme Judaique et Mahometan*, and later published and expanded
in English as *Nazarenus, or Jewish, Gentile and Mohometan Christianity*,[78]
Toland undertakes two ambitious and subversive projects, the results of
which are presented in the form of two letter, both of which take as their
point of departure the interpretation of relatively obscure texts. The second
letter, which did not form part of the original French work, is an "Account
of an Irish Manuscript of the *Four Gospels*; with A Summary of the ancient
Irish Christianity, before the Papal Corruptions and Usurpations."[79] As his
own title plainly indicates, Toland attempts to rewrite the history of Christianity in his native Ireland, rejecting Roman Catholicism as a temporary
imposition, using the aforementioned manuscript to provide clues for
his reconstruction of the country's religious history. The religio-political
implications of such a work are self-evident, but they broadly rely on
the canonical Gospels, and so it is the first letter which commands our
attention.[80] In this first letter, Toland promises a "succinct history of a
New Gospel, which I discovered in Amsterdam, in the year 1709."[81] The
discovery of a mere fragment of a text which mentions Jesus (not to mention his 'secret wife') remains sufficient today to make news headlines
around the world,[82] so one can imagine the interest among the intellectual class in eighteenth-century Christian Europe at the 'discovery' of a
whole 'New Gospel.' And when such a 'discovery' is purported to have
been made by Toland, the interest would be accompanied by some trepi-
dation. His critics were not disappointed.

The text Toland claimed to have discovered was "a Mohometan Gospel,
never before publically made known among Christians":[83] the *Gospel of
Barnabas*, which Toland judged to have carried some authority in the
Islamic world. Toland concedes that this would be no news to Christians
of learning, but, for most of those Christians, it seems fair to say that the
fact that a religious text was in some way authoritative among Muslims

---

[78] French and English versions of the work are collected in Champion, ed., *Nazarenus*.
[79] Toland, *Nazarenus*, 194–245.
[80] *Nazarenus*, 114–193.
[81] *Nazarenus*, 115.
[82] The reference here is to a reputedly ancient fragment referring to the 'wife of Jesus'.
The co-editor of the current collection has written (with entirely warranted scepticism)
about this very matter: see A. K. M. Adam, "A Fragment is a Fragment," *The Living Church*
(on-line), 26 Sep. 2012, accessed 05 Mar. 2013: http://www.livingchurch.org/a-fragment-is-
a-fragment.
[83] Toland, *Nazarenus*, 115.

would, at best, make it a scholarly curiosity: the occasion for a study in historical and religious error, perhaps, but not a constructive document for the purposes of Christian theology. As Toland outlines his argument in the Preface to *Nazarenus*, however, it becomes clear that he is advancing this text as the catalyst for the reconstruction of the "ORIGINAL PLAN OF CHRISTIANITY":[84] proposing, as he does, that the *Gospel of Barnabas* is capable of explaining the close historic relationship between elements in primitive Christian thought about Jesus, as he understood them, and Islamic views of Jesus.[85] The very name of Barnabas has apostolic currency, of course: Barnabas was the name of an Apostle and associate of Paul (Acts 14:14), to whom the *Epistle of Barnabas* (c. 135 CE) was traditionally attributed.[86] Toland draws his reader's attention to the Gospel's authorial claims in the Italian manuscript: "Barnaba Apostolo di Jessu Nazareno, chiamato Christo" ("Barnabas, the Apostle of Jesus of Nazareth, called the Christ").[87] Toland leaves the true identity of the author as an open question, but he is keen to distance the Gospel from the Epistle, which he agrees is "spurious."[88] Questions of apostolic authorship aside, even a tentative juxtaposition of primitive Christian and Islamic conceptions of Jesus was a perilous move: on the one hand, the recovery of primitive Christianity was the Holy Grail for many post-Reformation theologians; on the other hand, there was a strong tendency in Christian Europe to regard Mohammed as a religious imposter, and Islam an extreme Christian heresy.[89] So the idea that a "Mohometan Gospel" might point the way to the Grail would be unlikely to receive a warm reception. What was the substance of Toland's argument?

---

[84] *Nazarenus*, 114: part of the subtitle, on the frontispiece.

[85] Although the original language of the composition is disputed, the oldest known texts of *Barnabas* are an Italian manuscript dating from around the end of the sixteenth century, and a Spanish one from the eighteenth; see Jan Joosten, 'The *Gospel of Barnabas* and the Diatessaron', *Harvard Theological Review* 95 (2002), 73–74. Toland read the Italian version while it was still in Amsterdam. It was later sold to Prince Eugène of Savoy. The dates proposed for the original composition run from antiquity to the seventeenth century, but the majority of scholars prefer a late medieval or early modern date (Joosten, '*Gospel of Barnabas* and the Diatessaron', 73–74). For an English translation see *The Gospel of Barnabas*, ed. & trans. Lonsdale Ragg and Laura Ragg (Oxford, 1907).

[86] Ehrman, *Lost Christianities*, xiii.

[87] *Gospel of Barnabas*, quoted by Toland, *Nazarenus*, 143 n. 18.

[88] Toland, *Nazarenus*, 138. Not only does this leave open the *possibility* that the Gospel is authentically apostolic, it important for Toland to distinguish the two documents because of their different theological preoccupations.

[89] See, for example, Humphrey Prideaux, *The True Nature of Imposture Fully Display'd in the Life of Mahomet* (London, William Rogers, 1697).

Not all the European literature on Islam in the late seventeenth and early eighteenth centuries was hostile, and Toland had some of the more sympathetic at his disposal. One notable treatment of the genesis of Islam was penned by Henry Stubbe, one time librarian at the Bodleian Library, Oxford.[90] In his *Account of the Rise and Progress of Mahometanism*, Stubbe draws *comparisons* between certain features of Islamic theology—including an emphasis on the unity of God and a prophetic rather than incarnational conception of Jesus—and the theology of the Ebionites, typically taken to be an early Christian heresy.[91] On this latter view, God was one; Jesus was God's chosen messenger, but he was not, by nature, divine. In *Nazarenus*, Toland accepts the comparison between these seemingly disparate theological traditions,[92] while making an audacious attempt to find a textual grounding for the connection in the 'lost' Gospel of Barnabas. Toland thought he had ancient papal support in supposing the existence of an ancient Gospel of Barnabas,[93] while he was confident that, counterintuitive though it may seem, 'the *Gospel of the Mahometans* ... is in great part the same book.'[94] What remained was for Toland to try to link Barnabas with that early Christian community, the Ebionites, so that he could argue that "some of the fundamental doctrines of Mohometanism.... have their rise ... from the earliest monuments of the Christian religion."[95] He attempts this by mounting a circumstantial case that this 'New Gospel' testified to the beliefs and practises of an early Christian movement known in some historiographical traditions as 'the Nazarens', which Toland takes to be another name for the Ebionites.[96]

---

[90] For a more recent edition of his work, see Stubbe, *An Account of the Rise and Progress of Mahometanism*, ed. M. K. Shairani, (London: Luzac, 1911).

[91] The name derives from the Hebrew אביונים ('poor ones'). The evidence we have comes mainly from patristic sources, the earliest being Justin Martyr, but it is not always clear if the ancient sources are bearing witness to the same group of Jewish Christians: see 'Ebionites', *The Oxford Dictionary of the Christian Church*, ed. F. L. Cross and E. A. Livingstone, 3rd rev. ed. (Oxford: Oxford University Press, 2005); *Oxford Reference* (on line), 2009, accessed 11 Feb. 2013: http://www.oxfordreference.com/view/10.1093/acref/9780192802903.001.0001/acref-9780192802903-e-2214.

[92] Toland, *Nazarenus* (English), 152–153. On the connections between the work of Stubbe and Toland, see Champion, 'Introduction', 86.

[93] Toland, *Nazarenus*, 136–139.

[94] *Nazarenus*, 139.

[95] *Nazarenus*, 135.

[96] *Nazarenus*, 150–156. Whether this identification is historically sound has been disputed for centuries, with such luminaries of church history as Adolf von Harnack making the same judgement as Toland on the matter, while J. B. Lightfoot distinguished between the two movements (Cross and Livingstone, 'Ebionites').

Such conjectures about the continuity of Islamic doctrines and some early Christian movements were controversial enough, but Toland was not satisfied with drawing speculative connections between ancient religious communities and their texts. He sets himself against the perceived judgement of the Church fathers and argues that far from being a Judaising heresy, the Ebionites / Nazarens were the closest in historical and geographic proximity, and in religious spirit, to Jesus of Nazareth,[97] whose religious vision remained within the parameters of Mosaic law: "JESUS did not, as tis universally believed, abolish the law of Moses, neither in whole nor in part, not in the letter no more than in the spirit."[98]

Given the praise heaped on twentieth-century scholarship which has sought to locate the historical Jesus within the matrix of first-century Judaism, one should not underestimate the radicalism of Toland on this point concerning Jesus and the law. Interestingly, Toland insists that Jews from Nazareth, Galilee, were closely bound to the Jewish law and resisted the influence of Hellenistic culture. Whether this is a historically sound judgement is fiercely contested in rival reconstructions of Palestine at time of Jesus, and has been since at least the nineteenth century.[99] Toland thought that it was sound, and, in so far as Barnabas could have emanated from this community and impacted upon the Islamic world, Toland also considers it safe to conclude that Islam is a "sort of sect of Christianity, as Christianity was first esteem'd a branch of Judaism."[100] Toland therefore offers a radically antagonistic challenge to his contemporaries' notions about the historical relationship between Judaism, Christianity and Islam,

---

[97] Toland understands the term 'Nazarens' to refer to those Jews who followed the rabbi, Jesus, who became the focus of Christian devotion: "these Jewish converts were term'd Nazarens from JESUS of Nazareth" (*Nazarenus*, 151).

[98] *Nazarenus*, 135.

[99] For good general surveys, see Halvor Moxnes, "The Construction of Galilee as a Place for the Historical Jesus, Part I", *Biblical Theology Bulletin* 31 (2001), 27–37; and "Part II", *BTB* 31 (2001), 64–77.

[100] Toland, *Nazarenus*, 135. Toland tried to prove his case by comparing the picture in *Barnabas* with Islamic notions about Jesus, drawn in part from from the Qur'an ('Alcoran') of 'Mahomet', (139)—although there is no substantial engagement with the text of the Qur'an—and references to the Ebionites in ancient sources (136–152). There does indeed seem to have been an early Jewish Christian sect known as the Ebionites, but they were probably a second-century phenomenon (Ehrman, *Lost Christianities*, xi) which Toland conflated with the oldest Jewish-Christian movement. More recent scholarship has indicated that the Ebionites and the Nazoraeans (probably Toland's 'Nazarens') were distinct Jewish-Christian groups, possibly with their own gospels: William L. Petersen, "Ebionites, Gospel of the", in *Anchor Bible Dictionary*, ed. David Noel Freedman, Vol. 2 (New York: Doubleday, 1992), 261–262; and Petersen, 'Nazoraeans, Gospel of the', in *ABD* Vol. 4, 1051–1052.

with Muslims emerging 'as a sort of Christians, and not the worse sort neither, tho farr [*sic*] from being the best',[101] and all facilitated by this supposed textual common denominator: the Gospel of Barnabas.

Toland, scourge of intolerant theological exclusivism, was not about to insist that he had found the 'true and original' Christianity to which his own age must lay claim. On the contrary, he seizes on the diversity of early Christianity, and, instead of either trying to impose unity, or suggest that plurality undermines the integrity of the Christian religion, he argues that this diversity was "design'd in The Original Plan of Christianity."[102] The good news from the 'gospel of Toland' is summarised thus:

> FROM the history of the NAZARENS, and more particularly from the evident words of Scripture, I infer in this discourse a distinction of two sorts of Christianity, viz., those from among the Jews, and those from among the Gentiles: not only that in fact there was such a distinction (which no body denies) but likewise that of right it ought to have been so (which everybody denies)...I mean that the Jews, tho associating with the converted Gentiles, and acknowledging them for brethren, were still to observe their own Law...and that the Gentiles, who became so far Jews as to acknowledge ONE GOD, were not however to observe the Jewish law...[103]

According to Toland, there is creative theological potential in affirming diversity in primitive Christianity:

> I judge it to be most right and true, the genuine primary Christianity; and therefore producing the promis'd effects of the Gospel, GLORY TO GOD ON HIGH, PEACE ON EARTH, GOODWILL TOWARDS MEN...I have moreover prov'd, that the distinction of Jewish and Gentile Christians...reconciles PETER and PAUL about Circumcision and the other Legal ceremonies, as it does PAUL and JAMES about Justification by Faith, or...by Works; it makes the Gospels to agree with the Acts and the Epistles...but, what is more than all, it shows a perfect accord between the Old Testament and the New...[104]

Toland's historical treatment of Christian origins was almost certainly produced with a view to addressing the religio-political factionalism within post-Reformation Christendom: the acceptance of different modes of religious life, in some way centred on the figure of Jesus conceived as Messiah, was a live option among intellectuals willing to accept a minimalist

---

[101] Toland, *Nazarenus*, 116.
[102] *Nazarenus*, 117.
[103] *Nazarenus*, 117.
[104] *Nazarenus*, 119.

Christian theology as part of a religious and cultural consensus in European societies. Justin Champion offers the following summary statement of Toland's work on Christian origins, and tries to explain his likely aims:

> Having reconstructed the historical milieu of early Judaeo-Christianity, Toland then proceeded to reinterpret the scriptural accounts of disputes between Peter, Paul and James about the relationship between Jewish ceremony and the soteriological efficiency of faith, not as theological systems, but as practical injunctions about how different types of believer, (Jewish, Nazarene, Gentile) could co-exist in civil society... This was part of the reasoning behind advancing the *Gospel of Barnabas* as a Scriptural text that was used by Jewish-Christians and Muslims: Scripture was effective not for its doctrinal content (foisted by priests) but because it enables communities to live a virtuous life.[105]

If Champion's account is accurate, and I judge that it is, then Toland was adopting the moral-theological hermeneutic employed in the previous century by Benedict de Spinoza, where scripture serves the purpose of inculcating obedience to God, manifest in a life of virtue, rather that the revelation of any definitive doctrines about the nature of God.[106] Spinoza stuck doggedly to the biblical canon in his *Tractatus Theologico-Politicus*, whereas Toland was prepared, in principle, to allow minor texts in Islamic (and Jewish-Christian) tradition to count as Scripture, in so far as they testified to the possibility of authentic religious responses to God, inevitably shaped by their cultural embeddedness, and not gravely worse for it: "the true religion being one and the same in substance from the beginning, though in circumstances the Institutions of it at different times be different, and consequently more or less perfect."[107]

Toland's relatively pluralistic religious stance, with primitive Christianity serving as the blueprint, has seemed, to some, a thin disguise for what was little more than an attack on the canon, the Church, and the religious authority invested in both.[108] Indeed, in the earlier *Christianisme Judaique et Mahometan*, Toland advances his argument about the continuity of the earliest Christian communities with Judaism as a historical thesis,

---

[105] Champion, 'Introduction', 75, 77.
[106] Benedict De Spinoza, *Theological-Political Treatise*, trans. Samuel Shirley (Indianapolis, Ind.: Hackett, 1998), 164.
[107] Toland, *Nazarenus*, 154.
[108] For a condensed summary of responses to *Nazarenus* and Toland's replies, see Champion, 'Introduction', 89–96.

without "the veneer of pious *renovatio*."[109] Nevertheless, when he came
to rework the piece for a wider public, Toland presents his reconstruction
as part of a religiously affirmative thesis. It is difficult to establish with
any great certainty whether Toland's change in the presentation of his
ideas is indicative of a change in intellectual and theological ambition,
or whether he simply felt it expedient to try and infuse his theories with
the fulsome praise which typically attended discussion of primitive Christianity in more pious scholarship. Toland certainly would not be the last
self-declared friend of Christianity to feel the need to undermine exclusive
claims to theological truth in the course of, or prior to, advancing a more
positive, pluralistic religious stance.[110] Whatever Toland's motives, and
he had supporters as well as detractors,[111] his heterodox opinions were
based on a substantial edifice of independent and borrowed scholarship:
in *Nazarenus*, Toland's credibility as a critic of orthodox Christian theology rested on his credibility as a historian of the Church, as a reader and
utiliser of patristic sources, and as an enquirer into the provenance of
obscure texts. On all counts, Toland's critics found him hopelessly wanting, and some judged him downright deceitful in his scholarly practises.

According to one of his contemporary critics, James Patterson, Toland
had presented his readers with "a labyrinth of Amusements to blend Christianity with Mahometanism."[112] Patterson was far from amused, though
his consternation was largely directed at Toland's disregard for orthodox theology as a barometer for scriptural authority, rather than for the
Irishman's historical malpractice. The outstanding scholarly responses to
*Nazarenus* in English came from the Anglican cleric and classicist Thomas
Mangey, and the Welsh Non-Conformist minister Jeremiah Jones. The former blends scholarship and stinging polemic in a brief work which argues,
among other things, that the evidence provided by Toland for the antiquity
of Barnabas included papal decrees which were probably forged,[113] and

---

[109] *Nazarenus*, 69.

[110] Examples are bountiful, but a good one would be the provocative volume edited
by the late John Hick, *The Myth of God Incarnate* (London: SCM Press, 1977), followed by
his own *The Myth of Christian Uniqueness* (London: SCM Press, 1988). There seems little
doubt that such deflationary works formed part of a positive pluralistic religious vision in
such works as Hick's *An Interpretation of Religion: Human Responses to the Transcendent*
(London: Palgrave, 2004).

[111] One of his supporters was Martin Eagle, an expert on oriental languages (Champion,
'Introduction', 90–91).

[112] James Patterson, quoted in Champion, "Introduction," 91.

[113] Thomas Mangey, *Remarks Upon Nazarenus* (London: William and John Innys, 1718),
12–14. He is thinking specifically of the judgements of Pope Gelasius I.

that Toland even managed to misrepresent those, which originally repudiated any suggestion of the Gospel's authority.[114] The response by Jones offers a comprehensive alternative model for the use of historical-critical methods with integrity, and for pious Christian ends.[115] Originally published in 1726, Jones's effort runs to three volumes, and it became something of a classic on the historical and theological authority of the canon.[116] Jones takes Toland to task directly on a great many points. For example, in response to *Nazarenus*, Jones criticises Toland's parsimonious quotations from Barnabas, which Jones expands on by quoting from another study of the document, which shows more fully the extent to which the text reflects a developed Islamic view of the story of Jesus on such sensitive matters such as his death, to the point where Jesus is depicted in conversation with his mother assuring her that, contrary to popular belief, he had in fact escaped death: 'Believe me, my mother, for I positively affirm that I was never dead, for God has reserved me even to the end of the world.'[117] In addition to such heavy handed apologetics in the Gospel, Jones finds fault with Toland's extremely loose historical inferences in favour of the antiquity of Barnabas, on the basis of parallels between parts of this work and writings associated with certain Christian sects:[118] the presence of assuredly ancient fabrications in a text does not made said text assuredly ancient. Finally, like many critics of Toland's Church history, and this time focussing specifically on *Amyntor*, Jones criticises Toland's highly tendentious and selective quoting of patristic sources, including St Augustine, when compiling his list of apocryphal works and documenting their status in the Church.[119] Faced with such criticism, Toland responded angrily, claiming that he had been misrepresented, and that his "mature examination" of the document had led him only to posit its connection

---

*Remarks*, 13. Even if we accept the relevant Gelasian Decrees as valid, according to Mangey they may attest to *Barnabas's* existence but not its apostolic authorship, which they actually deny. And assuming that the Gelasian Decrees were forged, that would mean "The very Name of *Barnabas's* Gospel was therefore utterly unknown to the Ancients" (13).

[114] Jeremiah Jones, *A New and Full Method for Settling the Canonical Authority of the New Testament*, Vol. II (Oxford: The Clarendon Press, 1798), 66–67.

[115] Although according to Champion, the work was "conceived as a painstaking rebuttal of Toland" ("Introduction", 98).

[116] Champion, "Introduction," 93.

[117] Jones, *New and Full Method*, Vol. I, 165. Jones is relying on the extracts from an analysis of *Barnabas* by Bernard de la Monnoye.

[118] *New and Full Method*, Vol. I, 167–168.

[119] *New and Full Method*, Vol. II, 66–67.

with Islam, not to imply its apostolic authority,[120] although Toland's original work seemed to leave open that very possibility. In his reply to his critics, Toland is clear that this Gospel was "attributed to" Barnabas, "father'd upon him, and forg'd under his name"[121]—though even here Toland seemed unable to let go of the Gospel's antiquity.[122]

As with Morton Smith, approximately two and a half centuries later, Toland's critics were not content to express skepticism over the antiquity of the document he was using to reconstruct Christian origins. One French critic suggested Toland had presided over a "sham discovery,"[123] facilitating his subterranean war against Christendom. Beyond a shared interest in the apocrypha and a taste for religious controversy, however, we should not push the parallels between Toland and Smith's textual discoveries too far. Toland insisted he was no "false coiner,"[124] and that the authenticity of his discovery was "sufficiently known to all Europe."[125] On the defensive, Toland's claim for the renown of his find may have been rather grand; nevertheless, whereas the location of the text that Smith claimed to have discovered in Mar Saba remains a mystery, we know exactly where the Gospel of Barnabas referred to by Toland is kept: the Austrian National Library, Vienna.[126] Toland may not have been a scrupulously honest analyst of the textual witnesses for the antiquity of Barnabas, but he was not a 'false coiner'. The case against Smith, though far from conclusive, is likely to persist in the absence of independent textual verification.

It is difficult to measure, with any precision, the success of Toland's argument that religious pluralism was in some sense theologically normative for Christianity, though it seems safe to conclude that his converts were few in number. What he did do was to stir some Christian scholars from their "dogmatic slumbers,"[127] and show that it was not enough to catalogue apocryphal Christian works in the name of historical erudition.

---

120 Toland, *Mangoneutes: Being a Defence of Nazarenus* (London, 1720), 149.
121 *Mangoneutes*, 149.
122 *Mangoneutes*, 149.
123 de la Monnoye, quoted in Toland, *Mangoneutes*, 156.
124 *Mangoneutes*, 156.
125 *Mangoneutes*, 156.
126 Joosten, 'Date and Provenance', 201–202.
127 The phrase is borrowed from a much more famous and influential figure of the Enlightenment: Immanuel Kant's description of the impact of reading David Hume, when the latter disrupted his 'dogmatischen Schlummer' and stimulated a new phase in his 'spekulativen Philosophie': *Prolegomena zu einer jeden künftigen Metaphysik: die als Wissenschaft wird auftreten können*, 6th ed., ed. Karl Vorländer (Leipzig: Verlag Von Felix Meiner, 1920), 7.

If scholars wanted to maintain that the books included in the New Testament, and the Bible as a whole, possess some kind of authority which
distinguishes them from Christian texts outside the canon, then they had
an ongoing intellectual (perhaps even a religious) duty to define what
that authority consists in, and to demonstrate the privileged status of
the canon on publicly contestable grounds. The historical formation and
theological authority of the canon have been a significant focus of modern
biblical studies ever since.

### Conclusion: The Uses and Abuses of the Apocrypha

The pursuit of non-canonical textual witnesses to first century Christian
and Jewish communities, and the popularisation of such scholarship, is an
intellectual end in itself: adding to the sum of human knowledge, and illuminating the spiritual landscapes of times otherwise lost, for the interest
and information of an educated public. Scholars once based at the University of Glasgow have played a role in that enterprise.[128] And it is surely
true that for some students of the history of the canon, and the emerging Church that authorised it, there is a troubling sense of victor's justice
about the orthodox story: truth prevailing, truth triumphant, pernicious
error vanquished. With some justification, such students can sketch a picture of alternative Christian perspectives from the ancient world being
marginalised (or worse), and their texts suppressed, by a Church which
put unity before authentic religious commitment from all members of the
(extended) Christian family, and in doing so sought to control theological
legitimacy.[129] The historically precarious, highly contingent, fate of some
Christian texts, as discerned through the study of the intertwined histories
of the canon and the apocrypha, has surely helped to instil a degree of
humility in many reflective Christians, when they consider the meaning
they give to their commitment to the Bible as the 'Word of God', and how
that affirmation informs their relations with others for whom different

---

[128] See John M. G. Barclay, *Frequently Asked Questions on the Dead Sea Scrolls* (Glasgow:
Trinity St Mungo Press, 1998).

[129] The first recorded case of a Christian receiving capital punishment for their heresy was the Spanish ascetic Priscillian, whose Gnostic and Manichaean tendencies were
associated with the apocryphal gospels at his disposal, although, like other famous early
heretics (e.g. Marcion), the letters of Paul were a major influence; see Henry Chadwick,
*Priscillian of Avila: The Occult and the Charismatic in the Early Church* (Oxford: Clarendon
Press, 1976).

religious texts, Christian or not, are authoritative. On the use of the apocrypha as a weapon with which to attack the principles and values of the
established churches and their political bedfellows, however, the gains are
rather less obvious.

The claims for the apocrypha by Anglophone writers like Toland were
part of a wider movement of radical biblical criticism in the early British
Enlightenment. At least one major historical survey of modern New Testament studies has argued that the antagonistic nature of much of this work,
and the impression that such criticism was serving the idiosyncratic religious interests of heretics, or of political protagonist propagandists (such
as Toland) may well have been a factors in the process whereby historical
criticism of the Bible fell into disrepute in the English speaking nations,
and stimulated a pietistic backlash.[130] And on the question of religious
toleration, which forms the background to so much of Toland's work, his
rhetoric contribution pales in comparison to the mark left on intellectual
history by John Locke's *Letter Concerning Toleration*, whose theological
arguments for toleration are largely drawn from the canonical Gospels.[131]

British and Irish writers such as Toland anticipated many of the later
scholarly positions about early Christian diversity, and they did so in an
age when questioning the unity of the primitive Church was much more
problematic, theologically and politically.[132] Nevertheless, a more influential voice on the question of religious diversity (and conflict) in the early
Church was that of Ferdinand Christian Baur and the Tübingen school.
Baur did not rely on the apocrypha to make his case for early Christian
diversity and conflict, however, but identified the sources of that diversity and conflict in the canon itself.[133] Moreover, Baur's most subversive

---

[130] See William Baird, *New Testament Research*, Vol. 1, 56–57. The subversive use of
the apocrypha was just one of the provocations during this period, however, when the
miracles, morality and prophecies of the Bible all came under attack by British and Irish
scholars.

[131] Locke's first *Epistola de tolerantia* was quickly translated into English by William
Popple: see *John Locke: A Letter Concerning Toleration and Other Writings*, ed. Mark Goldie
(Indianapolis: Liberty Fund, 2010), 36–67. Locke's *Letter* appeared in the same year that the
Act of Toleration was passed: the legislation granted freedom of worship and assembly to
dissenting Protestants however, non-Trinitarian religion, such as that which permeates the
Gospel of Barnabas, was not covered by the Act.

[132] This was long ago recognised by, for example, D. Patrick, 'Two English Forerunners
of the Tübingen school', *Theological Review* 14 (1877), 562–603.

[133] A seminal work here was the long essay by Ferdinand Christian Baur, 'Die Christus-
partei in der korinthischen Gemeinde, der Gegensatz des paulinischen und petrinischen
Christentums in der ältesten Kirche, der Apostel Petrus in Rom', *Tübinger Zeitschrift für
Theologie* iv (1831), 61–206.

historical moves with respect to the canon were less concerned with the diversity of ancient witnesses excluded from the canon, and more with internal authority: not *introducing* texts into the history which unsettles, say, a Pauline view of the early Church (Toland's thesis), but questioning the apostolic authorship of the Pauline corpus itself.[134] Time and again in the history of scholarship on Christian origins, the seemingly all too familiar books of the New Testament are the primary sources of interpretive innovation and historical controversy.

Although no one argues for the ancient authenticity of the Gospel of Barnabas today, genuine textual discoveries have been found which do expand our knowledge of the early Christian context. Even here, though, the capacity of these texts to fundamentally challenge some 'mainstream' Christian attitudes is extremely doubtful. For all the hullabaloo about the so called 'Gnostic Gospels', and especially the Gospel of Thomas, when historians try to reconstruct the story of Jesus of Nazareth, which is central to almost any Christian identity, it is to the canonical Gospels, and most of all to the synoptic Gospels, that scholars turn.[135] Of course, the faith of most confessing Christians pays little heed to academic historical questions, and the content of their confession is likely go beyond anything that could be demonstrated firmly at the bar of historical reason. But for those who want to show that the canonical treatments represent a historically distorted range of early perspectives on Jesus, which must be corrected by appeal to other sources, the relative lack of weight given to the Christian apocrypha by historical Jesus scholars does not bode well for this line of argument. Historical scholars of primitive Christianity remain wedded to the New Testament canon as their primary sources, whereas the most culturally influential scholar in recent times to argue that the texts from Nag Hammadi represent the 'earliest Christian documents',[136] and should fundamentally change our view of Jesus and the original plan

---

[134] Baur, *Die sogenannten Pastoralbriefe des Apostles Paulus aufs neue kritisch untersucht* (Stuttgart: J. G. Cotta, 1835); and *Paulus, der Apostel Jesus Christi. Sein Leben und Wirken, seine Briefe und seine Lehre*, 1st ed. (Stuttgart: Verlag von Becher and Müller, 1845).

[135] One need only scan the primary sources used by such major scholars over the last forty years as Vermes, Sanders, Richard Horsley, Gerd Theissen, John Paul Meier, N. T. Wright, Dale Allison and Maurice Casey. Even Crossan, a scholar noted for his early dating of Thomas and other apocryphal texts, is much more dependent on Mark and the hypothetical Q source, i.e. material already imbedded in the canon: see his inventory of authentic sayings in *Historical Jesus*, xiii–xxvi.

[136] Dan Brown, *The Da Vinci Code* (New York: Doubleday, 2003), 322.

of the early Church, is Sir Leigh Teabing—the fictional historian in Dan Brown's the *Da Vinci Code*.[137]

The appeal to Christian diversity, supported by non-canonical sources, is often well intentioned: to challenge the theological authority of those who have appealed to canonical texts when acquiescing to (or supporting) such scandals as the institutions of slavery and apatite, of religious intolerance, the subordination of women, and the persecution of homosexuals. Progress has been made in parts of the Christian world in all these areas, but, in so far as scripture has played any role in challenging prejudice and unjust institutions, there seems little evidence that the breakthroughs have come from the insights of 'other testaments.'[138] If the books in the canon have been used to authorise intolerance towards a range of religious and social identities, which they surely have, then in so far as there is to continue to be correctives to such intolerances, they are more likely to depend on critical re-readings of the canon, or straight talking denials of the theological authority of the offending texts,[139] than on any attempt to crack open the canon in the hope that that the rehabilitation and introduction of discarded scriptures will save Christianity from itself.[140]

---

[137] Questions of gender are pressing here. Brown's fictional historian hypothesises, on the basis of the 'earliest Christian documents' that it was Jesus' intention that the Church be led, in the first instance, by Mary Magdalene, with Jesus thereby cast as the "the original feminist'," only to be thwarted by "sexist" Peter (325). From Toland to Brown, appeal to an "original plan" for Christianity, hitherto neglected by the church, is an irresistible (and, to many readers, attractive) rhetorical device, wielded by those who claim access to lost or suppressed documents, which a reputedly controlling church has tried (with considerable success) to wipe from historical memory.

[138] This phrase is stolen, out of context, from the subtitle of *Derrida and Religion: Other Testaments*, ed. Yvonne Sherwood and Kevin Hart (London: Routledge, 2004).

[139] A mere smattering of critical re-readings in the areas of gender and sexuality would include Elizabeth Schüssler Fiorenza's *Sophia's Prophet: Critical Issues in Feminist Christology* (New York: Continuum, 1994), and *In Memory of Her: A Feminist Theological Reconstruction of Christian Origins*, 2nd ed. (London: SCM Press, 1995); ed. Robert L. Brawley *Biblical Ethics & Homosexuality: Listening to Scripture* (London: Westminster John Knox Press, 1996); and Dale B. Martin, *Sex and the Single Saviour: Gender and Sexuality in Biblical Interpretation*, (London: Westminster John Knox Press, 2006). Outside the academy, a leading figure of the Anglican Church and global justice campaigner, Archbishop Desmond Tutu, passionately affirms the authority of the biblical canon while flatly repudiating texts which are said to authorise practises now routinely regarded as abominations (such as slavery), and those on much more contentious matters such as female ordination and homosexuality: all these themes are explored, in conversation with the Bible, in Tutu, with Douglass Abrams, *God Has a Dream: A Vision of Hope for Out Times* (London: Rider, 2004).

[140] Although the *New Testament*, produced by Taussig and his colleagues, represents a constructive attempt at such a revisionary project.

# SISTERHOOD IN THE WILDERNESS: BIBLICAL PARADIGMS AND FEMINIST IDENTITY POLITICS IN READINGS OF HAGAR AND SARAH

## Anna Fisk

The ambivalent relationship of feminist biblical scholarship is well expressed by Alicia Suskin Ostriker: "[i]f the Bible is a flaming sword forbidding our entrance to the garden, it is also a burning bush urging us toward freedom. It is what we wrestle with all night and from which we may, if we demand it, wrest a blessing."[1] For many feminist interpreters, wrestling a blessing from the biblical text means recovering the lost stories of the women who are mentioned only fleetingly amidst a narrative more concerned with a male God's dealings with the men of Israel. This constitutes a *reclaiming* of female biblical characters, celebrating their strengths and exploring their motives, giving voice where before there was silence. Yet when feminists foreground the women's story of Genesis 16:1–21 and 21:9–21 they may end up clasping a curse as well as a blessing. The story of Hagar and Sarah is challenging for those who want to emphasise positive images of women's relationships in the biblical traditions.

Hagar and Sarah[2] are significant in feminist biblical reception history, as mothers of nations who are granted important roles and developed characterization in the Genesis narrative. Hagar names God and is the first person in the Bible to see God and live. Sarah is enshrined in memory as the mother of the people of Israel. Yet these two female figures, who share a story and a husband, never talk to one another; the biblical narrative and subsequent interpretation places them in opposition to each other. Feminist religious discourse[3] has been accused of a tendency towards innocence, of wanting to present women in the best possible

---

[1] Alicia Suskin Ostriker, "A Triple Hermeneutic: Scripture and Revisionist Women's Poetry", in *A Feminist Companion to Reading the Bible*, eds. Athalya Brenner and Carole Fontaine (Sheffield: Sheffield Academic Press, 1997), 189.

[2] In Genesis 16, her name is 'Sarai,' but by chapter 22 it has changed to 'Sarah.' I use Sarai/Sarah (and Abram/Abraham) depending on which particular text is being discussed. When speaking of the stories as a whole, I use 'Sarah' and 'Abraham.' When considering secondary sources, I use the version of the name used by the writer to whom I am referring.

[3] The two projects of biblical scholarship and theology have been more readily and comfortably intertwined in the feminist strands of both disciplines.

light, and to explain away women's wrongdoing in terms of the unjust system of patriarchy. For black womanist thinkers, this is part of white feminism's refusal to accept itself as part of another unjust system—that of racism and imperialism—in universalizing 'women's experience' of patriarchy and not acknowledging the social and economic differences between women. Whilst feminist thought has, in the last twenty-five years or so, made significant strides in recognising and contending with 'the challenge of difference', this is an ongoing struggle, and white and Jewish feminist readings of Sarah display a residual anxiety and guilt over her treatment of Hagar, with shades of justification that may stretch beyond the confines of the text itself to touch on contemporary political relations. This is not only because today's pale-skinned reader may imagine Sarah as similar to herself, whereas the Egyptian Hagar is dark-skinned and other. It is also perhaps related to how the conflicted sisterhood between Hagar and Sarah has been deployed to symbolize the relationship between white feminism and black womanism, with the former made to acknowledge its own privilege, and complicity in the oppression of other women. Hagar— slave, surrogate and survivor—has been a paradigmatic figure in African-American womanist theology. Sarah's treatment of her has also been read as representative of privileged white women's oppression of women of colour.

The Genesis story, and its afterlives, is complicated. The 'other', excluded from the camp and from the blessing that God grants only to one of Abraham's sons, has in Christian interpretation been read as a justification of the slave trade and apartheid,[4] but also as a demonstration of the inferiority of the Jews. Any reading of Hagar and Sarah that aims to speak to contemporary identity politics needs to take into consideration the fact of Sarah's Jewishness in order not to reinforce both anti-semitism and white hegemony by continuing the trajectory of Christian appropriation of the Hebrew Scriptures, in which Abraham and Sarah become exemplary of white European Christian ideology. But to foreground Sarah's Jewishness is to lead us to another political and religious conflict of today's world, that which, since that "violent rupture that we know, by shorthand, as '9/11' ",[5] has come to define today's world. In Islam, Hagar is the foremother, and

---

[4] See Cain Hope Felder, *Race, Racism and the Biblical Narratives* (Minneapolis: Fortress Press, 2002).

[5] Yvonne Sherwood, "Binding-Unbinding: Divided Responses of Judaism, Christianity, and Islam to the 'Sacrifice' of Abraham's Beloved Son", *Journal of the American Academy of Religion* 72.4 (2004), 822.

it is her son Ishmael, not Isaac, who is the true heir of the one true God. Drawing on feminist scholarship and contemporary women's imaginative writing, this essay explores the various ways in which readings of Hagar and Sarah, as paradigmatic biblical women, speaks to contentious issues of contemporary identity politics.

## Hagar and Womanism

The monotheistic traditions of Judaism, Christianity and Islam all look to the figure of Abraham as "the founding father of an extended family of believers".[6] The mothers of his children take a central role, yet for many readers of the Hebrew Bible, the story of the conflict between Hagar and Sarah is unfamiliar, quickly glossed over in the emphasis on Abraham's great faith and his role as the father of God's chosen people. Susan Niditch makes the insightful point that the narrator of Genesis "works hard to rationalize and justify the emotions and actions of Abraham and Sarah" (cf. 21:12–13), whilst at the same time foregrounding Hagar and Ishmael's point of view.[7] However, the weight of religious tradition has meant that the story has tended to be read from Abraham and Sarah's perspective. It is in the reading of those who approach the text with a concern to emphasise the plight of the oppressed—such as liberation, feminist, African-American and postcolonial interpreters—that the story is seen from the viewpoint of Hagar and Ishmael. When read as Hagar's story, the Genesis text becomes a tale of slavery, exploitation, abuse and cruelty.

In *Texts of Terror*, her landmark work of feminist biblical interpretation, Phyllis Trible reads Sarah as a cruel mistress who takes the active role in Hagar's oppression. Sarah's harsh treatment of Hagar, which prompts her to run away, foreshadows the Exodus story, in an ironic reversal in which the Egyptian is persecuted and cast out by the Hebrew woman. The verb in 16:6, "Sarah afflicted her," is the same as that used to describe the Hebrews' suffering in Egypt. Yet, for Trible, Hagar is denied the liberation and loving sustenance that God provides to the people of Israel. Here it seems that God is on the side of the slave-owner. In the first episode, the

---

[6] Phyllis Trible and Letty M. Russell, "Unto the Thousandth Generation," in their (eds.) *Hagar, Sarah, and Their Children: Jewish, Christian and Muslim Perspectives* (Louisville, Kentucky: Westminster John Knox Press, 2006), 1.

[7] Susan Niditch, "Genesis", in Carol A. Newsom and Sharon H. Ringe (eds.), *The Women's Bible Commentary* (London: SPCK, 1992), 18.

divine messenger instructs Hagar to "return to your mistress, and submit to her" (16:9); As Trible notes, "the God who later, seeing the suffering of a slave people, comes down to deliver them out of the hand of the Egyptians (Exodus 3:7–8) here identifies with the oppressor and orders a servant to return not only to bondage but also to affliction".[8]

The Exodus paradigm of God's identification with and rescue of the Hebrew slaves is hugely significant in liberation theology, especially in its African-American guise. Thus the Hagar story forms a challenge to what Delores Williams terms "the liberation tradition of African-American biblical appropriation",[9] because here God does not help the African slave to escape; rather, she is told to return and submit to oppression. African-American slaves and their descendents have long identified with the slave-woman Hagar:

> For more than a hundred years Hagar—the African slave of the Hebrew woman Sarah—has appeared in the deposits of African-American culture. Sculptors, writers, poets, scholars, preachers and just plain folks have passed along the biblical figure Hagar to generation after generation of black folks.[10]

For example, Pauline Hopkins's 1902 novel is entitled *Hagar's Daughter*; the title character of Frances Harper's *Iola Leroy* is a slave cast out to raise her child on her own, compared to "Hagar of old".[11] Toni Morrison's *Song of Solomon* features a black woman named Hagar who is exploited by a powerful family.[12] Despite the reversal of the Exodus narrative in God's dealings with Hagar in Genesis 16, Hagar's story has remained paradigmatic for African-American women, in a manner quite distinct from the emphasis on liberation in male black liberation theology.

Renita J. Weems provides one of the earliest theological treatments of Hagar's story from a contemporary womanist perspective. In *Just a Sister Away: A Womanist Vision of Women's Relationships in the Bible*, she writes:

> For black women, the story of Hagar in the Old Testament is a haunting one. [...] Even if it is not our individual story, it is a story we have read in

---

[8] Phyllis Trible, *Texts of Terror: Literary-Feminist Readings of Biblical Narratives* (London: SCM, 1984), 16.

[9] Delores S. Williams, *Sisters in the Wilderness: The Challenge of Womanist God-Talk* (Maryknoll, New York: Orbis Books, 1993), 2.

[10] Williams, *Sisters in the Wilderness*, 2.

[11] Delores S. Williams, "Hagar in African American Biblical Interpretation," in Trible and Russell, *Hagar, Sarah, and Their Children*, 173.

[12] Ibid.

our mothers' eyes those afternoons when we greeted them at the front door after a hard day of work as a domestic. And if not our mothers' story, then it is certainly most of our grandmothers' story. For a black woman, Hagar's story is peculiarly familiar. It is as if we know it by heart.[13]

For Weems, Hagar's story expresses the need for women who are "abandoned, abused, betrayed, and banished" for "a sister who will respond with mercy".[14] Thus the role Hagar's story plays in informing the womanist theology of *Just a Sister Away* is to pose a challenge: Hagar needs the loving support of a sister, a need which is not met by Sarah.

In contrast, the work of Delores Williams uses the story of Hagar as a positive paradigm for the constructive effort of revisioning theology "from the point of view of black women's experience".[15] Like Weems, Williams draws parallels between Hagar's experience and that of African-American slave-women, including brutal treatment at hands of slave-masters, being raped and made pregnant by their owners, attempts at escape, and forced exile.[16] Where Williams departs from Weems is in her emphasis on Hagar's "personal and salvific encounters with God—encounters which aided Hagar in the survival struggle of herself and her son".[17] This, Williams argues, presents a paradigm quite distinct from the African-American model of exodus and liberation.[18] She writes, "God's response to Hagar's story in the Hebrew testament is not liberation. Rather, God participates in Hagar's and her child's survival [...]".[19] The angel's instruction to Hagar to return to Sarai is not collusion in her oppression; rather, it was to ensure her and her child's survival, as it would not have been possible for them to survive the trauma of birth in the wilderness.[20] When Hagar and Ishmael are cast out without sufficient means to survive, "God gave her new vision to see survival resources where she had seen none before."[21] Much of Hagar's story relates to black women's "predicament of poverty, sexual and economic exploitations, surrogacy, domestic violence, homelessness,

---

[13] Renita J. Weems, *Just a Sister Away: A Womanist Vision of Women's Relationships in the Bible* (San Diego, California: LuraMedia, 1988), 1.

[14] Ibid., 17.

[15] Williams, *Sisters in the Wilderness*, 3.

[16] Williams, *Sisters in the Wilderness*, 3.

[17] Ibid.

[18] Ibid., 4–5.

[19] Ibid., 5.

[20] Ibid.

[21] Ibid.

rape, single-parenting, ethnicity and meetings with God".[22] The last part
of Hagar's story describes her and Ishmael's independent life in the wilderness. For Williams, this parallels the experience of African-American
single-parent families, "in which a lone woman/mother struggles to hold
the family together" amidst unjust poverty.[23] Hagar finds the strength to
survive through her wilderness encounters with God, and this echoes the
testimonies of many black women who declare that "God helped them
make a way out of no way".[24]

For womanist theologians, Hagar's story also speaks to another aspect
of black women's experience: that of being marginalized and oppressed
by other women in positions of power. For Weems, Sarah's part in Hagar
and Ishmael's banishment is a "piercing portrayal of one woman's exploitation of another woman".[25] The story of Hagar and Sarah speaks to black
women's experience of being oppressed by other women firstly in terms
of the historical context that today's women have inherited. Weems
writes that the "painful memory" of slavery's "web of cruelty" continues
to "stalk the relationships between black and white women in America
even to this day".[26] The story of an African woman's oppression by her
slave-owning mistress "exposes the many hidden scars and ugly memories
of the history of relationships between racial ethnic and white women in
America".[27] Hagar's treatment by Sarah is "hauntingly reminiscent" of the
testimonies of enslaved African-American women, in which the brutality
of being raped by one's master was "compounded by punitive beatings
by resentful white wives".[28] Thus the story may remind white women in
the US of the horrific crimes on an enormous scale that is part of their
cultural inheritance.[29]

---

[22] Ibid., 5–6.
[23] Ibid., 33.
[24] Ibid., 5–6.
[25] Weems, *Just a Sister Away*, 14.
[26] Weems, *Just a Sister Away*, 7.
[27] Ibid., 16.
[28] Ibid., 7.
[29] Whilst the vast majority of womanist discourse on Hagar is from the United States, a slave-owning past is of course relevant to other western nations. As a British woman, my relationship to the slave-trade and colonialism of my nation may appear less direct than for American women, in that most of the Africans who were captured and sold into slavery by the British Empire were not brought to these shores, and the 20,000–30,000 slaves who were taken to Britain have been largely erased from the nation's collective memory. Yet my country's wealth and culture was built on slavery, and today I rub shoulders with the descendants of those African slaves: the African-Caribbean immigrants who chose to come to Britain, and there found racist oppression and economic exploitation.

Womanist insistence that the story of Hagar and Sarah parallels black women's oppression by white women is not a case of imposing the "sins of the fathers" and mothers onto contemporary women. The racist ideology upon which the slave-trade was founded continues to pattern the modern world and women's relationships with those of other ethnicities, and this includes the feminist movement, both in the past and in the present. Weems describes how the nineteenth-century suffragettes "pandered to the racist attitudes of white southerners [...] and they extolled the supremacy of white women over black men (and black women)".[30] Williams argues that when white feminism blames women's exploitation of other women on patriarchy alone, it pays "very little *serious* attention to assigning some of the responsibility to women for this historical phenomenon of women oppressing other women".[31] By reminding us of the history of slavery, the story of Hagar and Sarai may enable both black and white women

> to become conscious of the negative effect of their historic relations. When this is more clearly seen and anticipated, perhaps white feminists will become more conscious of the ways in which their life-work perpetuates the oppressive culture of white supremacy.[32]

Today, the tendency for white feminists "to speak as though theirs is the universal experience" is not simply thoughtless presumption. For Weems, it demonstrates white women's "persistent belief in their superiority and sovereignty over women of other races".[33] Jacqueline Grant puts this in no uncertain terms: not only is feminist theology inadequate for black women because it is "white", it is also "racist".[34] Audre Lorde's critique of white feminism, and its failure to acknowledge the differences between women, is particularly pertinent to the story of Hagar and Sarah:

> If white american [sic] feminist theory need not deal with the differences between us, and the resulting difference in aspects of our oppressions, then what do you do with the fact that the women who clean your houses and

---

[30] Weems, *Just a Sister Away*, 8. See also Barbara Andolsen's *Daughters of Jefferson, Daughters of Bootblacks: Racism and American Feminism* (Macon, Georgia: Mercer University Press, 1986) and Susan Thistlethwaite, *Sex, Race and God: Christian Feminism in Black and White* (London: Geoffrey Chapman, 1990).

[31] Williams, *Sisters in the Wilderness*, 184.

[32] Williams, *Sisters in the Wilderness*, 186.

[33] Weems, *Just a Sister Away*, 8.

[34] Jacqueline Grant, *White Women's Christ and Black Women's Jesus: Feminist Christology and Womanist Response* (Atlanta: Scholars Press, 1989), 195.

tend your children while you attend conferences on feminist theory are, for
the most part, poor and third world women? What is the theory behind
racist feminism?[35]

As well as race-relations, the story of Hagar and Sarai is applied to contemporary power structures of class and socio-economic hierarchies. Weems
claims that the power relationship between Hagar and Sarai concerns
"economic stratification of women as much as it is about the ethnic dis-
crimination of one woman against another. Translated into today's language, Hagar was a domestic; Sarai was her employer".[36] For Alice Ogden
Bellis, the story of Hagar and Sarah raises the question of how "how
privileged women [...] relate to the women who serve them, whether as
domestics in their homes, in public establishments such as restaurants
[...], or, at even greater distance, in third-world countries".[37] It reminds
privileged minority-world women of any ethnicity that, in "seek[ing]
justice for women, we must be careful not to do it at the expense of
others, especially those whose position in society is more marginal than
our own".[38]

Womanism challenges white, western, middle-class feminism to examine its own racist assumptions not to promote ill-feeling, but so that
"[w]omen learn to help each other see when and how they are instru-
ments of their own and other people's oppression".[39] The story of Hagar
and Sarah can aid this process: Weems argues that it is important not to
"deny the sorrow in this story [...] to ignore the lessons in this kind of
pain".[40] The parallel between Hagar and Sarah's story and contemporary
race-relations "warrants taking the enormous risk of opening up the deep
festering wounds between us and beginning to explore our possibilities
for divine healing".[41]

Yet many readings of Hagar and Sarah avoid this pain, by trying to
understand Sarah's motivation in emotional and relational terms. I have
not read any imaginative retelling of Sarah that presents her as an oppres-

---

[35] Audre Lorde, "The Master's Tools Will Never Dismantle the Master's House," in *This
Bridge Called My Back: Writings By Radical Women of Color*, eds. Cherríe Moraga and Gloria
Anzaldúa (Watertown, Massachusetts: Persephone Press, 1981), 100.

[36] Weems, *Just a Sister Away*, 9.

[37] Alice Ogden Bellis, *Helpmates, Harlots, and Heroes: Women's Stories in the Hebrew
Bible*, 2nd ed. (Louisville, Kentucky: Westminster John Knox Press, 2007), 66.

[38] Ibid., 62.

[39] Williams, *Sisters in the Wilderness*, 186.

[40] Weems, *Just a Sister Away*, 16.

[41] Ibid., 2.

sive tyrant, and even when interpreters emphasise Sarah's 'affliction' of Hagar, they withhold the moral condemnation that is readily meted out to Abraham. As Angela Carter has commented, women writers are kind to women. Perhaps too kind [...] I cannot think of any woman in any work of fiction written by a woman who is taken to [...] final revelation of moral horror. We forgive; we don't judge".[42]

## Morality in Readings of Hagar and Sarah

Feminist retellings of the Genesis text "forgive" rather than "judge" through presenting Sarai's sending Hagar to Abram in the context of friendship between the two women, rather than the relationship between a mistress and her slave. In Vanessa Ochs's midrash, Hagar remembers herself as a young woman who went to Abraham's bed "made giddy by the sisterly friendship Sarah offered".[43] In Sara Maitland's 1987 retelling from Sarah's perspective, Hagar and Sarah love each other, and Sarah encourages Hagar to sleep with Abraham to be "a mother twice over. A mother to Hagar [...] whose back she supported through the long night while the child was pushed laboriously towards life [...] A mother to Ishmael, because she called him to being, not by lust but by intelligence".[44] In this short story's section told from Hagar's perspective, she remembers Sarah telling her to give in to Abraham's desire, to "[g]et the old goat off both our backs. We need a child in the tents [...] an end to his obsession"; when Hagar refuses, because "she whored for no married men," "Sarah in a sudden fury told her that she was the mistress, that Hagar was hers, hers to do as she willed with".[45] This is the first time that Sarah had ever treated Hagar like a slave, and she responds with pride, "flaunting the long full curves of her buttocks and thighs, ask[ing] Sarah with impudence how her husband liked it best", and goes into his tent.[46]

A number of interpretations attempt to explain Sarai's harsh treatment of Hagar by emphasizing the pregnant Hagar's contempt for Sarai. They stress the devaluing of infertile women within the patriarchal

---

[42] Angela Carter, "Introduction" to her (ed.) *Wayward Girls and Wicked Women* (London: Virago, 1986), ix–x.

[43] Vanessa L. Ochs, *Sarah Laughed: Modern Lessons from the Stories and Wisdom of Biblical Women* (New York: McGraw-Hill, 2005), 17.

[44] Sara Maitland, *A Book of Spells* (London: Methuen, 1987), 115.

[45] Ibid., 106.

[46] Ibid.

culture of Genesis. For Susanne Scholz, Hagar's reaction to becoming pregnant shows that she has "internalized sexist oppression" in which women are valued only for their reproductive capacities.[47] In *The Women's Bible Commentary*, Susan Niditch reads Hagar's story intertextually, alongside other Genesis accounts of barren women and their rivalry with their fertile co-wives. She comments that "[c]hildless wives were humiliated and taunted by co-wives".[48] Norma Rosen also emphasises Hagar's pride in her midrash on Sarah's struggle with the near-sacrifice of Isaac. Sarah dreams of Hagar, "no longer handmaid, [...] decked in full Egyptian robes and tasselling. She stares outward, sybil-like, enthroned. In the perversity of dreams, she is now possessed of Sarah's former youth and beauty".[49] The desperate Sarah, eager for the secret of accessing God's mercy, asks Hagar what prayer she uttered when her own son was near death, himself sacrificed by Abraham. Hagar responds with pride, not pity: "I offer you aid, my former mistress. Not as a measure of my love, but of my power".[50] Remembering that Sarah desired the death of her son, Hagar tells her that God wants the death of hers.

Feminist revisioning of Sarah also explains her actions in terms of maternal love. In Naomi Graetz's retelling, Sarah is jealous of the time that Isaac spends with Ishmael, and thus Hagar rather than her, and she convinces Abraham to send them away by claiming that they will lead Isaac astray with their foreign gods.[51] In Maitland's 1995 story, Sarah tells herself that "[s]he had to defend her son. It was right to defend her son," but in the end, as a lonely old woman waiting to die, she knows "[t]here were no excuses".[52] This is because "even if it were true that a woman must defend her own children [...] there was something truer: all women are sisters [...] and no woman in defence of her own child may kiss another woman on the cheek [...] and send her and her child out into the desert to die".[53]

---

[47] Susanne Scholz, "Gender, Class, and Androcentric Compliance in the Rapes of Enslaved Women in the Hebrew Bible", *Lectio Difficilior: European Electronic Journal for Feminist Exegesis* 2004/1. http://www.lectio.unibe.ch/04_1/Scholz.Enslaved.htm

[48] Niditch, "Genesis", 17.

[49] Norma Rosen, *Biblical Women Unbound: Counter-Tales* (Philadelphia: Jewish Publication Society, 1996), 48.

[50] Ibid., 48.

[51] Naomi Graetz, *S/he Created Them: Feminist Retellings of Biblical Stories* (Piscataway, New Jersey: Gorgias Press, 2003), 39.

[52] Sara Maitland, *Angel and Me: Short Stories for Holy Week* (London: Mowbray, 1995), 20.

[53] Ibid., 21.

In other readings, the blame for Hagar's expulsion lies with Abraham. Tivka Frymer-Kensky notes that Abraham's words in the Genesis text, "[y]our slave-girl is in your power; do to her as you please" (16:6), are same as those used by the Levite when he offers up his concubine to be gang-raped and murdered (Judges 19:22–26): "[t]he phrase sounds evil and immoral" when the speaker abdicates responsibility for the person he is giving over to the hands of an enemy".[54] In Maitland's 1987 story, Abraham forces Sarah to expel Hagar and Ishmael: "Hagar could not afford to see the black bruises round Sarah's eyes and neck [...] she would rather die here in the desert than acknowledge that Sarah could not have said otherwise".[55]

Hagar and Sarah are presented as victims of patriarchy by a focus on Sarah's lack of power and status within a patriarchal system, both in a realist and textual sense. In Ellen Frankel's midrash, Huldah the Preacher comments "[s]uch is the nature of subordination—to compete with each other, since they can't override the master's power".[56] Jessica Grimes argues that patriarchal social codes are to blame for the conflict between Hagar and Sarai:

> both women are hurting. As is the case with hurting people they resort to hurting each other [...] because it is difficult and dangerous to pro-test that they feel betrayed by the patriarchal society. [...] Showing anger towards another woman is the only acceptable type of anger in a patriarchal society.[57]

Feminist scholarship argues that the text itself is fundamentally patriar-chal and biased against women. For Esther Fuchs, the narratives of the Hebrew Bible are intrinsically andocentric, in the sense that an "ideological aspect prevails in all literary characterization".[58] She argues that Genesis stories of rivalry between wives form part of a "literary strategy serving patri-archal ideology" especially in how the preferred wife is infertile, whereas

---

[54] Tivka Frymer-Kensky, *Reading the Women of the Bible* (New York: Schocken Books, 2002), 228–229.

[55] Maitland, *A Book of Spells*, 109.

[56] Ellen Frankel, *The Five Books of Miriam: A Woman's Commentary on the Torah* (San Francisco: HarperCollins, 1996), 18.

[57] Jessica Grimes, "Reinterpreting Hagar's Story", *Lectio Difficilior: European Electronic Journal for Feminist Exegesis* 2004/1. www.lectio.unibe.ch/04_1/Grimes.Hagar.htm

[58] Esther Fuchs, "The Literary Characterization of Mothers and Sexual Politics in the Hebrew Bible", in *Women in the Hebrew Bible: A Reader*, ed. Alice Bach (London: Routledge, 1999), 128.

the unfavoured wife is able to bear children.[59] This is seen as a "legitimation of polygyny",[60] because no one woman is presented as satisfying her husband's desires, and thus the man is justified in resorting to additional wives in order to satisfy his interests".[61] The text perpetuates the image of women as rivals also as a way of implying "that sisterhood is a precarious alternative to the patriarchal system".[62]

Yet it could be that feminist emphasis on the common lot of Hagar and Sarah, contending with the problem of rivalry between women rather than differing social status, echoes womanist critique of white feminist universalising of the experience of patriarchy. When the womanist theologian Jacqueline Grant describes "sisterhood" as a "crude joke" or the "conciliatory rhetoric of an advantaged class and race",[63] I think of Alicia Ostriker's poetic revisioning of Sarah, in which she tells Hagar to forget about differences in ethnicity and social class in order to manipulate her:

> She pretended to care for me
> Forget about our nationalities, forget
> About social rank, she would say
> We are women together
> That is what matters Hagar.[64]

Sarah's knowledge of their shared subjugation as women is overtaken by rivalry:

> Ignorant, servile girl
> We should be allies
> We are both exiles
> I tell her
> She smiles slyly
> And he is happy with her
> And I want to die
> Then it is my turn
> Behold the fruit of my womb
> Get out, I say.[65]

---

[59] Ibid., 160.

[60] Esther Fuchs, *Sexual Politics in the Biblical Narrative: Reading the Hebrew Bible as a Woman* (Sheffield: Sheffield Academic Press, 2000), 160.

[61] Ibid., 161.

[62] Fuchs, "Literary Characterization", 136.

[63] Grant, *White Women's Christ*, 196.

[64] Alicia Suskin Ostriker, *The Nakedness of the Fathers* (New Brunswick, New Jersey: Rutgers University Press, 1994), 73.

[65] Ostriker, *Nakedness of the Fathers*, 68.

It would be wrong, however, to suggest that feminist revisioning of Sarah is characterised by innocence; rather it seeks to explain her behaviour in emotional and relational terms, and it emphasises patriarchy rather than class as the driving social factor (the retellings of Ostriker and Maitland being notable exceptions). Sarah is rarely presented as an exploitative slave owner, perhaps because contemporary feminists cannot put themselves in the place of someone who unthinkingly oppresses another woman. Or perhaps because it hits too close to home, and the parallels between Sarah's power over Hagar and the economic privilege held by middle-class western feminists is not something that is easily admitted to and imaginatively engaged with.

Considering Hagar and Sarah's paradigmatic status, Letty Russell and Phyllis Trible ask "[h]ow can we get the two women and their children back together? Is there any way to overcome the hidden and not-so-hidden injuries of class, race, gender, economics, and politics that use our faith traditions to excuse continuing conflict?"[66] Similarly, a number of feminist retellings imagine an eventual reconciliation between them. In Karen Prager's midrash, Sarah seeks Hagar's forgiveness, and it is granted: "[l]et Isaac and Ishmael grow up as brothers. Each shall have two mothers and one father. You alone shall be my family".[67] But perhaps this is to "smooth over"[68] too quickly, in the name of sisterhood, the differences between privileged women and those from other social locations. That resolution is impossible within the Genesis text reminds us how difficult this is to achieve, and that we must not rush too quickly into proclaiming harmony. Katy Taylor, recalling Susan Thistlethwaite's description of herself as a "recovering racist",[69] describes white feminism's recovery as "perpetual rather than finite while we continue to live in a society in which racism is part of the air we breathe".[70] In encountering the stories of biblical women, feminists from privileged social locations would do better not to smooth over the conflict between Hagar and Sarah, or place all the blame on male patriarchy, in the hope of providing positive images of women's relationships across ethnic and social divides. As Letty Russell

---

[66] Letty M. Russell, "Children of Struggle", in Trible and Russell, *Hagar, Sarah, and Their Children*, 185.

[67] Karen Prager, "God's Covenant with Sarah", in *Biblical Women in the Midrash: A Sourcebook*, ed. Naomi M. Hyman (Northvale, New Jersey: Jason Aronson, 1998), 25.

[68] Thistlethwaite, *Sex, Race and God*, 86.

[69] Thistlethwaite, *Sex, Race and God*, 146.

[70] Katy Taylor, "From Lavender to Purple: A Feminist Reading of Hagar and Celie in the Light of Womanism", *Theology* 97 (1994), 355.

writes, "[t]he daily struggles of our own living teach us that a search for solidarity in struggle may engage the trajectory of the story more directly than rewriting the unhappy ending".[71]

## Hagar, Sarah and Jewishness

Some interpreters have warned of the dangers in stressing Hagar's African heritage and its relevance for contemporary oppression on the basis of race. Alice Ogden Bellis does not ignore issues of race—she insists that "the matriarchs should not be depicted as though they were what we call white [...] Biblical women are "women of color".[72] Yet she stresses that the ethnic divisions of the Hebrew Bible "are not the ones familiar to people living in the United States"[73] and thus we should not project "modern American racial tensions" onto Hagar and Sarah's story.[74] In the Hebrew Bible, there are no negative connotations applied to those of African descent or with darker complexions.[75] However, whilst issues of race should not eclipse how the story may speak to other modes of social oppression, it is perhaps all too easy for white readers to want to use the story's historical context, in which race is not the primary factor, as a way of overlooking how our reading is shaped by our own cultural location. To read the Hagar and Sarah narratives in the present day is to come to the text with an imagination and set of interests that have been shaped by modern discourses on race, whether we like it or not. When I read about Hagar and imagine her as a black woman, her blackness has not the same meaning it would have had to the composers and compilers of Genesis, but that does not render any less significant the intersection between Hagar's story and the concept of women of colour with which I approach the text. To my mind, what is more problematic about womanist appropriation of the conflict between the African Hagar and the Hebrew Sarah is the assumption of Sarah's whiteness, both in terms of the conflation of Jewishness with white hegemony, and the risk of reinscribing anti-Semitic attitudes in the name of countering racial oppression.

---

[71] Russell, "Children of Struggle", 186.
[72] Bellis, *Helpmates, Harlots, and Heroes*, 30.
[73] Ibid., 66.
[74] Ibid.
[75] Ibid., 29.

The problem with womanist identification of Sarah with white oppression is that Sarah is not a slave-owner of white European heritage: she is an ancient Hebrew, and if any modern ethnic category may be ascribed to her, it is that of a Mizrahi Jew.[76] Womanist interpretations of Sarah may reinforce white hegemony by continuing the trajectory of Christian appropriation of the Hebrew Scriptures, in which Abraham and Sarah become exemplary of white European Christian ideology. Furthermore, for Jewish women who identify strongly with Sarah as the mother of the Jewish people, the story itself is troubling in terms of Sarah's behaviour towards Hagar. Pamela Reis writes, "the Hebrew Bible was not only my people's book, it was my book. I felt tarnished by its depiction of God as complicit in Abraham and Sarah's callousness and by the story's failure to deprecate this couple's inhumanity toward their bondwoman and her son".[77] Adele Reinhartz and Miriam-Simma Walfish express how the story creates a conflict between the Jewish principle of justice and that of honouring the ancestors:

> For Jewish commentators through the ages, the biblical story of Hagar and Sarah forces a choice between two central principles: reverence for their Jewish ancestors, through whom God creates the nation of Israel, and concern for the powerless, which is enshrined in biblical and subsequent Jewish law. Whose side to be on, that of the revered matriarch whose son signified God's fulfilment of the covenantal promises to Abraham and resulted in the eventual appearance of the Jewish people on the stage of history? Or that of the beleaguered maidservant who suffered at that matriarch's hands, though her pregnancy had been engineered by the matriarch herself?[78]

However, there is a long tradition of circumventing this tension through the emphasis of Hagar as 'other' to the Jews. Judith Baskin's survey of the treatment of women in classical midrash demonstrates that rabbinic interpretation is generally positive about Sarah and negative about Hagar.[79] *Genesis Rabbah* 45:3 tells that Hagar was treated well by Abraham and Sarah, and that Sarah entreated her kindly to go to Abraham's bed and gave her the special position of Abraham's wife, rather than concubine. It also

---

[76] The Mizrahim—Jews who have descended from the Jewish communities of the Middle East—have historically been marginalised in Israeli politics and culture.

[77] Pamela Tamarkin Reis, *Reading the Lines: A Fresh Look at the Hebrew Bible* (Peabody, Massachusetts: Hendrickson Publishers, 2002), 55.

[78] Adele Reinhartz and Miriam-Simma Walfish, "Conflict and Coexistence in Jewish Interpretation", in Trible and Russell, *Hagar, Sarah, and Their Children*, 102.

[79] Judith R. Baskin, *Midrashic Women: Formations of the Feminine in Rabbinic Literature*. (Hanover, New Hampshire: University Press of New England, 2002).

narrates that Hagar betrayed Sarah's trust by saying to other women, "[m]y mistress Sarai is not inwardly what she is outwardly: she appears to be a righteous woman, but she is not. For had she been a righteous woman, see how many years have passed without her conceiving, whereas I conceived in one night!" (*Genesis Rabbah* 45:5). Baskin suggests that "the negative tenor of these texts" regarding Hagar is due to her status as an Egyptian, a foreigner: "[t]he otherness of the foreign woman evoked significant sexual anxiety in rabbinic discourse".[80] Hagar's choice to marry Ishmael to an Egyptian woman is seen as confirmation that Hagar had never integrated into Abraham and Sarah's culture and religion: "[t]hrow a stick into the air, and it will fall back to its place of origin" (*Genesis Rabbah* 53:15).[81]

Womanist interpretation has also stressed Hagar's cultural and ethnic distinction from the Hebrew family. In the Hebrew Bible, Hagar's wilderness encounters with God are unique: as Trible states, in her naming of God, "Hagar is a theologian. Her name unites the divine and human encounter: the God who sees and the God who is seen".[82] Abraham and Jacob name the place of the encounter, whereas Hagar names God, and in so doing she addresses God directly: "*You* are the God who sees me".[83] Delores Williams stresses the distinctness of Hagar's encounter with God as evidence of her rejection of the religious culture of her slave-owners. In Williams' interpretation, Hagar's name for God—"El Roi," "the God of seeing"—is very different from "the God of the slave holders Sarai and Abram"[84] and Williams links it with Hagar's Egyptian heritage, and the Egyptian myth of the eye of Ra.[85] This suggests to her an "image of the belligerent Hagar in the household of Sarai and Abram",[86] who held fast to her cultural heritage, and leads to the question, "Is Hagar's naming action a strike against patriarchal power at its highest level, since the ultimate head of this ancient Hebrew family was its patriarchal God? Was Hagar's naming of God an act of defiance and resistance as well as an expression of awe?"[87] By choosing a wife for Ishmael, a role that would ordinarily go to the male

---

[80] Baskin, *Midrashic Women*, 152.

[81] See also Reinhartz and Walfish, "Conflict and Coexistence", 101–125, for surveys of rabbinic interpretation which offer an ambivalent attitude towards Hagar and Sarah's guilt.

[82] Trible, *Texts of Terror*, 18.

[83] Trevor Dennis, *Sarah Laughed: Women's Voices in the Old Testament* (London: SPCK, 1994), 71.

[84] Williams, *Sisters in the Wilderness*, 25.

[85] Ibid.

[86] Ibid.

[87] Ibid., 26.

head of the family, Hagar further demonstrates her autonomy and also her wish not to "perpetuate the culture of Abraham and Sarah".[88]

When Christian feminist interpretation—both black and white—stresses the patriarchal character of Hebrew monotheism it runs the risk of supersessionism and a negative portrayal of Jewishness.[89] The language Williams uses in distinguishing between the religious experience of the Egyptian Hagar and the "patriarchal God" of the "Hebrew family" heightens this risk, particularly when read in parallel with her critique of African-American appropriation of the Exodus narrative on the basis that the Bible contains no injunctions for the liberation of the "non-Hebrew slave".[90]

Pamela Reis describes her experience of listening to a womanist presentation on Hagar and Sarah, in which Reis felt that "the speaker's vilification of Sarah went beyond the fringes of biblical exegesis into the outskirts of anti-Semitism".[91] However, Reis sometimes seems to project anti-semitism onto womanist critiques of race and class privilege, for example Williams' comment that Sarah's worries about inheritance were "economic"[92] is not to imply Jewish greed, as in Reis's interpretation; rather it refers to the economic reality of the time. However, if womanist criticism of Sarah refers to the Hebrews' preoccupation with 'chosenness', it risks reinscribing an ancient and visceral prejudice towards the Jewish people. If we are to interpret the story through the lens of contemporary racial categories and the history of slavery, then we could do also with remembering that Jews were taken as slaves and systematically murdered by European Christians, and, just as those of African descent are made 'other' by the white supremacy of contemporary western culture, so too are Jewish people.[93]

---

[88] Ibid., 32.

[89] For discussion of religious feminist anti-Semitism, see Judith Plaskow, "Blaming the Jews for the Birth of Patriarchy", *Lilith* 7 (1980), 11–17 and "Anti-Judaism in Christian Feminist Interpretation", in *Searching the Scriptures Volume 1: A Feminist Introduction*, ed. Elisabeth Schüssler Fiorenza (New York: Crossroad, 1993), 117–129; Susannah Heschel, "Anti-Judaism in Christian Feminist Theology", *Tikkun*, 5.3 (1990), 25–28.

[90] Williams, *Sisters in the Wilderness*, 146.

[91] Reis, *Reading the Lines*, 56.

[92] Williams, *Sisters in the Wilderness*, 27, quoted in Reis, *Reading the* Lines, 74–75.

[93] For discussion of anti-Judaism in postcolonial feminist interpretation, see Amy-Jill Levine, "Multiculturalism, Women's Studies, and Anti-Judaism", in *Journal of Feminist Studies in Religion* 19.1 (2003), 119–128; Amy-Jill Levine, Kwok Pui-lan, Musimbi Kanyoro, Adele Reinhartz, Hisako Kinukawa and Elaine Wainwright, "Roundtable Discussion: Anti-Judaism and Postcolonial Biblical Interpretation", *Journal of Feminist Studies in Religion*

Hagar is a character of the *Hebrew* Bible, and her encounter is with the Hebrew God. Hagar's story is read as inspirational by Jewish women such as Vanessa Ochs.[94] Furthermore, in anti-Jewish Christian tradition, the enslaved and rejected Hagar has been identified with the Jews as opposed to the Christians, the true heirs of the promise. This tradition has its origins in Paul's allegory of Sarah and Hagar in Galatians 4:21–31, in which Ishmael, Abraham's "child of the slave", "born according to the flesh" (4:22), corresponds to the Jews who oppose the followers of Jesus, "children of the promise, like Isaac" (4:28). Those who continue to keep the law remain in slavery, like Hagar and her children (4:25), and Paul paraphrases Sarah's words allegorically: "Drive out the slave and her child; for the child of the slave will not share the inheritance with the child of the free woman" (4:30). This allegory would come to be interpreted by the Church Fathers and subsequent generations[95] in a way that was "but one element" of "the negative perception of Jews as 'others'" that "has become one of the fundamental teachings of the Church and has had lethal consequences for Jews throughout history".[96]

The Genesis story of the conflict between Hagar and Sarah is one with complex afterlives, part of a wider drama of promise, sacrifice and blessing. As numerous scholars have commented, the episode of Hagar and Isaac foreshadows Abraham's near-sacrifice of Isaac; it also sets the scene for the *exclusivity* of the blessing that follows that sacrifice.[97] The residual anxiety and guilt that I read in feminist retellings of Hagar and Sarah as being more than discomfort with rivalry between women pertains not only to the issue of race in terms of African slaves and their descendents, but also to another ethnic conflict, one which concerns religion as well as race, and has a direct lineage from the Genesis story.

---

20.1 (2004), 91–132; Kwok Pui-Lan, *Postcolonial Imagination and Feminist Theology* (Louisville, Kentucky: Westminster John Knox Press, 2005), 93–99.

[94]  Ochs, *Sarah Laughed*, 15–24.

[95]  For a full discussion, see Letty M. Russell, "Twists and Turns in Paul's Allegory," in Trible and Russell, *Hagar, Sarah, and Their Children*, 71–97.

[96]  Irene Pabst, "The Interpretation of the Sarah-Hagar-Stories in Rabbinic and Patristic Literature. Sarah and Hagar as Female Representations of Identity and Difference," *Lectio Difficilior: European Electronic Journal for Feminist Exegesis* 2003/1. http://www.lectio .unibe.ch/03_1/pabst.htm

[97]  Sherwood, "Binding-Unbinding", 826.

## *Hagar, Sarah, and the Children of Abraham*

Whereas Sarah is the foremother in the Jewish and subsequent Christian traditions, in Islam it is Hagar. The Egyptian slave-woman's role in the Muslim tradition is not as an outcast, marginal to the main story and a source of suppressed guilt within the text and its afterlives. Rather, Hagar is alongside Abraham in his monotheistic mission, and she is the ancestor of all Muslims, Abraham's true heirs, "since it was her descendent, Prophet Muhammad, who restored Abraham's religion after the world had once again fallen away from the true faith and proper worship of God".[98] Hagar is never mentioned by name in the Qur'an, and her textual role in Islam is in the Hadith and Islamic exegesis of biblical and Jewish tradition.[99] In the Islamic version of Hagar's story, Abraham leads her and her son to a holy place in the desert, where she is initially afraid, but then trusts in God's will. When the small amount of water that Abraham gave to her runs out, she walks seven times between the mountains of Safa and Marwah. On her last climb up the mountain, she hears a voice and is greeted by the archangel Gabriel. With his wing he scrapes at the dusty ground until water gushes out. Hagar builds a dam to contain the water, and the more she drinks the more water flows forth.[100] She is told that this place, where she and Ishmael will dwell, will be the site of the House of God—Mecca—and that her son will help his father to build the Ka'bah.[101] Hagar's walk back and forth seven times constitutes a rite of the hajj, and thus she is "one of the pillars of Islamic consciousness".[102]

It is not the texts concerning Hagar and Sarah that establish the one true heir, his descendents blessed by the one true God, but those narratives from which the mothers are most conspicuously absent: Abraham's near sacrifice of his beloved son, described in Genesis 22 and Sura 37 of the Qur'an. As Yvonne Sherwood notes, "Abraham can no more sacrifice both sons than any one of the monotheisms can fully relinquish the precious

---

[98] Hibba Abugideiri, "Hagar: A Historical Model for 'Gender Jihad'", in *Daughters of Abraham: Feminist Thought in Judaism, Christianity, and Islam*, ed. Yvonne Yazbeck Haddad and John L. Esposito (Gainesville, Florida: University Press of Florida, 2001), 81–82. See also Riffat Hasan, "Islamic Hagar and He Family", in Trible and Russell, *Hagar, Sarah, and Their Children*, 149–167.

[99] Abugideiri, "Hagar", 83.

[100] Ibid., 86.

[101] Ibid., 87.

[102] Ibid., 88.

status of the only-one-ness".[103] Whilst the identity of the promise child is now set in stone in both the Jewish and Islamic traditions, in the latter it was once less certain—"the gentle son" is not named in the Qur'an, and in the early centuries of Islam there was a debate between Isaac traditions, with Syria as geographical focal point, and Ishmael-Mecca traditions.[104] In the Jewish tradition, anxiety about the identity of the blessed son lies beneath the Genesis text. It is most manifest in Genesis 21, in Sarah's casting out of Ishmael and his mother due to her concern for her son's inheritance. Sarah sees Ishmael with Isaac, laughing. This has been variously translated as 'playing' and 'mocking', but Trible emphasizes the verb as a pun on Isaac's name: "[f]or Sarah, Ishmael's laughing poses a threat because, by word association, Ishmael is "Isaacing".[105] It is the similarities between Abraham's two sons that provoke the anxiety of the younger one's mother. The lack of distinction of the two sons, in terms of the blessing and the sacrifice, is brought to the fore in ancient midrash, which describes "a *competition* between Ishmael and Isaac over which son is the most loving and beloved".[106] Yet in Genesis Rabbah 55: 7, the victor of this contest only becomes clear once God instructs Abraham to "take your son":

> God: Take your son
> Abraham: I have two sons
> God: Your only one
> Abraham: This one is the only son to his mother and this one is the only son to his mother
> God: The one you love
> Abraham: I love them both
> God: Isaac.[107]

In later Jewish and Muslim traditions, the identity of the blessed son having been established, but also threatened by the existence of the other faiths, the *other* son is disparaged: midrash becomes zealous about Isaac's superiority to Ishmael "[a]s early Christianity Ishmaelizes the Jews and Islam deflects the true line away from Isaac toward Ishmael".[108] The Muslim

---

[103] Sherwood, "Binding-Unbinding", 832.
[104] Sherwood, "Binding-Unbinding", 830.
[105] Phyllis Trible, "Ominous Beginnings for a Promise of Blessing", in Trible and Russell, *Hagar, Sarah, and Their Children*, 45.
[106] Sherwood, "Binding-Unbinding", 828.
[107] Ibid., 827.
[108] Ibid., 831.

tradition avows "the Jews claim that it was Isaac, but the Jews lie".[109] Here we see the language of vilification that has come to characterise Jewish-Muslim relations in the 20th and 21st centuries.

Sherwood describes Tony Blair's "bland response to 9/11", that "Jews, Christians and Muslims are all children of Abraham", as an example of "paternalistic political-e(a)se".[110] She contends that

> the genealogical and interpretive lines that extend from [Genesis and Sura 37] would have to say that, far from offering a tranquil scene of hospitality played out beneath the generous canopy of the Abrahamic, these narratives stage conflicts or cuts of identity along the lines of Isaac/Ishmael/Jesus. (These dividing lines should be vocalized not as the gentle British "stroke" but as the North American "slash").[111]

Aside from the smooth confidence of the language of politicians, in the years since 9/11, Afghanistan, Iraq, 7/7, continued conflict over the possession of the Holy Land, and all the related debates and localised violence that circle around them, many theologically-informed and well-intentioned attempts at improving interreligious relations have made appeal to the same Abrahamic origin of Judaism, Christianity and Islam. Feminist analysis has not attempted to soften the 'slashes' of the Abrahamic narratives in appealing to his fatherhood, because of a dislike of this ur-patriarch[112] and a deep suspicion of the logic of sacrifice that is at the heart of his narrative.[113] Instead, feminist appeals to interreligious dialogue through scriptural interpretation have foregrounded the mothers of Ishmael and Isaac.

In the introduction to their edited collection, *Hagar, Sarah and Their Children: Jewish, Christian, and Muslim Perspectives*, Letty Russell and Phyllis Trible comment that "[u]nto the thousandth generation and beyond, disputes and divisions among all the families descended from Hagar and Sarah continue to breed violence".[114] They hope that their book will contribute to the efforts against this continued religious hatred

---

[109] Ibid., 830.

[110] Ibid., 825.

[111] Ibid., 825.

[112] For example, see David M. Gunn and Danna Nolan Fewell, *Narrative in the Hebrew Bible* (Oxford; New York: Oxford University Press, 1993), 91–2 and Carol Delaney, *Abraham On Trial: The Social Legacy of Biblical Myth* (Princeton, N.J.: Princeton University Press, 1998).

[113] For example, see Joanne Carlson Brown and Carole R. Bohn (eds.), *Christianity, Patriarchy and Abuse: A Feminist Critique* (New York: Pilgrim Press, 1989).

[114] Trible and Russell, "Unto the Thousandth Generation", 24.

by "allow[ing] for shifts in meaning" through changing the focus from Abraham to Hagar and Sarah, and that identification of the patriarchal worldviews of the source texts will also "yield new interpretations" that may "compel continual wrestling rather than the certitude of single or set answers".[115] Their volume demonstrates the ambivalent struggle of religious feminist biblical interpretation which wants to subvert hierarchical and exclusive power dynamics; dynamics that, in these texts, are perpetuated by God. Considering the issue of God's 'partiality', Russell and Trible note that "Scripture yields no single answer to God's preferences, [but] does show that human beings yearn above all else to be among God's chosen".[116]

Eleanor Wilner's "Sarah's Choice", a poem that reverberates with the generations of interreligious conflict as instituted on Moriah, powerfully contends with the problem of 'chosenness'. Sarah rejects God's command that she sacrifice Isaac. She realises that "[y]ou can be chosen / or you can choose. Not both". Isaac says to her, " 'if we were not God's / chosen people, what then should we be? I am afraid / of being nothing.' And Sarah laughed."[117] Remembering her earlier crime, she decides to leave early in the morning, to find Hagar and seek reconciliation. Isaac asks how he should greet Ishmael:

> "As you greet yourself," she said, "when you bend
> over the well to draw water and see your image,
> not knowing it reversed. You must know your brother
> now, or you will see your own face looking back
> the day you're at each others' throats."[118]

## Paradigms and Encounters

In early 2008, I took part in a residential programme for Muslim and Christian women, hosted by the faith-based retreat centre in the Yorkshire Dales at which I was living and working at the time. The event, led by Dilly Baker and Wahida Shaffi and sponsored by the Christian Muslim Forum, was entitled 'Women at the Well', and used the story of Hagar and Sarah as a theme for interreligious discussions. The geographical and

---

[115] Ibid., 24–25
[116] Trible and Russell, "Unto the Thousandth Generation", 25.
[117] Eleanor Wilner, *Sarah's Choice* (Chicago: University of Chicago Press, 1989), 23.
[118] Ibid.

social context of the workshop was the discord between 'modern' western values and 'Muslim culture'[119] in British political and media discourse, and the ethnic divisions that have come to characterise the conurbation of West Yorkshire. The far-right hothouses of anti-Muslim feeling (for example the English Defence League and the British National Party) and radical Islamism are dominated by men, yet it is women who are often used to symbolise the discord between 'modern', 'secular' western values and 'Muslim culture',[120] from women's clothing such as the burqa or the hijab, to so-called 'honour killings', and women's status in Sharia law.[121] This conflict was a subtext of this interfaith 'encounter', which worked on the premise that the relationship between Hagar and Sarah, and Muslim and Christian women's identification with them, would inspire connection rather than deepen divisions. In terms of communication between the participants and relationships formed over those few days, it seemed to work. Yet I remember feeling some discomfort at the time, both with my role as 'Christian woman' (the programme stipulated a deep-rootedness in one's religious tradition, whereas I was very much *un*rooted) and subsequent identification as 'Sarah'. My youth and my various life experiences thus far had led me to identify more with Hagar than with Sarah.

Taking into account the various ways that the figures of Hagar and Sarah have been used to apply to contemporary relations and the power relations therein, Amy-Jill Levine cautions that there are problems with paradigmatic readings. She argues that, whilst "typological impulses and empathic reclamations" that "encourage group identification with one character" may be "empowering", they can be damaging when they result in "group rejection of the other".[122] Levine quotes Elizabeth Castelli's point that allegory is "distinguished by both violence and foreclosure", and that typological reading "intensifies" the reader's selection of "narrative elements to highlight and therefore elements to dismiss."[123] Whilst "[e]mpathic reclamation" may "lead to a new appreciation of both self and other," Levine suggests that readers from a position of privilege may,

---

[119] Here the deployment of quotation marks is to denote that these terms, however overused, are problematic, but there is not the space to explore them here.

[120] As above.

[121] See Fauzia Ahmed, "Still 'In Progress?'—Methodological Dilemmas, Tensions and Contradictions in Theorizing South Asian Muslim Women", in *South Asian Women in the Diaspora*, eds. Nirmal Puwar and Parvati Raghuram (Oxford: Berg, 2003), 43–66.

[122] Amy-Jill Levine, "Settling at Beer-lahai-roi," in Haddad and Esposito, *Daughters of Abraham*, 15.

[123] Ibid., 17.

overcompensating out of a sense of guilt, interpret "the previously marginalized, the 'other'" as "invariably right and good".[124] This did seem to come into play during the Christian-Muslim retreat based on Sarah and Hagar: in the feedback session some of the Christian women commented that there seemed to be more space for the Muslim participants to talk about their experiences than there was for the Christian women. The Muslim women's identification with the rejected Hagar may have compounded the guilty overcompensation that white, liberal women feel towards those who are ethnically and religiously 'other' in British society. Taken as a whole, the event left me with more questions on the usefulness of scriptural paradigms than it did answers.

The ambivalence of identification may be read in the novelist Sara Maitland's reflections on her interpretation of the story of Hagar and Sarah:

> For years I have heard Sarah's voice; for years I have strained my ears to hear it, identified with it. Not just I think the sharing of names, though that should not be discounted. It is easy for a woman like me to hear the voice of a woman like her; two women, of different time, place, space, race, but two women of privilege, articulate, sophisticated, adept, self-controlled. Women, even, of power, by class, education, marriage, status. I hear her voice too easily, Hagar's too furtively.[125]

Maitland's words here suggest to me a way of contending with the problematic elements of reading biblical women as paradigmatic for women today. Identification with biblical women may be refigured as an encounter with an other, an encounter that reaches across what Maitland calls "the timeless space between the boundary of myth and history".[126] In the reading encounter with the biblical women Hagar and Sarah, to read their story is also to be *read by* the story, and we bring to the biblical text the 'text' of our own social, cultural and personal experience.[127] As such, the encounter works both ways, recalling Hagar's difficult Hebrew phrase in Genesis 16:13, *the one I see and the one who sees me.* We see the text and the text sees us, but relating to the biblical characters in this way should not mean that we collapse our own identity in theirs; identification should resist regarding oneself as identical. In this vein, Letty Russell writes,

---

[124] Ibid., 18.

[125] Maitland, *Book of Spells*, 113.

[126] Sara Maitland, *Women Fly When Men Aren't Watching* (London: Virago, 1993), 82.

[127] See Ingrid Rosa Kitzberger (ed.), *Autobiographical Biblical Criticism: Between Text and Self* (Leiden: Deo, 2002).

the story of Hagar and Sarah endures, not only as a cautionary tale of inhospitality, competition, and patriarchal domination, but also as a story of blessing in which God's welcome is discovered in the wilderness. Many generations continue to find that their lives are read by the story as they seek to move beyond the enmity and constraints that flow from the misuse of difference to welcome the stranger.[128]

Hagar's role as the "archetypal stranger" may call us to enact the biblical ethic of hospitality. This does not mean a denial of the differences between Hagar and Sarah, because "it is the challenge of difference, strangeness and 'otherness' that calls for the practice of hospitality", which "responds to difference through reciprocity and solidarity with strangers rather than through fear and exclusion".[129] This is a continued challenge: we remain in the wilderness, but there are lessons to be learnt there. Here in the wilderness we may, like Hagar, encounter hope, as we face up honestly to where we have come from, and as we seek a vision of where we are going.

---

[128] Russell, "Children of Struggle", 195.
[129] Ibid., 193.

# ATHALIAH OF JUDAH (2 KINGS 11):
## A POLITICAL ANOMALY OR AN IDEOLOGICAL VICTIM?

### Wabayanga Robert Kuloba

Athaliah is introduced in the political historiography of the Hebrew Bible as a family member of King Ahab[1] (2 Kgs 8:18, 26), wife of King Jehoram of Judah (2 Kgs 8:16–18) and mother to King Ahaziah of Judah (2 Kgs 8:25–26). My study examines the ideological frameworks of power and gender in the story of Queen Athaliah. Athaliah is caricatured in the Deuteronomic narratives as a monstrous woman who killed off all her male grandchildren for selfish political interests. Her ascension to the throne of Judah after the death of her son (King Ahaziah) is clearly perceived as illegitimate and anomalous. Brutally overthrown and then assassinated after seven years of leadership, she is replaced by the 7 year-old Joash who becomes King of Judah. In the narrative, the plotters against Athaliah are given a heroic gloss, while Athaliah is the demonised figure.

The story of Athaliah is preserved in the ideological context of the Deuteronomic narratives. Like all Deuteronomic narratives, there are a number of factual, logical and thematic mutilations and inconsistences in Athaliah's story, which promote a certain ideological propaganda. Proverbially speaking, the Bible story presents a history of a hare against the hyena; and indeed, until hyenas get their own historians, the hare shall always remain the hero!

This study is aimed at interrogating the ideological facets that inhibit the Bible text and that are responsible for the heroic outlook of the 'hare' against a female politician and leader. The study shall be guided by the following questions: Did Athaliah merit succeeding her son Ahaziah? What ideological custom does Athaliah contravene? What are Athaliah's merits

---

[1] The exact parentage of Athaliah is not clear from the Bible. In 2 Kings 8:26 and 2 Chronicles 22:2 she is called the daughter of Omri. But in 2 Kings 8:18 and 2 Chronicles 21:6, she is referred to as the daughter of Ahab. The Lucianic branch of the LXX tradition eliminates the contradiction by reading 2 Kings 8:26 as 'Ahab.' Josephus also calls Athaliah the daughter of Ahab. See Winfried Thiel, "Athaliah," in *Anchor Bible Dictionary*, ed. David Noel Freedman (London: Doubleday 1992), 511. T. Ishida, "The House of Ahab," *Israel Exploration Journal* 25, no. 2/3 (1975): 135–137. Also, H. J. Katzenstein, "Who Were the Parents of Athaliah," *Israel Exploration Journal* 5, no. 3 (1955): 194–197.

in the political space of Judah? The study will involve a close reading of
2 Kings 11. The Bible shall be *read against the grain*, a method employed
by David Clines in his book *Interested Parties*.[2] Information from extra-
biblical sources, especially archaeology and histories of the contemporary
Ancient Near East relevant to the subject of study shall be utilised.

The text is nuanced with at least two ideological stereotypes: the ideology of motherhood, which holds women as mothers; and the ideology
of political legitimacy, which is concerned with the questions of Davidic
ancestry and the appropriate gender for political leadership. Athaliah is
preserved in the narrative as the woman who violates and conflicts with
both these archetypal customs. Her behaviour is atypical of the customs
that the Bible narrator approves. The text shall be divided and analysed in
two sections. Section 1 shall study the first three verses (1–3), while section
2 shall examine the rest of the text (verses 4–20).

### 2 Kings 11:1–3

In section 1, Athaliah rises to power and reigns for almost seven years.
However, her rise and reign are not only portrayed as extempore, impul-
sive, and illegitimate but also murderous and offensive to the political
custom of Judah, which upholds Davidic kingship. Athaliah is introduced
in this section as the mother of King Ahaziah of Judah, who upon receiving news of her son's demise, is moved to exterminate "all the male members of the royal family" (כָּל־זֶרַע הַמַּמְלָכָה).[3] Athaliah is bent to utterly
destroy (תְּאַבֵּד) not just the extended family members of the fallen King,
but also Ahaziah's own children—Athaliah's grandchildren. זֶרַע הַמַּמְלָכָה
is constructed differently from other incidences like Ezekiel 17:13 and Jeremiah 41:1 where we have זֶרַע מְלוּכָה. The noun זֶרַע denotes male offspring (Gen 4:25). The same root word is used for semen (זֶרַע) in Leviticus
22:4. In Greek it is σπερμα, which is translated sperm in English. הַמַּמְלָכָה
זֶרַע apparently refers to only the male offspring of the dynasty, as indeed,
female children like Jehosheba were not killed. This story obscures

---

    [2] David J. A. Clines, *Interested Parties: The Ideology of Writers and Readers of the Hebrew
Bible*. (Sheffield: Sheffield Academic Press, 1995).
    [3] King Ahaziah had been entrapped in Jehu's coup against Jezebel in the Northern
Kingdom of Israel. He was wounded, and eventually died at Megiddo before reaching
Jerusalem (2 Kgs 9:27).

Athaliah's political merit and interests by accentuating the act of killing of the royal seed.

This section also introduces Joash, King Ahaziah's infant son who survived Athaliah's murderous intentions. In verse 2, Jehosheba, who was apparently the daughter to King Joram and Athaliah and sister of King Ahaziah stole (תִּגְנֹב) Joash away from "among the King's sons that were being slain" by Athaliah. For over six years, as Athaliah reigned over the land (מֹלֶכֶת עַל הָאָרֶץ), Joash was in the custody of Jehoiada the Temple Priest.

### 2 Kings 11:4–20

Section 2 begins from verse 4 and runs to verse 20. It entails the coup against Athaliah, which is celebrated in the narrative as a redemptive measure to cleanse and restore the throne of Judah to the rightful and legitimate heir. The coup was organised by Jehoiada the priest in the seventh year of Athaliah's rule. The scene of the plot is the temple where Jehoiada conspired with the military officials and secured their loyalty in an oath to revolt against Athaliah. Treaty making is written differently in verse 4, where we have the preposition *l*. The construction[4] וַיִּכְרֹת בְּרִית לָהֶם is different from וַיִּכְרֹת . . . עִם (1 Sam 20:16; Hos 12:2). It indicates a "granting of treaty" or "coming to terms" (cf. Deut 7:2; Josh 9:15, 15; 2 Sam 5:3; 1 Kgs 20:34). In this text Jehoiada is taking a superior status over the military guards. Covenants (בְּרִית) were strong commitments made among people or between gods and people in the ancient Near East. Breaking a covenant had devastating consequences (Isa 24:5–6; Jer 22:8–9). Jehoiada's covenant is accompanied with an oath of loyalty and allegiance to Jehoiada and the success of the coup. Joash, here defined as the King's son (בֶּן הַמֶּלֶךְ) is presented to the generals as the legitimate heir to the throne of his father Ahaziah. The military generals are instructed to ensure maximum security for the King and are under oath to ensure that the coup succeeds. Jehoiada presents the military with the noble weapons that have been kept in the temple. They are weapons allegedly used by King David—the legendary military and political leader, whose dynastic heritage is challenged by Queen Athaliah. Joash is already described as the King, and King's son,

---

[4] This form appears mainly in situations where former enemies are changing allegiance and loyalty to the master (former enemy). The master grants them (לָהֶם) the treaty to instil confidence and a sense of security.

in verses 11 and 12 respectively. He is protected by armed guards and is stealthily crowned, anointed and blessed as King over Judah.

Verses 13–14 reintroduces Athaliah whose attention is drawn by the applause at the coronation. She is mentioned by name in juxtaposition with Joash, here called 'King', "standing by the pillar as per the custom" (מִשְׁפָּט). The honour accorded to Joash repudiates Athaliah in all aspects, and renders her credibility to the throne of Judah illegitimate. The category of people here named as עַם הָאָרֶץ is ambiguous. In his recent article, John Tracy Themes has discussed different interpretational issues associated with this term. However, in Athaliah's context, Themes thinks that it is "designed to communicate and emphasize the actions of the dethronement, the destruction of the Baal temple, and the joyful accession of the new king, without assigning particular relevance to the actors."[5] I will however not ignore what Themes calls a technical interpretation,[6] where עַם הָאָרֶץ denoted a distinct social group in the kingdom of Judah, whose activity at the time of dynastic crisis is recorded several times in 2 Kings. They intervened after the assassination of Amon (2 Kgs 21:23–24) and the death of Josiah (2 Kgs 23:30) to elevate a proper Davidic lineage to the throne (cf. 2 Kgs 14:21). Jeremiah (1:18, 34:19, and 37:2) juxtaposes the people of the land with other strata of society, and Ezekiel 22:29 berates them for their oppression of the poor, the destitute, and the sojourner; these contexts suggest that they were an elite group of citizens,[7] and probably Jehoidah was one of them or acting in their interests. Only a small fraction of the people of the land were active participants in their communities; "these were naturally the wealthy who by dint of their influential position could direct public affairs, as they did so often during monarchic upheavals in Judah."[8] עַם is also used to mean the army (Num 31:32; Josh 10:7, 11:7; 1 Sam 11:11; 1 Kgs 20:10). This would suggest that the army's support, allegiance and loyalty had been firmly secured and promised to the young King.

The coup devastated Athaliah. She tore her clothes over what she called a conspiracy (קֶשֶׁר) against her regime. קֶשֶׁר is a word that often appears in situations of political conflict and intrigues that often result in the assas-

---

[5] John Tracy Themes, "A New Discussion of the Meaning of the Phrase *Am Hā'āres* in the Hebrew Bible," *Journal of Biblical Literature* 130, no. 1 (2011): 123.

[6] Ibid., 110, 123.

[7] See also Mordechai Cogan and Hayim Tadmor, *II Kings: A New Translation with Introduction and Commentary*, 1st ed. (N.Y.: Doubleday, 1988), 129.

[8] Ibid.

sinations of reigning kings.[9] In the case of Athaliah, the narrator disowns the word by putting it in Athaliah's mouth. The narrator does not regard Jehoiada's coup as the conspiracy, but Athaliah herself. The narrator may infer that Athaliah is using קֶשֶׁר inappropriately as it does not actually apply to her case since she is just an imposter.

According to the narrative, the military, under Jehoiada's command, drag Athaliah to the gate and then assassinate her. Jehoiada then leads a covenant-making ceremony. This is followed by the rhetorical destruction of the altars and statues of Baal as a way of cleansing the land and the throne, re-dedicating them back to the rightful respective authorities. In verse 19, the new king is moved from the Temple area and taken to the palace. He is enthroned on the throne of the kings. The procession to enthrone the King takes the way of the gate of the guards, apparently the main entrance to the palace. The narrative ends with verse 20, which describes the political climate of Jerusalem after the coup as quiet, with the people of the land happy because Athaliah has been slain.

## Analysis

Richard D. Nelson has observed that throughout the events that lead to the Athaliah's overthrow, God does not do or say anything.[10] The prophetic voices, so audible in previous chapters, are missing in this text. "The word of God (דְּבַר יְהוָה), which is the prime mover of events"[11] as Nelson puts it, is replaced by the word of Jehoiada the priest, who is the chief architect and perpetrator of the coup.

The text clearly presents two idiosyncratic ideas about Athaliah. She is the woman who kills her own children and grandchildren, the seed of a royal family, and she is the woman who ascends to the political throne of Judah and reigns in place of kings. Athaliah is generally an antagonist to the socio-political customs of Judah. She is ambitious, but her ambitions are depicted as atypical of her gender and the narrator is disapproving of her behaviour. By describing the alleged killing of her grandchildren, the narrator biases the reader's attitude against Athaliah.

---

[9] It is however interesting to comment on how the writer of the Athaliah story has positioned the word קֶשֶׁר in relation to how it is used elsewhere. In other stories, the narrator owns the word in describing the events in a certain political conflict. For example, in 1 Kgs 16:16, 20 and 2 Kgs 12:21, 14:19, 15:30, 17:4.

[10] Richard D. Nelson, *First and Second Kings* (Atlanta: John Knox Press, 1987), 212–213.

[11] Ibid., 213.

Athaliah's story is framed against the backdrop of two ideologies: the ideology of motherhood and the ideology of the legitimate ruler. The term 'ideology' has many definitions; in this essay, I utilise David Clines' definitions of the term. As part of his indices of the denotations and connotations of 'ideology', Clines defines the concept as "ideas that serve the interest of a particular group especially a dominant group",[12] and "ideas that are wrongly passed off as natural, obvious or commonsensical."[13] Thus, if we take the Hebrew Bible writers as advancing their own ideological arguments, then "their text is a realization of their ideology, a performance of their investment in their ideology; one could say that ideology is 'inscribed' in their texts."[14] Along with writers, Clines emphasizes that "readers too have ideological investment in what they choose to read, how they incorporate or fail to incorporate what they read into their own structure of opinions, how they report on what they have read and how they recommend or insist to others that they read the same works."[15]

In relation to the narratives surrounding Athaliah, Clines work is useful in ascertaining that there is a dominant group, whose ideological context is favoured by the text, representing Athaliah as contravening patriarchal norms. Clines' view rightly points out the limitations of the ancient readers who would appreciate the writer's context and, in turn, demonise Athaliah, so much so that Athaliah is voiceless in her literal rendition.

Athaliah as Ahaziah's mother would have been expected to be modest, affectionate and matronly especially at this sombre moment. She falls short of the qualities of the other biblical mothers like Eve, Rachel, Hannah and Naomi, among others, who protected and loved their offspring. Athaliah is not the woman of Proverbs 31:28–29. The text is tactfully brief, but clearly designed to imprint on the reader the idea that Athaliah was the heartless grandmother who kills her own flesh and blood in her greed for political power.

Athaliah's political activism is not unusual in the context of the ancient Near East, where queens and queen mothers regularly played significant political roles. Rivkah Harris (2003) and Hennie J. Marsman (2003) have demonstrated that royal women played a very significant role in the administration of the kingdoms of the Ancient Near East. For the purposes of situating Athaliah in her proper political context, a few examples

---

[12] Clines, *Interested Parties*, 10.
[13] Ibid.
[14] Ibid., 23.
[15] Ibid., 23–24.

from her own contemporary context may unmask a different picture of Athaliah.

It was normative for royal women especially queens and queen mothers to engage in ancient political systems through different roles. Different communities had different names for these royal women. For example, in Mari, a queen was called *šarratu*, a feminine form for *šarru* "king," (which is semantically related to the Hebrew שַׂר meaning prince or king (cf. 2 Sam 10:3, 19:6; 1 Kgs 9:22) and whose feminine form is hypothetically שָׂרֶת or שָׂרָה.). In Assyria, the queen was called *aššat šarri* "wife of the king."[16] In Ugarit, the queen was called *mlkt*,[17] which attests to the Hebrew root מלך.

Egypt had female Pharoahs at different points in history. For example Sobeknefru (1798–1794 BCE), was the last Pharaoh of the 20th dynasty. She used the title of Kingship and is acknowledged in the list of kings.[18] Hatshepsut (1479–1458 BCE) succeeded her husband Thutmose II, and reigned with the insignia of a king.[19] Sammuramat, wife of Shamshi-Adad (823–810 BCE) ruled as a regent in Assyria for 5 years after the death of her husband and continued to exercise influence in the reign of her son Adad-nirari III;[20] while queen Shibtu deputised Zimri-Lim of the Mari in his administration. Her roles included the writing of royal correspondences, acting as King in the absence of Zimri-Lim, supervising various departments, including the administration of the palace and the temple.[21]

In some societies, kings used dynastic marriage to strengthen the political control of their vast empires. For example, among the Mari, Zimri Lim used dynastic marriages to secure his legitimacy. Wherever he married off his daughters, he vested them with political authority to act out their "father's hegemony."[22] These daughters were in effect serving as ambassadors of their dynasty and certainly regulated the centre of gravity of national and international politics both within and without kingdoms. It was the same practice in the early dynastic period of Assyria (2600–2350 BCE), where Baranamtara wife of Luglanda of Lagash acted as a

---

[16] Hennie J. Marsman, *Women in Ugarit and Israel: Their Social and Religious Position in the Context of the Ancient near East* (Leiden: E. J. Brill, 2003), 326.

[17] Ibid., 334.

[18] Ibid., 350.

[19] Ibid., 351.

[20] Ibid., 347.

[21] Ibid., 329.

[22] Ibid., 331.

significant diplomatic figure between Assyria and other kingdoms like Adab.[23] Baranamtara was, in essence, a foreign affairs minister.

Queens and queen mothers also played key roles in political successions. They always fronted sons of their choice as kingly candidates, through whom they would exercise power. For example, Ahatmilku, the wife of Niqmepa, king of the Ugarit in the thirteenth to fourteenth centuries BCE, set her young son Ammistamru II against his older brothers for succession to the Ugaritic throne.[24] In Assyria, Naqi'a-Zakûtu, the wife of King Sennacherib, after successfully influencing her husband's choice of Esarhaddon, their younger son, continued to exercise a strong influence in Sennacherib's government.[25] Other queens acknowledged in this study are: Adad-Guppi of Babylon (6th Century BCE),[26] who died a heroic death while accompanying the Babylonian army led by her grandson, prince Belshezzar;[27] and Atossa, the wife of Darius I, King of Persia (6th Century BCE).[28] This motif is also evident in the Hebrew Bible. Zafrira Ben-Barak (1994) has well articulated the status and roles of the Biblical queen mothers in the making of Kings. Bathsheba's role in the succession of Solomon to the throne of David (1 Kgs 1:13ff) against other elderly sons of David is well accentuated in 1 Kings. Also, Hamutal fronted Jehoahaz as king against his elder brother Jehoiakim (2 Kgs 23:31, 36.), while Nehushta set up the 8-year-old Jehoiachin against the 21-year-old Zedekiah (2 Chron 36:9–11).[29]

From the above evidence, it can be deduced that, in distinction to the Hebrew Bible, the women in the rest of the Ancient Near East were politically active. The Bible stories, which are ideologically constructed, do not however reflect the actual events in the politics of ancient Judah and

---

[23] Ibid., 327–328.

[24] Michael Heltzer, *Internal Organization of the Kingdom of Ugarit* (Wiesbaden: Reichert, 1982), 183.

[25] Rivkah Harris, *Gender and Aging in Mesopotamia: the Gilgamesh epic and other ancient Literature* (Oklahoma: University of Oklahoma Press, 2003), 115.

[26] C. J. Gadd, "The Harran Inscriptions of Nabonidus," *Anatolian Studies* 8 (1958): 311–312.

[27] Harris, *Gender and Aging in Mesopotamia*, 116.

[28] H. Tadmor, "Autobiographical Apology in the Royal Assyrian Literature," in *History, Historiography and Interpretation: Studies in Biblical and Cuneiform Literatures*, eds. H. Tadmor and M. Weinfeld (Jerusalem: Magnes, 1983), 56–57.

[29] See Zafrira Ben-Barak, "The Status and Right of the Gebira," in *A Feminist Companion to Samuel and Kings*, ed. Athalya Brenner (Sheffield: Sheffield Academic Press, 1994), 178–182.

Israel. I suggest that the factual manipulations and mutilations of female leadership suit the ideological motivations of the narrators.

In the Biblical literature, it would be expected that the word מלכה be used as title for kings' wives, but this is not the case. The only occurrences of this title are in relation to foreign queens (1 Kgs 10:1, Esth 1:9, Song 6:8) or a Hebrew woman residing in a foreign court like Esther (Esth 2:17, 22). In limited cases, the word שגל is used denoting a king's wife (Neh 2:6 and Ps 45:10). It is related to the neo-Assyrian title *ša ekalli*, which literally mean she-of-the-palace.[30]

There is scant information about the institution of גְּבִירָה (*gebirah*)[31] in the Bible narratives. The word *gebirah* in this case stood for both queens (King's consorts or wives) and queen mothers (cf. 1 Kgs 11:19 and 15:13). The distinction between the political significance of queens and queen mothers is not clear, but we might suppose they played more or less similar duties. Information about these women is fragmentary. They are only preserved as names with almost no political roles mentioned.

Though the 'Dtr redactor' has great antipathy to women in politics, in the narratives he approves the behind-the-scenes political activities of queens like Bathsheba, daughter of Eliam (2 Sa. 11:3) and the wife of David and mother of King Solomon; Hamutal, the daughter of Jeremiah of Libnah (2 Kgs 23:31) mother of King Jehoahaz and Zedekiah; and finally Nehushta, the daughter of Elnathan (2 Kgs 24:15) mother of King Jehoiachin. All these women are significantly associated with the Davidic dynasty and are daughters of Jerusalem.

The *gebirah* in Israel and Judah was a woman of high political stature. There are a number of clues to this effect in the Bible: in 1 Kings 2:19, King Solomon meets Bathsheba and makes her sit on his right side.[32] Jehu executes 42 men who had gone to pay allegiance to the *gebirah* in Israel (2 Kgs 10:13). In the lamentation of the mother in Ezekiel 19, Greenberg thinks it could be Hamutal who is referred to in the lament.[33] In the story of King Jehoiachin, Nehushta, the *gebirah* is mentioned immediately after the king, as exiles sent into Babylonian captivity (2 Kgs 24:15).

---

[30] Marsman, *Women in Ugarit and Israel*, 338.

[31] The word גְּבִירָה has principally three meanings in the Bible and the ancient Near East: (1) mother or wife of the reigning sovereign (cf. 1 Kgs 11:19; 2 Kgs 10:13, Jer 29:2; 1 Kgs 15:13; 2 Chr 15:16, Jer 13:18. (2) A female ruler, governess (cf. Isa 47:5, 7); and (3) a mistress in relation to maidservant (cf. Gen 16.4, 8, 9; 2 Kgs 5:3; Ps 123:2; Prov 30:23, Isa 24:2).

[32] See also Ben-Barak, "The Status and Right of the Gebira," 173.

[33] Moshe Greenberg, *Ezekiel 1–20: A New Translation with Introduction and Commentary*, The Anchor Bible (Garden City, N.Y.: Doubleday, 1983), 354–359.

Also Jeremiah 13:18 ("say to the king and the *gebirah*: take a lowly seat, for your beautiful עֲטָרָה [crown] has come down from your head") suggests the high stature and importance of the *gebirah*. Like the king, she also wore עֲטָרָה.[34]

Given this background, one can say that Athaliah, as the *gebirah*, was a politically significant woman. After the demise of her son, she was potentially a suitable candidate to secure the political leadership, and indeed ruled successfully and peacefully over the kingdom for six years. However, the narrative does not give legitimacy and credibility to the *gebirah*. To the narrator, the sole legitimate heir must be royal seed, the male offspring and sons of the royal family. Athaliah is presented as a usurper of the political seat and a murderer of rightful heirs to the throne of David. Political conspiracies and assassinations were a common practice in ancient Israel and Judah, as also in other communities. Politically ambitious people killed their potential rivals for ascensions and consolidations. King David destroyed the family of Saul during the early years of his reign, sparing only the lame Ishboshet (cf. 2 Sam 9, 21), while Solomon killed Adonijah due to the latter's politically sensitive request to the former. Solomon also tried to kill Jeroboam, but the latter escaped (1 Kgs 11:40), and King Baasha eradicated the whole family of Jeroboam (1 Kgs 15:29), among others. In these political strivings, men were at the heart of the struggle for succession. Eliminating one's opponent was a sign of strength. In Athaliah's story, a woman's political advancement against men has been rendered mischievous and foreign.

It is important to note that the narrative presents several factual and logical contradictions. To begin with, the text presupposes that the Davidic weapons allegedly stored in the temple had existed for over 170 years. The chronological timeline of the kings of Judah indicate that King David existed between 1010 and 970 BCE, while Athaliah reigned between 841 and 835.[35] Over this long period of time, if in existence, these weapons certainly would have been affected by corrosion and had, by this time, become archaic tools. There was no reason why the military of Judah could not use the modern iron weapons they had at the time. I am inclined to argue that the clause on Davidic weapons serves to gloss the ideological motifs in the story. Davidic weapons evoke nostalgic sen-

---

[34]  Ben-Barak, "The Status and Right of the Gebira," 174.
[35]  Kenneth Kitchen, *On the Reliability of the Old Testament*, (Grand Rapids: William B. Eerdmans, 2003).

timents of noble Davidic warfare. Athaliah, who is framed as the enemy of the Davidic dynasty is deposed from the throne and killed using these weapons—weapons David used to defeat all his enemies and build the dynasty (cf. 2 Sam 7).

It is hard to validate the accuracy of the narrator's accusation against Athaliah given the background that Jehu had already massacred the brothers of Ahaziah (אֲחֵי אֲחַזְיָהוּ) when they had gone to pay homage to Queen Jezebel in Israel (2 Kgs 10:13–14). The assertion in verse 1 that Athaliah rose up to destroy the entire royal family is not logically consistent with death of אֲחֵי אֲחַזְיָהוּ in the hands of Jehu.

The discovery of the Tel Dan Inscription in Israel was a watershed in the study of ancient Israelite politics. Though the inscription is fragmented, among other things, the writer of the royal inscription boasts of having killed kings from the house or dynasty of David. He also states that the Aramean King crowned him. Scholars like J. W. Wesselius think that the writer of the inscription was Jehu.[36] Admittedly, in 2 Kings 10, Jehu staged a coup that brought him to power at the time Israel was at war with Aram. Jehu killed Jehoram king of Israel and inflicted heavy wounds on Ahaziah king of Judah that eventually killed him. Jehu proceeded to Jezreel from where Jezebel was assassinated. The entire Omrid family was reportedly eradicated by Jehu. In 2 Kings 10:13–14, Jehu killed 42 brothers of Ahaziah. These, needless to say were sons of David's dynasty, and potential political successors to the throne of Judah. The narrative is silent about Ahaziah's personal family life and the number of sons he had, which leaves us with the possibility that only the infant Joash survived at the time of his death in Megiddo.

With the death of Ahaziah and the massacre of his brothers at the hands of Jehu, the political succession of Judah was in balance. Athaliah was the most politically experienced person in the immediate vicinity. She had been queen and probably king's consort, and now queen mother—the *gebirah*. As noted earlier, *gebirahs* were significant in ancient Near Eastern politics. They were political advisers to kings, administrators, cultic leaders, and enjoyed a commendable degree of political privileges and prestige. Virtually no information is provided by the Dtr. writer about Athaliah's political roles prior to the death of her son Ahaziah.

---

[36] J. W. Wesselius, "The First Royal Inscription from Ancient Israel: The Tel Dan Inscription Reconsidered," *SJOT* 12, no. 2 (1999): 175–76.

I argue that the overthrow of Athaliah was a move of resistance against a foreign gender that had infiltrated the politics of Judah. In the understanding of the men of Judah, notably the priests of Anathoth like Jehoiada, it was more legitimate to be ruled by a small boy than a woman. Joash at the age of seven was very young and his only political act at that time was to sit on the throne as a *symbol* of legitimate male authority. He did not wield any significant political authority and influence. The political mechanism of Judah was in the hands of Jehoiada the priest and his loyal guards who had organised the coup.

Although Athaliah is acknowledged as ruling the land, the 'Dtr redactor' tactfully omitted details regarding her coronation and enthronement. Athaliah is presented as a leader without the support and the will of the people. There is no information about her seven year reign. Her rule is not granted full legitimacy.[37] There is neither an opening nor closing formula given as is the case with all other heads of the Crown either in Judah or Israel. What is left of her in the narrative is only her name as her identity and the evils she allegedly committed and the punishment she suffered, which further highlights the intention of the writer to fragment or distort Athaliah's political image.

It is not misplaced to state that despite the factual flaws and logical incoherencies in the text, Athaliah's political actions to clinch power were a fundamental change in the political historiography of Deuteronomic literature. It was a resistance against patriarchal political monopoly in ancient Judah. It is important to note that although the text does not detail Athaliah's political life over the seven years, the text does not baldly suggest that Athaliah was a bad leader. Kings in the category of Saul, Abijam, Jehoram, Ahaz and Jehoahaz among others, caused suffering to their subjects or received prophetic disproval and condemnation or were rejected by Yahweh. Athaliah is nevertheless penned off negatively on grounds of the protocol that patriarchal authorities approve. The narrators used the patriarchal ideological yardstick in examining Athaliah's political legitimacy.

Although there is great antipathy to women in politics in the Bible, the narratives admit queens and queen mothers into the game as long as they remain behind the scenes in their political activities. Such women include Bathsheba, daughter of Eliam (2 Sam 11:3) and the wife of David and

---

[37] See also Cogan and Tadmor, *II Kings: A New Translation with Introduction and Commentary*, 133–134.

mother of King Solomon; Hamutal, the daughter of Jeremiah of Libnah
(2 Kgs 23:31) mother of King Jehoahaz and Zedekiah; and finally Nehushta,
the daughter of Elnathan (2 Kgs 24:15) mother of King Jehoiachin. The
Hebrew Bible approves the role queens and queen mothers played in
political successions. They always fronted sons of their choice—through
whom they would exercise power, as kingly candidates, as was also the
case in the rest of the Ancient Near East. Queen Athaliah in her quest and
ascension to the throne took a full-blooded political activism. Instead of
supporting male candidates, she treated them as political rivals and killed
all male kingly candidates and pronounced herself ruler over Judah. Athaliah's actions according to the texts are foreign to the Deuteronomist's
values and violate the rules of the game.

In the Hebrew Bible, the land of the forefathers is for men and it is
given by the supreme God, Yahweh. Both the land and its occupants are
Yahweh's. The men are appointed as Kings by Yahweh himself as His cus-
todians. He assigns them with the responsibilities of keeping justice, cultic
purity and protecting the political and cultural integrity and interests of
the land. God Himself is the Supreme King over the people and the land.
He reserves the powers to appoint and dismiss his subjects (kings) the
way He sees fit. The relationship between Yahweh, Kings and the people
is pyramidal and hierarchical in design, with women and children being
at the bottom of the pyramid or hierarchy. Women are expected to give
birth and nurture children. They are to be motherly and protective to the
children under their care. Men are supposed to protect women and children in society.

Jehoiada, the military and עַם הָאָרֶץ (people of the land) are presented
in the text as risk bearers and true patriots. They are devoted to defending
the customs of their land, which include restoring the Davidic dynasty.
Using the 'right' weapons, they removed and killed off their female leader
and replaced her with the 'legitimate' heir, who though only seven years
of age, was the right gender. Athaliah, despite great leadership ambitions
like other women in her Near Eastern context ends up a victim of an ideology that did not appreciate the leadership of a woman.

In the final analysis, it is not out of place to ask to what extent does
the Bible reflect the realities of the ancient Israel and ancient Near East? I
suggest that scholars should treat the Bible as a world in itself, a world created in the writers' ideological image. Athaliah's story is not a dead story
buried in the Hebrew texts. It stretches its ideological influence out to
wherever and whenever it has been read. In the context of the Bible texts,

the story of Athaliah is outstanding because it contravenes two ideological principles of Davidic kingship and male authority. She is an anomaly in the listing of the kings of Judah. The ideological caricature of Athaliah's motherliness presents her as the woman who kills her own children and grandchildren, for political ambitions. In some communities, which still hold to a strong patriarchal bias, such as in my own experience of the mix of Ugandan politics and popular religion, Athaliah's story conflicts with the ideological motif of male authority. In this case, the ideological framework in which Athaliah is preserved continues to eschew her political merit and rights.

# THE BABEL COMPLEX:
## TAKING A TURN AROUND THE TOWER AND THE CITY

### Samuel Tongue

*… and they left off building the city.*[1]

*A migrational, or metaphorical city, thus slips into the clear text of the planned and readable city.*[2]

Genesis 11:1–9 sees the Babelian workforce come up against a planning problem. When the "LORD comes down to see the city and the tower, which mortals had built"[3] the proposed further work does not meet YHWH's stringent planning-permission legislation. It is this stringency that so animates biblical commentators: exactly why did YHWH come down and confuse the builders? Were the builders attempting to take heaven by force, manufacturing a siege-engine on the grandest of scales? Or were they trying to construct a symbol of unity amongst the disparate nations and tongues after the post-diluvian terrors of the flood? Or were they simply trying to create a secure urban habitation for themselves? Whatever the reason, the project had to be abandoned and the project managers became so confused that they were not even sure what their own city was called.[4] Eventually, the people are scattered "across the face of the whole earth", taking their blueprints with them.

But we have not abandoned the project. In this article, I want to explore how this city/text, left unfinished in the early chapters of Genesis, becomes

---

[1] Gen. 11:9b All English biblical quotations are from the NRSV.

[2] Michel de Certeau, *The Practice of Everyday Life*, trans. Steven Rendell (Berkeley: University of California Press, 1984), p. 93.

[3] Gen. 11:5.

[4] There are a number of interlinked etymologies for 'Babel' which might not be the name of the city at all. Claus Westermann views 11:9 ("Therefore it was called Babel, because there the Lord confused the language of all the earth; and from there the Lord scattered them abroad over the face of all the earth") as a 'secondary etiology' and thus an accretion to the basic motif, which is "that people want to demonstrate their greatness in a work of their own hands" (p. 554). In fact, he argues, the word בלל (translated as *confusion*) only has a slight resemblance to Babel, "an indication of the cultural level at which such amateurish 'popular etymologies' occur; they are frequent in the early layers of the Old Testament." He also suggests that cuneiform *Bab-il* ('Gate of God') is perhaps only another popular etymology. Claus Westermann, *Genesis 1–11: A Commentary* (Minneapolis: Augsburg Fortress Publications, 1994), pp. 553–54.

a migrational metaphor in the imagining of cities that boast their own ambitious towers, particularly New York and Paris.[5] By linking these iconic cities with Babel, we can examine how this biblical text and its interpretation haunt some of our own urban constructions. Engaging some of the work of Roland Barthes, Michel de Certeau and Jacques Derrida, and read alongside biblical scholars Claus Westermann and Gerhard von Rad, I will analyse and extend the reach of what Barthes calls the 'Babel-complex'. Examining how the biblical story lives on as an imaginative blueprint in the commentary around architectural feats such as the Eiffel Tower and The World Trade Center (which has become a space in which the 'Freedom Tower' is now being constructed), enables me to move between the textual rendering of Babel, the psycho-social discourse around the meaning of such towers, and their material construction and destruction. As Danna Nolan Fewell notes;

> Theories of language, philosophy, politics, and ethics; architectural innovations; critiques of technology; visions of empires; denunciations of urbanization; images of postmodern life; arguments for ethnic diversity and segregation; and condemnations of human arrogance have all looked to Babel for symbolic shade and shelter.[6]

Babel is a copious city/text able to provide habitation for a number of theories, ideas, and readings. For the purposes of this article, I will examine how vision and visuality are particularly important parts of the Babel-complex. For a reader and traveller such as Certeau, society is characterized by

> a cancerous growth of vision, measuring everything by its ability to show or be shown and transmuting communication into a visual journey. It is a sort of *epic* of the eye and of the impulse to read. The economy itself, transformed into a 'semeiocracy', encourages a hypertrophic development of reading. Thus, for the binary set production-consumption, one would substitute its more general equivalent: writing-reading.[7]

---

[5] There is not enough space in this article to also encapsulate London's new 'Shard', the tallest tower in Western Europe standing at 310m (1,016ft), boasting offices, restaurants, the *Shangri-La Hotel*, private residencies and a £24.95 experience designated 'The View from the Shard', a "multi-sensory journey to 244m (800ft) above one the greatest cities on earth...[where you'll be] drawn into the tapestry of London...[and] the past, present and future of London will be unfurled beneath you [...]." www.theviewfromtheshard.com, accessed 8th February 2013.

[6] Danna Nolan Fewell, "Building Babel," in *Postmodern Interpretation of the Bible: A Reader*, ed. A. K. M. Adam (St. Louis: Chalice, 2001), pp. 1–2.

[7] Certeau, *The Practice of Everyday Life*, p. xxi.

With this in mind, I shall argue that the signifying view from Babel combines both the views out across the cities and into the distance, and also the gaze upward from street level toward these looming structures; such signifying views are species of reading and writing. As Certeau notes, "'The city', like a proper name . . . provides a way of conceiving and constructing space on the basis of a finite number of stable, isolatable, and interconnected properties."[8] Towers become viewpoints from which to scan across this seemingly unified city. The proper nouns New York and Paris are Babels, names that hide the necessary and untranslatable confusions from which they are imagined. These are cities that shimmer between real places and imagined spaces and both have towers, present and absent, that dominate the horizons of their citizens' imaginative gaze. Certeau notes that climbing the highest point in a city offers a "seeing the whole, of looking down on, totalizing the most immoderate of human texts."[9]

Babel is thus a name to conjure with. As Fewell observes, "we only have to speak its name, and a structure appears in our imaginations, an archaic skyscraper ascending toward, but never reaching the heavens, conjuring images of confusion, scattering, and even failed ambition."[10] Perhaps a perfumer or designer might not want to add such a name to their redoubtable list of international outlets (*New York, Paris, London . . . and Babel*). Confusion and failure do not sell. Yet Babel bubbles and babbles in our cultural imaginary; Jacques Derrida conjures with the name asking "in what tongue was the tower of Babel constructed and deconstructed? In a tongue within which the proper name of Babel could also, by confusion, be translated as 'confusion'."[11] Using a proper name conceals the improper emptiness at the choric non-centre of words; the proper name is also always 'confusion' but pretends otherwise, like Babel itself, concealing a messy fusion of myth, dream, and imagination and bricks, mortar and slime.[12] I shall unpack how the construction of secure proper names (through the writing of a city/text) are part of the Babel-complex where confusion must not confound for too long. Foundations must hold. In

8 Ibid., p. 94.

9 Ibid., pp. 91–92.

10 Fewell, "Building Babel," pp. 1–2.

11 Jacques Derrida, "Des Tours De Babel," in *Acts of Religion*, ed. Gil Anidjar (New York & London: Routledge, 2002), p. 104.

12 The KJV renders Gen. 11:3 as "And they said one to another, Go to, let us make brick, and burn them thoroughly. And they had brick for stone, and slime had they for mortar" [*sic*]. The NRSV is much more in line with planning regulations where it changes 'slime' (הַחֵמָר) to 'bitumen'.

effect, New York and Paris can be read from the ruined summit of Babel's tower as city-texts that, in the light of Certeau's and Barthes' work become readable as 'proper names' only with such a view from the top.

The imagined Tower becomes a launching site for some vertiginous uses, theological, artistic, and political *bricolages* across the centuries that do not pay heed to the tower/city/text's 'original' use-value. Paradoxically, this is how the Babel-complex survives, over-living (*sur-vivre*) any original context, a 'cultural epistle'[13] addressed to 'everyman' and 'nobody'. As Certeau muses,

> the role of this general character (everyman and nobody) is to formulate a universal connection between illusory and frivolous scriptural productions and death, the law of the other. He plays out on the stage the very definition of literature as a world and of the world as literature. Rather than being merely represented in it, the ordinary man acts out of the text itself, in and by the text, and in addition he makes plausible the universal character of the particular place in which the mad discourse of a knowing wisdom is pronounced.[14]

For my argument, the 'scriptural production'[15] of Babel exhibits or stages a strange kind of fecund uselessness. 'Everyman and nobody' can turn this uselessness to their own ends, finding in this particular text the confusions, the 'mad discourse', from which a kind of knowing can be produced. Biblical critics, politicians, terrorists, right-wing Christian evangelicals, poets, cultural theorists, architects, and so on (everyman and nobody), add a brick or two, chip away at the mortar, or bring the tower crashing down, building or breaking the meaningful connections to this text. Babel is a migrational metaphor overlaid on our own cities. Reading the city and reading the biblical text (always already bricked in by centuries of commentary and rewriting) realizes the interchange between literature as world and world as literature. Deciding on what these cultural epistles mean reflects our reading and viewing positions.

---

[13] As Christopher Meredith writes, "The labyrinthine supermarket, the phallic skyscraper, the ships we describe as 'she'—these are not just physical constructions but cultural epistles. We 'read' these epistles, or ones like them, over ourselves every day; they inscribe themselves upon us. And so while spaces concretize our ideas about who we are as a society, they are also a means of reminding ourselves, persuading ourselves, or forcibly telling ourselves stories about our own individual identities." Christopher Meredith, "The Lattice and the Looking-Glass: Gendered Space in the Song of Songs 2:8–14", *Journal of the American Academy of Religion*, 80. 2 (June 2012), p. 2.

[14] Certeau, *The Practice of Everyday Life*, p. 2.

[15] For Certeau, part of the scriptural economy functions as the "multiform and murmuring activity of producing a text and producing society as a text." Ibid., p. 134.

According to the Genesis legend, humankind was scattered across the face of the earth. Let us then begin our analysis of the Babel-complex at a point in Western Europe in a city that boasts a very modern tower: Paris.

### The Eiffel Tower: A Hateful Blot of Ink on the City/Text

Erected as the entrance arch to the 1889 World Fair (itself organised to coincide with the centennial of the French Revolution), the Eiffel Tower already has more than a whiff of Babelistic interpretation about it: the Hebrew בלל (*balal*) is seen by some interpreters as a pun on the Akkadian *bab-ilu*, a 'gate of/to God' that is constructed amidst humanity's rebellious and potentially revolutionary self-confidence. However, just as with Babel's Tower, Gustave Eiffel's feat of engineering was contentious from the beginning. A group of leading artists objected at the time that,

> [w]e, writers, painters, sculptors, architects and passionate devotees of the hitherto untouched beauty of Paris, protest with all our strength, with all our indignation in the name of slighted French taste, against the erection ... of this useless and monstrous Eiffel Tower ... To bring our arguments home, imagine for a moment a giddy, ridiculous tower dominating Paris like a gigantic black smokestack, crushing under its barbaric bulk Notre Dame, the Tour Saint-Jacques, the Louvre, the Dome of Les Invalides, the Arc de Triomphe ... all of our humiliated monuments will disappear in this ghastly dream. And for twenty years ... we shall see stretching like a blot of ink the hateful shadow of the hateful column of bolted sheet metal.[16]

Eiffel's Tower, they argued, would change Paris for ever, casting a long shadow over its beautiful 'untouched' cityscape. It was a modernist monstrosity, characterised as useless yet still polemically linked with the uncultured barbarism of industry ('a gigantic black smokestack') able to affect humiliation on all over which it cast its 'hateful shadow'. Crucially, the protestors liken this shadow to a 'blot of ink', a seepage of the modern into their aspic daydream of Paris, the city/text becoming blurred, confused, and unreadable through the terms of their aesthetic taste.

It was the Tower's perceived uselessness that prompted Eiffel to respond, scrupulously listing all the notably scientific uses of the Tower:

---

[16] Henri Loyrette, *Gustave Eiffel*, (New York: Rizzoli, 1985), qtd., p. 174. Guy du Maupassant, a key member of this 'Committee of the Three Hundred' (one member for every metre of the tower), would lunch in the restaurant at its peak: "It's the only place in Paris, he used to say, where I don't have to see it." Qtd. Roland Barthes, "The Eiffel Tower," in *A Barthes Reader*, ed. Susan Sontag (New York: Hill and Wang, 1983), p. 236.

"aerodynamic measurements, studies of the resistance of substances, physiology of the climber, radio-electric research, problems of telecommunication, meteorological observations, etc."[17] For Roland Barthes, these attempts to swathe the Tower in utilitarian functionality are ridiculous "alongside the overwhelming myth of the Tower, of the human meaning which it has assumed throughout the world…[Utility is] nothing in comparison to the great imaginary function which enables men [*sic*] to be strictly human."[18] Barthes goes on to diagnose

> a true Babel complex: Babel was supposed to *serve* to communicate with God, and yet Babel is a dream which touches much greater depths than that of the theological project; and just as this great ascensional dream, released from its utilitarian prop, is finally what remains in the countless Babels represented by the painters, as if the function of art were to reveal the profound uselessness of objects, just so the Tower, almost immediately disengaged from the scientific considerations which had authorized its birth…has arisen from a great human dream in which movable and infinite meanings are mingled: it has reconquered the basic uselessness which makes it live in men's imagination.[19]

It is the very emptiness of the Tower, the airy spaces framed by its struts and girders, that gives it its life as a 'pure signifier' allowing people to fill it with meaning; indeed, the rhetoric of use "never does anything but shelter meaning."[20] What is interesting here is that Barthes understands literature (*écriture*—the same word for 'scripture' in French) as providing the imaginative blueprint that predates such towering technological and architectural (archi-textual?) structures; as he puts it "it is frequently the function of the great books to achieve in advance what technology will merely put into execution."[21] The Babel-complex then, with its roots in the 'ascensional dream' of constructing a route between heaven and earth, becomes something more, a celebration of 'uselessness', a dream-space in which the imagination can begin to write.

However, Gen. 11:1–9 is a difficult blueprint for such a modern edifice as the Eiffel Tower and it is important to note that Barthes, by assigning a theological use-value to the 'original' Tower, emphasising that it was supposed 'to *serve* to communicate with God', falls into the very monological trap he has already sketched for others. Although he moves quickly

---

[17]  Ibid., p. 239.
[18]  Ibid.
[19]  Ibid., p. 240.
[20]  Ibid.
[21]  Ibid., p. 242.

to underline that Babel signifies more than *theological* utility, he misses
the fact that the biblical commentaries and paraphrases that add an ever-
thickening gloss to the Tower have always marked the confusion inherent
in its blueprint. I want to argue that the text of Gen. 11:1–9 was always
already 'useless' in the Barthesian sense, allowing different themes and
emphases an imaginative life. If the Babelians left off building the city
and the tower, commentators flock to these useless ruins which, like the
Eiffel Tower, "offer for consumption a certain number of performances, or,
if one prefers, of paradoxes, and the visitor then becomes an engineer by
proxy [...]."[22] The visitor becomes an engineer of commentary, of writing.
If one is able to climb high enough, the altitude offers an "incomparable
power of *intellection*: the bird's-eye view, which each visitor to the Tower
can assume in an instant for his own, [giving] us the world to *read* and
not only to perceive; this is why it corresponds to a new sensibility of
vision [...]."[23] The new sensibility offered by the Eiffel Tower is the view
of the city/text as "a corpus of intelligible forms."[24] The ascensional dream
becomes a way of reading from a towering position.

In keeping with Barthes' diagnosis of the Babel-complex, I suggest that
it is the biblical writing that prepares us to imagine such vistas. And,
although I want to argue that the commentators' views from the top of
their textual towers attempt to offer a 'corpus of intelligible forms,' Babel
is even more complex than Eiffel. Confusion remains. In Derrida's own
exploration of the Babel-complex in language and translation, 'Des Tours
de Babel', *Des* can mean 'some' or 'of the' or 'from the' or 'about the' and
*Tours* could be towers, twists, turns, or tropes as in a 'turn' of phrase.[25] The
commentator-engineers are visitors and tourists, passers-by in the city/
text, turning their own phrases and not creating fixed abodes.[26] In fact,

---

[22] Ibid., p. 248.

[23] Ibid., p. 242.

[24] Ibid., p. 243.

[25] Cf. Translator's Note, Derrida, "Des Tours De Babel," p. 134.

[26] Derrida is aware that "From its height Babel at every instant supervises and surprises
my reading: I translate [and yet] there could be no translation of translation [...]. Recalling
this strange situation, I do not wish only or essentially to reduce my role to that of a pas-
ser or passerby. Nothing is more serious than translation." The passerby hears the original
"pleading for translation. This demand is not only on the side of the constructors of the
tower who want to make a name for themselves and to found a universal tongue translating itself by itself; it also constrains the deconstructor of the tower: in giving his name,
God also appealed to translation, not only between the tongues that had suddenly become
multiple and confused, but first *of his name*, of the name he proclaimed, given, and which
should be translated as confusion to be understood, hence to let it be understood that it
is difficult to translate and so to understand." Ibid., p. 118.

the process seems to be more like adding to a cairn, happened upon in the hills and started with some unsearchable intention, but continuing a tradition of human intervention, a marking or orientation in the landscape. Or, to put it differently within the city limits, their writing is similar to a graffiti or a scratching in stone that contributes to making the cityscape readable but not monological.[27] As Certeau writes, "the walking of passers-by offers a series of turns (*tours*) and detours that can be compared to 'turns of phrase' or 'stylistic figures'. There is a rhetoric of walking. The art of 'turning' phrases finds an equivalent in an art of composing a path (*tourner un parcours*)."[28] Marks in the city/text are part of these compositions. The 'useless' tower (*tour*) in the city of Babel becomes an imaginative site through which to take a turn (*tour*).

At this stage in my analysis of the Babel-complex, we have touched upon how the inherent 'uselessness' of Babel-like towers contributes to their position in the human imagination as material structures that embody a number of different themes: scientific modernism, artistic freedom, mythological depth. In addition to this productive uselessness, another key element is how such towers offer a 'new sensibility of vision', a position which provides the intellectual position from which to read the city/text. However, these positions are only arrived at by rhetorical turns and tropes; there is always another path up the tower before one gets to the all-encompassing viewpoint. One of the paths that has been composed through the city, alongside and up to the Tower is the idea that the biblical Babel marks a great and punishing disaster. Here I turn to a selection from these commentators and passers-by who have chipped their own names into the Tower's brickwork as they attempted the climb. Whence comes this idea and how does it migrate into contemporary manifestations of the Babel-complex? How does such a powerful God's-eye view become, paradoxically, a source of such anxiety?

### A View from the Top with 'The Faces of Oxen and the Horns of Stags'

If the Eiffel Tower was seen as a blot of shadowy ink on the city/text of Paris, the myriad interpreters of Gen. 11:1–9 see in the shadow of Babel a Rorschach-like smudge across Genesis and beyond. Rather than provid-

---

[27] In Glasgow, for example, aside from the often cryptic codes of graffiti on the walls, the older kerbstones have initials chiselled into them to denote the stonemason and yard from whence they came. In addition, some sites have poetry placed in strategic and thought-provoking spots. All add to the murmur of reading the social and physical landscape.

[28] Certeau, *The Practice of Everyday Life*, p. 100.

ing anything like a reception history of Babel, I will nevertheless examine some of the blueprints (or 'cultural epistles') that eventually manifest themselves in how we read our own towering architectures and cultural compositions. These blueprints are also palimpsests of the migrational metaphors of Babel in the contemporary world, theological sketches underlining how part of the Babel-complex is also Babel's place as a symbol of humankind's depravity, a technological extension of human limits that merits punishment and destruction.

Many interpretations of 11:1–9 take this to be a story of humankind's hubris and pride, trying to build a tower high enough to storm heaven, and become, at the very least, equal with God. As we shall see in some of the alarming rhetoric that surrounded the destruction of the Twin Towers in 2001, Islamic and Christian fundamentalists were united in seeing this act as a divine punishment directed at the immoral heart of the United States and the Tower of Babel was a motif that quickly circulated. However, as Tina Pippin underlines,

> cultural representations of Babel/Babylon are rather anachronistic; in Genesis 11 there is no mention of perversion…, and the city is not even completely built, for when God scatters them, 'they left off building the city' (11:9). But the art of Babel is certainly not literal; what is important is to tell a good story, one with which spectators will connect.[29] (57)

How, then, does the tower come to be linked with punishment when the biblical text is so reticent in assigning a singular motivation to the builders' project?

Part of the difficulty is that, according to Claus Westermann, the motif of Babel is always already doing (at least) two things at once. The redactor of this narrative has used the Babel story to construct two separate etiological meanings around the building of a city/tower and the origin of the plurality of tongues. In Westermann's hands, the tools of source criticism can scrape away at the text and highlight the two blocks the Yahwist is using but it cannot prise them apart—the mortar is too strong. As he argues "the sequence of vv. 7 and 8 shows that the motifs of the confusion of language and the dispersion of humankind have been deliberately joined at a later stage […]."[30]

> 'Come, let us go down, and confuse their language there, so that they will not understand one another's speech.' [two sentences joined here] So the

---

29 Tina Pippin, *Apocalyptic Bodies: The Biblical End of the World in Text and Image* (London and New York: Routledge, 1999). p. 57.
30 Westermann, *Genesis 1–11: A Commentary*, p. 552.

Lord scattered them abroad from there over the face of all the earth, and they left off building the city.[31]

It does not necessarily follow that the 'confusion of tongues' leads to the scattering of the people. As this narrative comes hard on the heels of the 'table of nations' in Gen. 10 that charts the descendents of Japheth, Ham, and Shem "by their families, their languages, their lands, and their nations,"[32] plurality is already very much in evidence. Westermann reads 11:1–9 as regarding "the repeal of this plurality as endangering humankind."[33] The attempt to unify the divinely sanctioned post-diluvian plurality ("the nations spread abroad on the earth after the flood")[34] must be resisted. It is upon reflection at seeing the work of the people that YHWH muses that "nothing that they propose to do will now be impossible for them."[35]

Westermann sees here a link with Job 42:2 where Job admits that "I know that you can do all things, and that no purpose of yours can be thwarted"; the balance between Creator and Creature must be maintained. Thus "it is against human presumption, albeit only feared, that God must intervene."[36] Westermann concludes that this narrative indicates a transition "from nomadic to sedentary life. But with the note 'with its summit touching the heavens' the city envisaged takes on a completely new meaning; it serves to present ambition."[37] There is no storming of the heavens but if we follow Barthes and Certeau, this ambition is the mastery of a god's eye view, a totalizing vision that reduces the labyrinthine confusion of the citizens' rhetorical turns to a useful and (even if only for a moment) all-encompassing singular.

For Gerhard von Rad, writing earlier and also noting that the motif of storming heaven is not mentioned in the biblical text,

> one will observe a subtlety of the narrative in the fact that it does not give anything unprecedented as the motive for this building, but rather something that lies within the realm of human possibility, namely, a combination of their energies on the one hand, and on the other the winning of fame, i.e., a naïve desire to be great [and secure]... These are therefore the basic forces of what we call culture.[38]

---

[31] Gen. 11:7–8.
[32] This coda is repeated at Gen. 10:5, 10:20, and 10:31.
[33] Westermann, *Genesis 1–11: A Commentary*, p. 552.
[34] Gen. 10:32.
[35] Gen. 11:6.
[36] Westermann, *Genesis 1–11: A Commentary*, p. 551.
[37] Ibid., p. 554.
[38] Gerhard von Rad, *Genesis: A Commentary*, 4 ed. (London: SCM Press, 1963), p. 145.

With the building of "a great city and a tower, they began to erect a monumental architectural work"[39] and their "joy in their inventiveness—they
use asphalt for mortar—is shown in the Hebrew text by the appropriate
puns:"[40] החמר היה להם לחמר[41] (*heimer hiyah lehem homer*).

Yet the joy in the creative work of the Babelians/Babylonians is short-
lived. Westermann suggests some darker ambiguities at the heart of the
word מגדל (*migdāl*) which "describes generally the fortress of a city and is
often mentioned together with the walls, e.g., 2 Chron. 14:6, Isa. 2:15 [...].
It can be applied too to the fortifications as a whole. But the word can
also designate a wooden structure (watchtower) in the vineyard, Isa. 5:2."[42]
Where the tower and the city being constructed on the plains of Shinar
might be seen as the mythological beginnings of 'culture', a blueprint
for human creativity, this מגדל might also be a shoring up of defences,
a military outpost or surveillance platform in a hostile environment. The
Tower can become a watchtower, a line of sight that only allows certain
meanings into its purview, "the only blind point of a total optical system
of which it is the centre [...]."[43] Security and culture seem to arrive hand
in hand. However, von Rad also suggests that

> this interpretation is debatable, for the saga *contains no data whatever about
> the actual purpose of the building (profane building? religious building?)*. The
> meaning would then have more to do with mankind's transition to a collec-
> tive ability to bear arms. But then one would also have to assume that the
> saga was related to remote knowledge about a gigantic building in Babylon,
> and that was particularly the ziggurat Etemenanki. In any case, the saga
> views such a development of power as something against God, rebellion
> against the Most High, as Babylon in many passages of the Old Testament
> is mentioned as the embodiment of sinful arrogance (Isa. 13:19; 14:13; Jer.
> 51:6ff.). It appears indeed that the oldest version of the narrative represented
> the building of the tower precisely as a danger and threat to the gods.[44]

For early commentators in this vein of power and threat, it is Nimrod,
grandson of Ham and hunter turned tyrant who presides over the enforced

---

[39] Ibid., p. 144.
[40] Ibid.
[41] *Biblica Hebraica Stuttgartensia*. Robert Alter suggests that a literal rendering of 11:3
"would read something like 'brick bricks and burn for a burning.' This fusion of words
reflects the striking tendency of the story as a whole to make words flow into each other.
'Bitumen,' *heimar*, becomes *homer*, 'mortar.'" Robert Alter, *Genesis: Translation and Commentary* (New York: W. W. Norton & Co., 1996), p. 47.
[42] Westermann, *Genesis 1–11: A Commentary*, p. 547.
[43] Barthes, "The Eiffel Tower," p. 237.
[44] Rad, *Genesis: A Commentary*, p. 147. My emphasis.

labour of the tower-builders. According to Josephus, Nimrod persuades the Babylonians that it is through adherence to his power that they shall prosper; "He also said he would be revenged on God, if he should have a mind to drown the world again; for that he would build a tower too high for the waters to be able to reach! and that he would avenge himself on God for destroying their forefathers!"[45] The notion that Babel signifies a militaristic rebellion against a sovereign YHWH has deep roots.

If the Yahwist brings together the two etiologies of geographical dispersion and linguistic confusion within the Genesis narrative it is this double-structure that also contributes to the Barthesian 'uselessness' of the tower looming over Babel and its commentators. Westermann concludes that whatever use this edifice had, and whether or not it was linked to Israelite experience of Babylonian ziggurats, the basic motif is "that people want to demonstrate their greatness in a work of their own hands."[46] The Babelians are working at their name ("let us, each one, write our names upon the bricks and burn them with fire" [Pseudo-Philo *Biblical Antiquities*]), carving out a proper name in the plain of Shinar where a "name in the sense of fame, a name that one makes for oneself by one's deeds . . . is only possible in a rather large community. It is the significance of the deeds for the community that gives them recognition and meaning; that is what is meant by the 'name'."[47] Making a name is part of making culture. As Brian Murdoch highlights, the Vulgate's translation of Gen. 11:4 links name

---

[45] Flavius Josephus, *The Antiquities of the Jews*, trans. William Whiston (Project Gutenberg, 2009). Available at www.gutenberg.org/files/2848/2848-h/2848-h.htm. Accessed 20th December 2012.

[46] Westermann, *Genesis 1–11: A Commentary*, p. 554. Westermann links this with prophetic condemnation of Babylon, such as Isa. 14:12–14:

> How you are fallen from heaven,
> O Day Star, Son of Dawn!
> How your are cut down to the ground,
> You who laid the nations low!
> You who said in your heart,
> 'I will ascend to heaven;
> I will raise my throne
> Above the stars of God;
> I will sit on the mount of assembly
> On the heights of Zaphon;
> I will ascend to the tops of the clouds,
> I will make myself like the Most High.'
> But you are brought down to Sheol,
> To the depths of the Pit.

[47] Ibid., p. 548.

and fame: *celebremus nomen nostrum* ('make known/celebrate a name for ourselves').[48]

Celebrating, defending, or marking a proper name is then a key part of the Babel-complex. Indeed, it is in this facet that Derrida traces the idea of God's punishment against the Babelians "incontestably for having wanted to make a name for themselves, to give themselves the name, to construct by and for themselves their own name, to gather themselves there ('that we no longer be scattered'), as in the unity of a place which is at once a tongue and a tower, the one as well as the other, the one as the other."[49] Derrida reads the שׁמה in vv. 8–9 through French biblical scholar André Chouraqui's translation: "They cease to build the city. Over which he proclaims his name: Bavel, Confusion, for there, YHWH confounds the lip of all the earth."[50] YHWH breaks, deconstructs, overturns the 'name and lip' of men, imposing and forbidding translation at the same time. Just as the Babelians are celebrating unifying their name, YHWH overthrows the symbol of the name with his own name and ensures plurality. Indeed, by the time the *Apocalypse of Baruch* (c. 100 CE and preserved only in the 6th-century Syriac Vulgate) is superimposed over the Babel motif, these men "who built the tower of strife against God" (2:6–7) are not only cast into plurality but are envisioned on a plain in heaven, "dwelling thereon, with the faces of oxen, and the horns of stags and the feet of goats, and the haunches of lambs" (2:3–5). Through trying to ascend to a vision of heaven, these men have been reduced to a strange stitch-work of animal parts; they can no longer look on their own bodies as 'corpora of intelligible forms'.

With the above analysis in mind, we can now add more facets to our understanding of the Babel-complex. Even though the text itself does not provide a definitive meaning on the purpose of Babel's tower, its Barthesian uselessness or emptiness has tended toward a number of interlinked interpretations. The ambition of a unifying perspective (against the divinely sanctioned plurality of nations) is coupled with the marking and making of 'the proper name', a cultural identity which also offers sure foundations and unified ways of reading and writing to avoid confusion. This development of cultural power also displays its own anxieties, linking the construction of the city/text with an armoured fortress and watchtower. Part

---

[48] Brian Murdoch, *The Medieval Popular Bible: Expansions of Genesis in the Middle Ages* (Cambridge: D. S. Brewer, 2003), p. 127.

[49] Derrida, "Des Tours De Babel," p. 107.

[50] Qtd. Ibid., pp. 107–8.

of such anxiety is that the Babel-motif has been strongly read for many centuries as a spectacle of divine punishment. How does this aspect of the Babel-complex map onto the terrifying scene of destruction that occurred in Manhattan on 11th September 2001, a spectacle that has become distilled into the 'proper name' of 9/11? How do the absent towers haunt the skyline and imaginations of New Yorkers and the post 9/11 world?

### The Twin Towers: 'The Tallest Letters in the World'

In the *Practice of Everyday Life*, Michel de Certeau climbs to the 110th floor of the World Trade Center and records how such a perspective organises his reading of the city:

> A wave of verticals. Its agitation is momentarily arrested by vision. The giant mass is immobilized before the eyes. It is transformed into a texturology in which extremes coincide—extremes of ambition and degradation, brutal oppositions of races and styles, contrasts between yesterday's buildings, already transformed into trash cans, and today's urban irruptions that block out its space. [...] A city composed of paroxysmal places in monumental reliefs. The spectator can read in it a universe that is constantly exploding. In it are inscribed the architectural figures of the *coincidato oppositorum* formerly drawn in miniatures and mystical textures. On this stage of concrete, steel and glass, cut out between two oceans (the Atlantic and the American) by a frigid body of water, the tallest letters in the world compose a giant rhetoric of excess in both expenditure and production.
>   To what erotics of knowledge does the ecstasy of reading such a cosmos belong? Having taken a voluptuous pleasure in it, I wonder what is the source of this pleasure of 'seeing the whole,' of looking down on, totalizing the most immoderate of human texts.[51]

Certeau notes how the spectator, whether tourist or engineer, becomes a reader, a voyeur, elevated above the plurality and confusion of the streets; New York is reduced to a corpus or texturology of intelligible forms. Such a viewpoint transforms the pedestrian into a visionary. In a now painfully poignant aside, Certeau notes how "a poster, sphinx-like," offers an enigmatic message: "It's hard to be down when you're up."[52] As with Barthes, Certeau notes that through the "scopic drive" such architectural feats materialize "the utopia that yesterday was only painted. The 1370 foot high tower that serves as a prow for Manhattan continues to construct the fic-

---

51  Certeau, *The Practice of Everyday Life*, pp. 91–92.
52  Ibid., p. 92.

tion that creates readers, makes the complexity of the city readable, and immobilizes its opaque mobility in a transparent text."[53] As Westermann and von Rad understood it, the biblical Babel marks a complex transition from nomadic tribalism to ambitious cultural and urbanizing materialism, whilst also hinting at militaristic or strategic defence. In much of the cultural history of the Babel myth, the result of such a transition, or 'making a name', is the divine punishment of plurality and/or dispersion. How then is Babel superimposed over the Twin Towers, even in their absence, and how does this analysis contribute to our diagnosis of the Babel-complex?

Allan Wexler, an architect and conceptual artist who had vigorously defended the building of the Twin Towers (completed in 1973) was interviewed by the *New York Times* a day after the 9/11 attacks. In a direct allusion to biblical precedents he said, "I always saw it as a sort of Tower of Babel or Jacob's Ladder...an attempt to penetrate through the cloud layer and attempt enlightenment."[54] Wexler's analysis links the Towers to Certeau's visionary aspect of the Babel-complex. Yet here the 'erotics of knowledge' is not of the scopophilic's voyeurism over a unified city but a different ecstasy: enlightenment. However, Wexler also understands the inherent Barthesian 'uselessness' of the Towers, their ability to be read as signifiers "in which movable and infinite meanings are mingled, [reconquering] the basic uselessness which makes [Babel] live in men's imagination."[55] As Wexler notes, most people saw the World Trade Center as "a static, bland structure. But it was so neutral that it became a barometer that transformed minute by minute by minute. By photographing it four times a day, it radically changed each time."[56] He goes on:

> I would tell my students that it was really the urban stage of the world. People used it as a forum, and now, unfortunately, politically as well. [...] It is now stronger as a monument. We'll never forget it. It will live in our memories. It's like the grassy knoll. It becomes a metaphysical structure at this point.[57]

---

[53] Ibid.
[54] Tara Bahrampour, "Reverberations: An Inspiration Lives on in His Mind," *The New York Times* 2001. http://www.nytimes.com/2001/09/30/nyregion/reverberations-an-inspiration-lives-on-in-his-mind.html. Accessed 20th December 2012.
[55] Barthes, "The Eiffel Tower," p. 240.
[56] Bahrampour, "Reverberations: An Inspiration Lives on in His Mind."
[57] Ibid.

An almost blank canvas, a stage, a forum and now a 'metaphysical structure'; in this sense, like the scriptural Babel, the World Trade Center has
become a readable absence, a metaphysical structure that one may climb
in order to take a turn around the top and render a commentary on the
view. The absence of the Twin Towers themselves does not undermine
the power of their vertical 'writing'—the tallest letters in the world do
not need to exist but continue to be read, an evident sign that the Babel-
complex runs deep in the psyche.

Historian Graham Davison, who takes a special interest in the history
of cities, charts some of the ways in which Babel was superimposed over
New York in the days preceding and following the attacks. As he argues,

> in the global competition for tourism and investment cities are judged by
> how well they manage to project an image of their power and success. A city
> that is not proud of itself is not likely to attract the confidence of others. But
> long before the emergence of the post-modern city, the cities of the ancient
> world had learned the same lesson.[58]

The Babel-complex takes another turn, this time toward materializing as
economic capital and financial confidence. A Tower at the heart of a city
not only offers a totalizing view out to the plains or up into the heavens
but is also a symbol of power, asserting itself on both the visual and imaginative horizon. Such a Tower is meant to be seen.

However, as Davison explains, even though the intellectual persuasions
of the last two hundred years have seriously undermined the attitude that
disaster is a direct consequence of divine wrath, the destruction of the
Twin Towers of the World Trade Center produced

> a wave of apocalyptic visions across the world, including in America. In the
> Islamic world, indeed through much of the Third World, the secularising,
> relativising spirit was much less evident. The evils of the western city—its
> luxury, waste, licentiousness and pride—are now, thanks to the satellite and
> the internet, visible for all to see. It is the particular conjuncture of three
> factors—the massive concentration of power and wealth in the financial
> capitals of the West, its increased visibility throughout the rest of the world,
> and the renewed vitality of fundamentalist religion, including a conviction
> that pride invites divine retribution—that underlies the new sense of vul
> nerability experienced by many city-dwellers in the wake of 9/11. [...] In the
> eyes of the rest of the world, and even sometimes in their own eyes, their
> manifest pride and power makes them morally vulnerable.[59]

---

[58] Graeme Davison, "The Fallen Towers: Pride, Envy and Judgement in the Modern
City," *The Bible and Critical Theory* 1, no. 3 (2005): pp. 14.1–14.2.

[59] Ibid., pp. 14.4–14.5.

The Tower has gone virtual, a migrational metaphor and metaphysical structure, that can be seen across a globalised, interconnected world through all of the technological extensions of vision. For Barthes, the 'uselessness' of the Eiffel Tower was also part of its appeal, a 'great ascensional dream, released from its utilitarian prop.' As we have seen, the Babel city/text offers little sure foundation for the Sodom and Gomorrah-like visions of punishment that proceed in its interpretive history; the motives for its construction are obscure. However, with the attacks on New York, both Islamist terrorists and the Christian Right shared the view that the World Trade Center's destruction and huge loss of life was a direct result of the moral depravity and cultural ambitions of the United States.[60]

In a televised interview between prominent televangelists Pat Robertson and the late Jerry Falwell two days after the attacks, Falwell opined that he believed "the pagans, and the abortionists, and the feminists, and the gays and the lesbians who are actively trying to make that an alternative lifestyle, the ACLU, People For the American Way, all of them who have tried to secularize America. I point the finger in their face and say 'you helped this happen'."[61] However, in Falwell's twisted revivalist logic, all this death and destruction was an opportunity, a "kind of brokenness that no one could conjure, only God could bring upon us. And, that is to me the most optimistic thing that I see today as I look across America."[62] Falwell's ability to see 'across America' from his own theological tower brought a statement from the White House, with George Bush distancing himself from Falwell's comments; Falwell was forced to apologize, stating that "the only label any of us needs in such a terrible time of crisis is American."[63] In keeping with Falwell's own Babel-complex, he retreated into the proper name of the label 'American', a national signifier of security and identity.

Where Falwell and Robertson saw the attacks as a vengeful yet ultimately beneficent strike from a Christian God uniquely concerned with America's national destiny, Osama bin Laden gave his own reading of the 'metaphysical structure' of the World Trade Center. In a video addressing the American people, the al-Qaida leader rhetorically linked his experiences

---

[60] Ibid., p.14.5.
[61] The full transcript is available at http://www.commondreams.org/news2001/0917-03.htm. Accessed 19th December 2012.
[62] Ibid.
[63] Gustav Niebuhr, "A Nation Challenged: Placing Blame; Falwell Apologizes for Saying an Angry God Allowed Attacks," *New York Times* 18th September 2001. www.nytimes.com. Accessed 19th December 2012.

of "the injustice and tyranny of the American-Israeli alliance against our people in Palestine and Lebanon"[64] during the 1982 Lebanon War to his inspiration to engineer an attack on the World Trade Center: "As I watched the destroyed towers in Lebanon, it occurred to me to punish the unjust the same way [and] to destroy towers in America so it could taste some of what we are tasting and to stop killing our children and women."[65] In an earlier video, broadcast in November 2001, he argued that the "Twin Towers were legitimate targets, they were supporting US economic power. These events were great by all measurement. What was destroyed were not only the towers, but the towers of morale in that country."[66] In Bin Laden's logic, the towers were filled with "supporters of the economical [sic] powers of the United States who are abusing the world. Those who talk of civilians should change their stand and reconsider their position. We are treating them like they are treating us."[67]

For both fundamentalist parties, the Towers were filled with human beings who could be grouped without confusion under the proper name of 'Adversary', inviting divine retribution. Where the Babel-complex I have been exploring thus far seeks to 'make a name' by building high enough to instil a new sensibility of organizational vision, for the fundamentalist, gazing up at the Tower itself is a means of unification that reflects their own nightmarish dreams; there is the enemy, contained and immobilized in a punishable singularity. And yet, if we read Genesis again, against the grain of these punishing nightmares, it is difficult to decide on the class, the race, the sexuality, the gender, the sex, and so on, of these builders; all the signifiers that we take for granted when reducing an Other to a manageable unity are absent. As Tina Pippin writes, what is clear is that the builders

> seem to be part of a unified movement and language. Then they all get scattered, which means 'my people and tongue' are in there somewhere. So identification of the enemy Babylon is not clear; in fact I find myself cheer-

---

[64] "God Knows It Did Not Cross Our Minds to Attack the Towers," *The Guardian* 2004. Available at www.guardian.co.uk/world/2004/oct/30/alqaida.september11. Accessed 19th December 2012.

[65] Ibid.

[66] David Bamber, "Bin Laden: Yes, I Did It," *The Telegraph* 11 November 2001. Available at www.telegraph.co.uk/news/worldnews/asia/afghanistan/1362113/Bin-Laden-Yes-I-did-it .html. Accessed 19th December 2012.

[67] Ibid.

ing for their plight like it is some Olympics of architecture, the ultimate prize of which is heaven.[68]

'My people and my tongue' are in the pluralities of the dispersed peoples walking the confusing streets, composing turns of phrase that can contribute to the babble that offers the possibility of drowning out singular and fundamentalist interpretations of 'scriptural' texts. If we can diagnosis some of the negative elements of the Babel-complex, what other visuality/texturology complex might we be able to utilise?

*Babel, Babble, Bible; Tongues, Twists, Towers: Conclusions and Confusions*

Taking a turn around the city and the tower, I have analysed some of the elements that extend Roland Barthes' thinking about what constitutes the visuality of Babel-complex. By providing a tentative index of these elements, I argue that the Babel-complex offers a way of understanding the 'semeiocracy' of the reading/writing process through reaching for an elevated vision that can lead to a mono-logical unifying of complexity, parallel with the construction of a 'proper-name'; for example, Paris becomes a unified city/text by being imaginatively viewed from the Eiffel Tower itself (world) or its literary equivalent, such as Victor Hugo's *The Hunchback of Notre Dame* (literature) or the imagined Babel blueprints.

This finding and founding a 'proper name' or 'making a name for ourselves' is also a process of cultural alignment and foundational security. Writing a city/text is a defensive practice that attempts to delineate the borders and edges of the knowable. The Tower can thus signify cultural ambition at the same time as displaying an anxiety toward such ambition. In this way, the Tower, whether literal or literary, is also a mode of surveillance, 'over-veiling' the threat of confusion and otherness, from within and without.

Such a unifying, totalizing vision from above can also be mirrored by the gaze from below. With the Twin Towers, different antagonists reduced them, and the people within them, to singular signifiers in order to justify their destruction. As a 'migrational metaphor' it is also critical to remember that in the dialectic between world and literature, literature and world, people are moving, living, and taking their turns, their detours.

---

[68] Tina Pippin, *Apocalyptic Bodies: The Biblical End of the World in Text and Image* p. 61.

The city/texts/towers are constructed by and through real bodies; as Tina Pippin identifies, "the imaginary ruins of Babel—and Eden—fill the Western cultural canvases. Babel and bodies are both part of the scene in art; the bodies are building, fleeing, or being plucked off the tower by God."[69] Towers only find meaning through the part they play in performing and extending imaginative and bodily limitations.

Although I have focussed my analytical efforts on the ways in which the Babel-complex is a form of reading and writing that organises an interpretive view over a city/text, the next stage in expanding the parameters of this complex would be to look at the other etiology that Claus Westermann identified in the redacted work of Gen. 11:1–9; the origin of the plurality of tongues. This part of the Babel story has generated even more religious and cultural commentary than the motif of city and tower building. Umberto Eco traces how the fall into plural tongues inherent in the Babel myth is seen as opening a vast gulf between humankind's many vernaculars and the original Adamic language, the language of creation itself where a single utterance could bind word and thing indissolubly. Eco notes that there are a paucity of known representations of the Tower of Babel before the so-called Cotton Bible of the 5th or 6th century. Following this, the 'Caedmon manuscript' from the end of the 10th century sketches a tower replete with industrious workmen; an 11th century ivory relief from the cathedral at Salerno depicts a skyscraper-like tower covered in builders. However after this date, Eco discerns

> a flood of towers. It is a flood, moreover, that has its counterpart in a vast deluge of theoretical speculation about the confusion of tongues. It was only at this point that the story of the confusion came to be perceived not merely as an example of how divine justice humbled man's pride but as an account of a historical (or metahistorical) event. It was now the story of how a real wound had been inflicted on mankind, a wound that might, in some way, be healed.[70]

Moving from images of punishment to the ways in which Gen. 11:1–9 has been read as a meta-critical event in the history of language, further explorations of the Babel-complex must take into account how the multiplicity of languages and the plurality and *différance* at the heart of each language system con-fuses the migrational metaphor of Babel further. From this

---

[69] Ibid., p. 59.
[70] Umberto Eco, *Serendipities: Language and Lunacy*, trans. William Weaver (London and New York: Harcourt Brace and Company, 1998), p. 28.

angle, Babel is the imagined "unity of a place which is at once a tongue and a tower, the one as well as the other, the one as the other."[71] If those aspects of the Babel-complex I have traced here are concerned with the ambitious construction of a reading position, a gods-eye view over the city/text (and the concomitant anxieties from occupying such a position), the next stage is to look at the tongues inherent in the tower and to ask what kind of universal languages (economic, political, cultural) are now being imposed over our city/texts, the texts in which we move and walk and write and live, composing our own paths. What necessary complexities do they elide and keep out of sight? By exploring the babble of relations between contemporary Babels and their scriptural ur-text we can understand how biblical narratives, as *écriture*, form part of our semiocracies, uselessly available, like an Eiffel Tower that "attracts meaning, the way a lightning rod attracts thunderbolts; for all lovers of signification, it plays a glamorous part, that of a pure signifier, i.e. of a form in which men unceasingly put *meaning* (which they extract from their knowledge, their dreams, their history), without this meaning thereby ever being finite and fixed: who can say what the Tower will be for humanity tomorrow?"[72]

---

[71] Derrida, "Des Tours De Babel," p. 107.
[72] Barthes, "The Eiffel Tower," p. 238.

# "THE STRONG RIGHT ARM THAT HOLDS FOR PEACE": PICTURING NATIONAL IDOLATRY[1]

A. K. M. Adam

If irony suffuses the relation of U.S. politics to the religion from which it claims Constitutional autonomy,[2] that irony intensifies a hundredfold when the focus of that relation falls on the status of the Bible. While the Bible itself bespeaks a monarchial theocracy where civil and cultic laws interweave comfortably, the U.S. Constitution draws a bright line of separation between the secular republic and the kingdom of heaven. Nonetheless, the Bible retains talismanic significance in U.S. political culture; much as politicians must nowadays sport a flag badge on every public occasion, they must also quote from, appeal to, and swear on the Bible (the Bible in which Jesus himself forbids oath-taking, whether either by heaven, for it is the throne of God, or by the earth, for it is his footstool, or by Jerusalem).

The multidimensional irony of the Bible's status in U.S. politics comes to the fore particularly in connection with the Ten Commandments, the talismanic centre for the talismanic book. As a *précis* of the Torah, the Commandments provide a convenient foundation-stone for Christian ethics without inconveniently-detailed Levitical precepts for worship and purity; most of the Commandments are relatively easy to keep, at least on a simple reading. Churches that eschew any possibly-distracting decorative iconography in their worship space frequently display the Commandments prominently as an edifying alternative to stained glass or plaster saints. And Jesus seems to have regarded them as a satisfactory synecdoche for the whole Torah in his dialogue with the rich young man (Matt 19:16–30 and parallels). For this and numerous other reasons, the Ten Commandments occupy a prominent place in the imagination of the U.S. public.

---

[1] I present this essay, an exercise in biblical political theology, in honour of my friend and colleague Yvonne Sherwood.
[2] The classic treatments by Reinhold Niebuhr (*The Irony of American History*, New York: Charles Scribner's Sons, 1952) and Martin Marty (*Modern American Religion, Volume 1: The Irony of It All, 1893–1919*, Chicago: University Of Chicago Press, 1997).

The apparent simplicity of the Commandments obscures a great many controverted aspects of their history and significance. For example, the Commandments appear in slightly different forms in Exodus and Deuteronomy, and different interpretive traditions divide the commandments differently. The simplicity of the Ten Commandments evaporates as one considers them more closely—but their ideological value as a simple, foundational, and universal basis for national life overrides any intricacies of enumeration, of interpretation, or of particularity.

However complex the tradition history of the Ten Commandments may be, their appeal to the popular imagination lies in their lucid clarity. So to begin a reflection on the how the Commandments—and more narrowly, the first three Commandments—inhabit and interrogate the distinctively American investment in their transcendent status, the focus should fall first on the Commandments in question.

### The Unique, Invisible, Useless Lord

First, in the narrative context of the Book of Exodus, these commandments are addressed not to a nation-state, but to a caravan of people wandering in the Sinaitic wilderness. At least in the imagination of the scribal tradents who compiled the Pentateuch, the relevance of these Commandments doesn't depend on an established civil government enacting their precepts into public policy, nor on each individual adopting them as a personal code. The Commandments are addressed to a people, a particular community, and this community holds together as a people in relation to the words Moses dictates to them.

"I am the LORD your God, who brought you out of the land of Egypt." God begins by announcing the Divine Name; where careful English translations say "the LORD," the Hebrew specifies God's own name—at which, according to tradition,[3] all the world stands still, all sound is hushed, the praise of God in heaven and the mysterious wheels of the chariot cease spinning, as God pronounces the unspeakable Name. God announces the Name, and explains that God's identity is made known in saving this

---

[3] "Said R. Abbahu in the name of R. Joḥanan: When God gave the Torah no bird twittered, no fowl flew, no ox lowed, none of the *Ophanim* [the wheels of the divine chariot] stirred a wing, the Seraphim did not say 'Holy, Holy', the sea did not roar, the creatures spoke not, the whole world was hushed into breathless silence and the voice went forth: I AM THE LORD THY GOD"; *Midrash Rabbah* vol. III, Exodus xxix 9; S. M. Lehrman trans., H. Freedman and M. Simon, ed. (London: Soncino Press, 1939), 345.

people from slavery—in the words of Psalm 77, "with a strong arm God redeemed the children of Jacob and Joseph" (Ps 77:15), a verse we will revisit at a later part of this essay. For the moment, it suffices to bear in mind that the Name itself is understood as a command in the Judaic tradition;[4] the bare fact of *knowing God* activates an ethical obligation whose details emerge in the subsequent verses.

The First Commandment emphasizes that this is not a random encounter between nomadic herders and a post-Chaldaic deity. The God who, in the Decalogue, teaches Israel how to live is the same God who delivered them from slavery in Egypt; God has already extended divine mercy to Israel as a basis for Israel trusting in God. "Deliverance" now constitutes a further revelation of God's identity, so that everything else to be learned about God should cohere with this demonstration of freedom.

"You shall have no other gods before me." The force of the prepositional phrase "before me" (*'al-panay*) has been much debated over the millennia; one would think that the prohibition would work just as effectively without it. "Before me" has been construed in various ways, from "over against me" to "in preference to me"[5]—but whatever the precise nuance of "before me," the across-the-board sense is that any other allegiance must be set aside in favor of Israel's allegiance to the Lord. God is not arguing that other deities don't exist; the next commandment goes on to allow that they must be real in some sense, since God commands that his followers not bow down to them or worship them.[6] Allegiance to this God takes precedence over any other possible priority; any other deity,

---

[4] The Judaic tradition treats the first commandment simply as the announcement of God's identity, and rolls the exclusivity clause in with the prohibition of idolatry. According to Exodus Rabbah, "God's voice, as it was uttered, split up into seventy voices, in seventy languages, so that all the nations should understand. When each nation heard the Voice in their own vernacular their souls departed, save Israel who heard but were not hurt" (*Midrash Rabbah* vol. III, Exodus v 9; 86); no nation can claim ignorance of God.

[5] Childs notes that Rashi reads this preposition as bearing the same sense here as in Numbers 3:4, "during the lifetime of" or "as long as X lives"; *The Book of Exodus*, The Old Testament Library (Philadelphia: The Westminster Press, 1974), 402.

[6] The distinction between "bowing down" and "worshiping" served the early church as a guide when some who apostatized under persecution argued that they had only *pretended* to worship. Origen considers the possibility that "those who deny Christianity on oath at the tribunals or before they have been put on trial do not worship but only bow down to idols when they take 'God' from the name of the Lord God and apply it to vain and lifeless wood." *Exhortation to Martyrdom* 6, in R. A. Greer, trans. and ed. *Origen*, Classics of Western Spirituality (Mahwah, NJ: Paulist Press, 1979), 45. Cf. also Christopher Rowland, "Living With Idols," in *Idolatry: False Worship in the Bible, Early Judaism, and Christianity*, ed. Stephen Barton (London: T & T Clark, 2007), 163–176.

any other possible rival for the people's commitment, must give way to the Lord God who brings Israel out of slavery.

The next commandment, then, explicitly requires not only that the people of God commit themselves completely to the Lord, but that they follow through on that promise of loyalty. God's unwillingness to allow anyone or anything to intervene between God and humanity comes to expression in the commandment, "You shall not make for yourself an idol"; they may not participate in any of the plausible, popular, culturally-acceptable practices that infringe on this unique commitment to God. That rules out the obvious: making and adorning statues that depict other deities (golden calves, for instance). It further rules out such representa-tions of the Lord God as might confuse anyone into worshipping the cre-ated instead of the creator, or such representations as satiate our curious imaginations with definitive details on topics where God has not seen fit to supply knowledge. The God of Sinai specifically does not want anyone to think that God looks like an elderly, bearded white patriarch; Moses is the only person in Scripture who gets a direct glimpse of God, and even then he only shalt see God's back parts (though presumably God's back parts look *divine*).

Instituting a theme that resounds thereafter through all of Scripture, God resolutely condemns any human endeavor that encroaches on God's unique self-representation. The Golden Calf episode in Exodus 32 stands out as an example, not only because it displays the chosen people indulg-ing in a festival of idolatry *while Moses is still on the mountain*, receiving the Torah, but especially because Aaron assures the people, "*These* are your gods, O Israel, who brought you out of the land of Egypt" (Ex 32:8)—to which God responds, as it were, "*No way*, Mosheh." However much God's people demand a God according to their own terms, they may not arro-gate to themselves the prerogative to characterize God as suits them; they may not devise domesticated deiti-ettes to solace their longing to lay hold of holiness for their own ends with emblematic representations of the Lord.[7]

---

[7] The stated emphatic ban on worship of foreign gods goes hand-in-hand with an appar-ent horror for the practice—which the prophets ascribe distinctively to other nations and their deities—of sacrificing children. While recent scholarship has complicated the topic of human sacrifice in ancient Israel, the Bible provides testimonies that the willingness of a culture to shed the blood of its children to demonstrate allegiance to their god con-stituted one of the focal points of self-definition. The Akedah marks a turning-point in God's interactions with Abraham; Jephthah won a battle for God's people at the cost of his daughter's life; Saul vowed to sacrifice anyone who tasted food before a decisive battle. At

The commandment explains that the basis for the exclusive allegiance is God's "jealousy," often interpreted as though God were a suspicious, envious figure, hiring sleazy detectives to catch God's people in a motel with strange gods. The lexicography of "jealousy"/"zeal" is complicated, but it is so in large part because subsequent usage has made and reinforced a divergence between possessive, manipulative *envy* (on one hand) and all-encompassing devotion (on the other). Both in Hebrew (*qanaʾ*) and Greek (*zêlos*), the fiercely strong attachment that the word denotes can bear either a positive or negative connotation. Perhaps the best way to capture the ambivalence of the modifier in English is "intense," an adjective whose vernacular usage reflects both the focused magnitude of God's concern and the somewhat uncertain coloration of that concern. The jealous zeal of which Exodus speaks here, thus, is not an expression of suspicious insecurity, but this zeal identifies God as "utterly ardent, uncompromising," unwilling for anything or anyone to come between God and the people God loves.

Finally, the third commandment forbids invoking God for ungodly purposes. The commandment seems to be directed specifically against lying (though the ninth commandment addresses this as well), or against swearing by God's name in a false cause. The context of this commandment, though, warrants a broader interpretation, and its proximity to the commandment against bearing false witness in 20:16 suggests that this verse concerns something different, something more pertinent to the preceding verses. In the context of the warnings against idolatrous polytheism, that difference seems to entail claiming God's authority for purposes that are not God's. Those who aim to live by the commandments are not free to profane God's name by ascribing to God's will, God's wisdom, that which they intend for their own aims. Just as God will not allow God's people to revere the Golden Calf or to honor it as their deliverer, so God rejects false prophets who claim "Thus says the Lord" when they themselves have devised the prophecies. Indeed, interpreters have appropriately discerned

---

some point, the prophets' certainty that the God of Israel abhors such sacrifices attained hegemony, and became associated with prohibitions of idolatry in general. A more extensive treatment of national idolatry would have to take up the topic of the blood sacrifice of a nation's youth in service to the emblem of national identity ('giving up one's life for the flag'), in dialogue with Jon Levenson's *Death and Resurrection of the Beloved Son* (New Haven: Yale University Press, 1993); the essays which comprise *Human Sacrifice in Jewish and Christian Tradition*, eds. Karin Finsterbusch, Armin Lange, and K. F. Diethard Römheld (Leiden: Brill, 2007); Henri Hubert and Marcel Mauss, *Sacrifice: Its Nature and Function* (Cohen and West, 1964); and of course, René Girard's theoretical corpus.

a further sense to this commandment, that is, forbidding any *magical* use of God's Name; whereas in many cosmologies, possession of a god's or a spirit's name gives one power over that subject, the God of the Decalogue cannot be compelled by such devices.[8]

To summarize, then, the first three commandments articulate a theology by which Israel (and its heirs) align themselves with a God who claims priority over all other interests or motivations, whom they may not draw down from heaven in any tangible, visible form, nor may they substitute for this invisible God a more congenially accessible champion. They may not dress up their own intents and purposes by wrapping them in God's radiance. The God of the Decalogue is uniquely authoritative, cannot be fashioned after our own image (*pace* Feuerbach), and cannot be controlled: God is absolute, aniconic, and useless.[9] God is not instrumentally accessible to humanity. God's people cannot honor their God by soft-pedaling God's uncompromising will, or by making God over in their image, or by bossing other people around as though knowing God's name wins them God's unique authority. They honor the God who brought them out of slavery into freedom by the practice of adhering to the way of life that this God commands, by standing firm for God.

### Compulsory Idolatry in Politics

As you may have ascertained from this description, the characteristics of the Decalogue's God comport poorly with priorities of an empire. Reasonable observers may disagree about whether the present U.S. regime should count as a pretender to 'empire'; at the very least, though, recent history points to ways in which a nation formed with a powerful ideology

---

[8] The Greek Magical Papyri exemplify this sort of instrumental invocation of a divine name throughout the collection (and the name of Jesus functions benignly for the church in this way, in the Acts of the Apostles 3:6, 4:30, 16:18; in vain for extra-ecclesial exorcists at 19:13); contrariwise, the *Catechism of the Catholic Church* exegetes the third commandment as (among other things) a rejection of manipulative uses of God's Name (cf. Part III, Section 2, Chapter 1, Article 2, I:2149, II:2155). The sequence by which the prohibition of the instrumental use of God's name follows the prohibition of idolatry coheres with the abhorrence of human sacrifice—which stands as the most extreme gesture by which one might influence a god's actions.

[9] In describing God as "useless," I rely appreciatively on the distinction between "using" and "enjoying" that Augustine articulates in detail in the opening chapters of Book I of *de Doctrina Christiana* (and that David Jones makes a hallmark of beautiful art in the essays in Harman Grisewood, ed. *Epoch and Artist* (London: Faber, 1973), especially "Art and Sacrament" (143–179) and "The Utile" (180–185).

of that state's unique, exceptional status can modulate from expecting general respect for civil authorities (on one hand) to veneration of numinous national entities in a mode that challenges these commandments (on the other). The transition from dutiful respect to misplaced reverence is facilitated by several factors. In part, people understandably long for a more available, more obviously effectual God, a God whom one can rally to support urgent causes. In another part, such a transition serves the obvious interests of the state and its ruling caste. Other parts of the transition serve the selfish interests of particular persons and organisations. However one distributes the causes, they combine to engender an atmosphere in which the state draws to itself allegiance, iconic sanctity, and effectuality that—according to the Commandments—properly pertain only to the LORD.

Commandments against venerating any transcendent power other than Moses' God stand diametrically opposed to the peculiar blend of patriotism and (professedly) Christian devotion that dominates the United States' political discourses. While popular opinion in the U.S. holds that the nation should base its policies on Christian values (or, more liberally, 'Judaeo-Christian' values), the shared behavioral norms of the citizenry institute an allegiance that trumps the commandments that themselves distill the elements of the way of life to which God called Israel— namely, allegiance to the Stars and Stripes, the national flag of the United States. Public events involve a ritual incantation of the National Anthem addressed to a flag; political candidates cannot afford to be seen without some form of a flag ornamenting their attire (typically, a lapel pin for male candidates);[10] and schoolchildren in public education are commonly required to recite an oath of loyalty to the flag.

To underscore the prevalence of vexillolatry in U.S. public life, in 2002 a panel from the 9th Circuit of the U.S. Court of Appeals ruled in the case of Newdow vs. the U.S. Congress, in which the plaintiff argued that his daughter ought not be exposed to recitation of the 'Pledge of Allegiance' to the flag, on the grounds that it includes an affirmation that the nation's unity exists 'under God' (which affirmation would constitute a form of pressure to acknowledge the existence of that God).[11] The

---

[10] As noted in *Time* magazine, which in 2008 appositely compared the display of a flag pin to the 'shibboleth' of Judges 12:5–6; http://www.time.com/time/nation/article/ 0,8599,1820023,00.html; accessed 18 February, 2013.

[11] Newdow v. United States Congress, Elk Grove Unified School District, et al., 542 U.S. 1 (2004), http://www.constitution.org/usfc/9/newdow_v_us.htm (accessed 18 February 2013).

9th Circuit determined that state-sponsored recitation of the pledge in public schools violated the establishment clause; it's impossible, they reasoned, to identify the U.S. as a nation "under God" without promoting a religious agenda. Politicians of almost every stripe rushed to demonstrate their pious patriotism by insisting that professing loyalty to "one nation, under God" need not conflict with the Constitution's insistence against any "law respecting an establishment of religion, or prohibiting the free exercise thereof." Positions ranged from the embarrassing *de minimis* claim that such a short phrase couldn't do any ideological harm[12]—it didn't mean much of anything (which raises the question, "Why then include it?")—to Chief Justice Rehnquist's concurring that "[t]he phrase 'under God' in the Pledge seems, as a historical matter, to sum up the attitude of the Nation's leaders, and to manifest itself in many of our public observances,"[13] to overwhelming votes in the House and Senate to the effect that the words "under God" ought to be retained in the Pledge, anyway.

Whereas most pundits advocated positions grounded in one of the obviously apposite civil-theological lines of argument,[14] I want to call attention to the oddity that so many Jewish and Christian public figures were advocating a pledge of *allegiance* to a *national flag*. The U.S. flag stands in a direct line of descent from the insignias, emblems, and standards by which nations invoked totemic deities in battle—to the extent that two millennia ago, faithful believers were willing to lay down their lives rather than venerate, or even *tolerate*, these representations of rival gods. Tertullian rejected the regimental standards of the Roman Army as "rivals of Christ" ("Vexillum quoque portabit aemulum Christi?");[15] and when a Roman procurator brought flags that honored Caesar into the city of Jerusalem—not into the *Temple*, mind you, but only within the city limits—a crowd of Judeans staged a five-day demonstration to have the standards removed:

---

[12] Judge Fernandez took this position in considering Newdow v. United States Congress.

[13] Elk Grove Unified School Dist. v. Newdow—02–1624, (Chief Justice Rehnquist); http://www.supremecourt.gov/opinions/03pdf/02–1624.pdf (accessed 17 March 2013).

[14] It is startling at how few public commentators noted the oddity of permitting a compulsory recitation of the Pledge on the grounds that that public affirmation of a transcendent God doesn't mean enough to give offense to an atheist.

[15] Tertullian, *de Corona* XI.

[Pilate] took a bold step in subversion of Jewish practices, by introducing into the city the busts of the emperor that were attached to the military standards, for our law forbids the making of images. It was for this reason that the previous procurators, when they entered the city, used standards that had no such ornaments. Pilate was the first to bring the images into Jerusalem and set them up, doing it without knowledge of the people, for he entered at night. But when the people discovered it, they went in a throng to Caesarea and for many days entreated him to take away the images. He refused to yield, since to do so would be an outrage to the emperor; however, on the sixth day he secretly armed and placed his troops in position, while he himself came to the speaker's stand. This had been constructed in the stadium, which provided concealment for the army that lay in wait. When the Jews again engaged in supplication, at a pre-arranged signal he surrounded them with his soldiers and threatened to punish them at once with death if they did not put an end to their tumult and return to their own places. But they, casting themselves prostrate and baring their throats, declared that they had gladly welcomed death rather than make bold to transgress the wise provisions of the laws. Pilate, astonished at the strength of their devotion to the laws, straightaway removed the images from Jerusalem and brought them back to Caesarea.[16]

When that procurator threatened to execute the protesting Judeans, they volunteered to be killed, rather than permit these idolatrous emblems to remain within the city of Jerusalem.[17] Likewise, on another occasion, the introduction of shields bearing an offensive inscription into Herod's Palace provoked a popular outcry which was not resolved until Pilate, on instructions from Tiberius, ordered the shields to be removed not simply from the palace, but from Jerusalem itself.[18] In these cases and more, the people of God refused to soft-pedal the significance of gestures that seemed to becloud the unique standing of their aniconic God, even at the risk of their lives.

Now, one must concede without hesitation that the military-totemic policies of the Roman Empire entailed a pervasive paganism inimical to Judaism and Christianity; contemporary national standards are not as obviously antithetical to the uniqueness of Israel's God. On the other hand, Pontius Pilate was not asking the Jerusalemites to *pledge allegiance* to the

---

[16] Josephus, *Ant.* XVIII.iii.1. *Jewish Antiquities, Books XVIII–XIX.* Translated by Louis H. Feldman. Loeb Classical Library. William Heinemann, 1965.

[17] Josephus, *War* II.ix; *Ant* 18.iii.

[18] Philo, *Embassy to Gaius*, 299–305. For a careful analysis of exactly what was at stake in these incidents, cf. Helen Bond, "Standards, Shields, and Coins: Jewish Reactions to Aspects of the Roman Cult in the Time of Pilate," in *Idolatry: False Worship in the Bible, Early Judaism, and Christianity*, 88–106.

standards; nonetheless, the people resisted the very presence of the iconic representation of imperial power within the holy city. In the twenty-first century, on the other hand, a unanimous vote of the U.S. Senate affirmed the premise that U.S. Christians ought to pledge their allegiance *to the flag*, and to the republic for which it stands.[19]

In 2006 the U.S. House of Representatives passed a proposed amendment to the Constitution that reads, "The Congress shall have power to prohibit the physical desecration of the flag of the United States."[20] The single word "desecration" merits particular attention, because that word distinguishes the amendment from merely conventional prohibitions of unwelcome political expression. Although Congress members debated the various possible senses of the word, they generally harked back to a Texas statute (subsequently overturned by the Supreme Court) that specified that '[f]or purposes of this section, "desecrate" means deface, damage, or otherwise physically mistreat in a way that the actor knows will seriously offend one or more persons likely to observe or discover his action.'[21] When Rep. Bobby Scott proposed amending the amendment to specify 'burning' instead of 'desecration', he explained that the motion was necessary because the term 'desecration' was insufficiently specific—not because the flag was not sacred.[22] In other words, this proposed amendment presupposed that the flag of the United States is in some sense sacred; and that claim of sanctity stands diametrically opposed to the teaching of the Decalogue, as the citizens of Jerusalem knew, and as Christian conscripts into the Roman army knew.

It will be said that the flag's sanctity is figurative: "Of course no one regards the flag as the manifestation of a transcendent divine national entity, and the flag doesn't signify the genius of the President or the totemic protector of an army division." But a figure of speech is never

---

[19] On the problematic of pledging allegiance, see also Michael Baxter's "God Is Not American: Or, Why Christians Should Not Pledge Allegiance to 'One Nation Under God'," in Brent Laytham, ed. *God Is Not…* (Grand Rapids: Brazos Press, 2004), 55–75.

[20] The amendment passed the House of Representatives by a vote of 286 in favour to 130 opposed, but failed by one vote to pass in the Senate (66 in favour, 34 opposed) ("Proposing an amendment to the Constitution of the United States authorizing the Congress to prohibit the physical desecration of the flag of the United States" http://clerk.house .gov/evs/2005/roll296.xml, "On the Joint Resolution (S.J.Res.12 as Amended )" http://www .senate.gov/legislative/LIS/roll_call_lists/roll_call_vote_cfm.cfm?congress=109&session=2& vote=00189; accessed 18 February 2013).

[21] "Flag Protection Constitutional Admendment," http://thomas.loc.gov/cgi-bin/cpquery/ T?&report=hr131&dbname=cp108&, accessed 18 February 2013.

[22] "Flag Protection Constitutional Admendment."

*simply* a figure, never just a metaphor. As it turns out, the vehemence with which politicians leapt to defend the state's interest in inculcating obedient allegiance to the flag, and to define the flag as a sacred object that one might be punished for treating impiously, bespeaks a more than merely metaphorical sensitivity at this point; as Muriel Morisey points out, 'This is conceivable only if we appreciate that the American flag is the equivalent of a sacred religious icon, comparable to Christianity's crucifix, Judaism's Torah and the Koran of Islam. No court has designated patriotism as a religion for Establishment Clause purposes, but in every other significant respect it operates as a religion in American culture.'[23] One need not alter the Constitution to justify a metaphor.

As the priorities of civil powers have permeated U.S. Christianity, it becomes harder and harder to make a theological case against the imperial ethos. The church feels a powerful temptation to accommodate, indeed in some quarters even embrace, the image of the United States as an visible, effective anointed agent for realizing divine purposes. In the name of realism, in the name of deference to honoring those who endure the mortal consequences of war (consequences that everyday public discourse treats as a sacrifice),[24] strident voices demand that Christians profess their loyalty to a national ensign, and observe national festivals that the government establishes as though they were feasts of holy martyrs. The combined interests and sensitivities—however innocent, however commendable—of state power, of patriotic citizens, of grief-stricken families, and of corporate advantage converge in a cultural system we

---

[23] Morisey, 'Flag Desecration, Religion, and Patriotism', *Rutgers Journal of Law and Religion* 9.1 (2007), 2.

[24] Unfortunately, public figures tend to describe soldiers' death in war as "the ultimate sacrifice." Especially since the commandment against idolatry forbids making sacrifices to other gods, the strong association of death in military service with the U.S. flag sails precariously close to instantiating the sort of sacrifice of the first-born male that the Law and the prophets condemn. Characterizing military casualties as 'sacrifice' both points toward the casual idolatry bound up with the service of the state, and specifically repudiates the theological significance of the cross and the Eucharist.

In the interest of even-handedness, I should acknowledge that the U.K. has experienced its own spasms of comparable political theology, as an Aylesham man was arrested for posting videorecordings of a burning poppy on a social networking site (as an expression of antipathy to Remembrance Day observances; http://www.guardian.co.uk/uk/2012/nov/12/kent-man-arrested-burning-poppy accessed 13 February 2013), and Northern Ireland is at this writing beset by conflict over how frequently the Union flag will be flown at Belfast's city hall. And of course, blasphemy is still illegal in the United Kingdom; cf. Yvonne Sherwood, *Biblical Blaspheming: Trials of the Sacred for a Secular Age* (Cambridge: Cambridge University Press, 2012).

may identify as *Sacramerica*.[25] In Sacramerica, the national pride of the United States blossoms into a displaced messianic hope that subordinates the God of the Decalogue to the sentimental consolations and pragmatic policy interests of a vast congregation of baseball fans, apple-pie eaters, and fireworks admirers.

Lest you think that anti-American rhetoric has carried the argument too far, and lest the tone of this essay grow too grim, let the reader take an excursus to an instructive illustration from a century ago. This image richly rewards our critical attention, and vividly exemplifies my claim that Sacramerica constitutes an antithetical spiritual alternative to the God of the Decalogue.

This illustration comes from an advertising campaign originated by Artemis Ward, one of the pioneers of the modern advertising industry. Ward made 'Sapolio' a brand name second only to Ford in popular recognition and cultural currency[26] by publicity stunts, jingles, mass-transit placards, and full-page advertisements in literary magazines. One such advertisement found its way into my family's collections several years ago.[27]

How does this advertisement pertain to the United States' paradoxical embrace and defiance of the first three Commandments? Let me count the ways. Being a biblical scholar, I'll begin by commenting on the words. First, then, "the strong right arm that holds for peace" in this poster belongs not to the God of peace who redeemed the children of Jacob and Joseph (as in Ps 77:15), who drove out the nations, but planted Israel, who afflicted the peoples, but set Israel free by the divine right hand and arm, for God delighted in them (Ps 44:2f). Instead, the advertisement ascribes this mighty arm to a feminine embodiment of Sapolio. The advert implicitly characterises the inhabitants of the Philippines, Cuba, and Puerto Rico at the turn of the twentieth century as "dark," "dirty," and "uncivilized" relative to the United States; Sapolio and the U.S.A., it suggests, will take

---

[25] A quick search of the internet suggests that I may have originated this phrase when (in 2005) I first gave the lecture on which this essay is based, so with an entrepreneurial zeal befitting an expatriate Sacramerican, I hereby lay claim to full intellectual-property rights to the term: "Sacramerica" ©2005 A. K. M. Adam.

[26] Donald S. Tull, "A Re-Examination of the Causes of Decline in Sales of Sapolio," *Journal of Business* 28 (1955) 128–37, as cited in Susan Mizruchi, "Becoming Multicultural," *American Literary History* 15 (2003), 47.

[27] The page on which this advertisement appears is inconveniently undated, but the US flag waving over Cuba implies that the images dates from the short window of time between the Spanish-American War and Cuban independence, hence between 1898 and 1902 (which dates correspond with Artemis Ward's campaigns on behalf of Sapolio).

Figure 1.  Advertisement, Sapolio Soap.

care of that with their cleansing, civilizing imperial mission.[28] The advertising copy associates Sapolio's cleansing mission with light-bringing, Finally, the text warns us that "imitations disappoint,"[29] or as God might have said through Moses, "Thou shalt have no other soap before me."

The iconography of the advertisement speaks even more emphatically of Sacramerican displacement of God. The composition is dominated by a superhuman female figure very similar to the Statue of Liberty, carrying a sword, draped in a flag, enlightening the world with her bar of soap.[30] The globe as Sapolio imagines it comprises only the U.S. and Cuba, Puerto Rico, and the Philippines; Mexico (which the illustration depicts as almost the same area as Cuba) vanishes into the ocean, and Canada doesn't exist visually (nor do Europe, Asia, or Central and South America). This American idol portrays the self-image of the U.S. projected to a heavenly scale; this is the god of whom Feuerbach and Durkheim warned their readers. Lady Sapolio wears a Phrygian cap, the vestigial signifier of the Mithraic mysteries. She is no mere human, recommending her favourite brand of soap to a neighbour; she represents a divine power for purification and liberation, with a peace-making strong right arm.

If anyone thinks that the religious infrastructure of this ad is simply incidental, they may want to consider such other Sapolio advertisements as that placed in the *Century* magazine of 1904 which links Sapolio with the "very peculiar, very strict" 6,000-year-old ceremonial law of "the Hebrew race". Thus it declares Sapolio "kosher"—in English and in Hebrew characters.[31]

---

[28] While the racism that equates dark skins with uncleanness lies outwith the purview of this essay, the convergence of commercial racism with imperialism and warped Christian theology have been amalysed brilliantly by Willie James Jennings in *The Christian Imagination: Theology and the Origins of Race* (New Haven: Yale University Press, 2011) and J. Kameron Carter in *Race: A Theological Account* (Oxford: Oxford University Press, 2008).

[29] Evidently Sapolio does not respect the oft-repeated Pauline admonition to "Be imitators of me" (1 Cor 4:16, 11:1; 1 Thes 1:6).

[30] At the time of this advertisement, the United States will only recently—28 October, 1886—have dedicated the statue of "Liberty Enlightening the World" as a gift from France. The Statue of Liberty herself carries a tablet—albeit not a tablet of Ten Commandments—whereas the Sapolionic goddess holds a sword, and in a visual allusion that readers must be expected to recognise, Sapolio enlightens the world not with Liberty's high-held torch, but with a luminous bar of soap.

[31] Figure 8, p. 52 of Mizruchi. The advertisement text reads, "For more than 6,000 years the Hebrew race has obeyed a sanitary law, very peculiar, very strict, but highly to be respected. Things pure with respect to that ceremonial law are called Kosher... This fact should give it preference over all doubtful soaps—among Gentiles as well as among Jews...."

It is a measure of how thoroughly Sacramerica is ascendant in U.S. culture that an advertisement which represents a superhuman figure who bestows light and health to a chosen people while attired in the garb of a participant in a mystery cult doesn't strike most acculturated viewers as odd. The point isn't that any of them would explicitly *endorse* a claim that the personified ablutionary regimen of U.S. commercial imperialism should be worshipped as God. The point is that an advertiser could confidently invoke an image that comprehensively displaces the God of the Decalogue—without fear that U.S. Christians would take offense, without expecting that displacement to hurt his sales.[32] In an atmosphere like this, how can one proclaim the Decalogue so as to bring into focus the antithesis of Sacramerica with God's unique, aniconic, useless identity?

Whatever else cultural activists and biblical interpreters may do, we need to take seriously the extent to which Sacramerica names not just a set of pernicious assumptions about the United States' role as liberator, law-giver, and commercial agent to the world. More than that, Sacramerica names a *signifying practice*, a repertoire of premises and, especially, actions that express, affirm, reinforce, and disseminate particular sorts of meaning.

What work does the term "signifying practice"[33] do in this context? The term develops from the disciplines of semiotics and cultural criticism, where it points to ways that people express important claims about themselves and the world not only by talking or writing, but by the ways they behave, by the ways they interact with others. Cultures, subcultures, dominant and resistant groups articulate their identities in the ways that people dress, the ways that people address one another, the type of cars they drive or their decision to ride a bicycle or take public transport. We can take the example of religious vocations as a highly-visible signifying practice, wherein every article of clothing, every meal, every prayer, every gesture combines to express a particular kind of life given over to the praise and service of God. More often, though, people participate in signification less self-consciously, more by elective affiliation, with many fewer

---

[32] In a similar vein, President George W. Bush and his speechwriters used habitually to allude to passages from Scripture in his speeches, substituting "America" (or equivalents) for the attributes or actions of divinity. See the examples cited by David James Duncan in "What Fundamentalists Need For Their Salvation" in *Orion*, July/August 2005 <http://www .orionmagazine.org/index.php/articles/article/156/ > (accessed 27 March 2012).

[33] For further amplification of this term, see A. K. M. Adam, "Poaching On Zion: Biblical Theology as Signifying Practice", in *Reading Scripture With the Church*, A. K. M. Adam et al. (Grand Rapids: Baker Academic, 2006), 17–34.

formal expectations and obligations; in so doing, they float along with
the significations made available by mass culture and socially-dominant
institutions.

Thus, if one regards the characteristic features of Sacramerica as a signifying practice, then Sacramerican practice amounts to more than just a
set of explicit verbal claims about the U.S. and its manifest destiny. As a
signifying practice, it entails a certain confluence of patriotism, political
theory and theology, messianic hope, personal and corporate interest, and
historic loyalties that go beyond debatable claims that that nation should
exercise its wealth and military power in one or another way. It includes
the axiom that one must vote, that liberal democracy constitutes a political order unexceptionably superior to other alternatives, that the way to
resolve all conflicts is to hold a vote of some sort, hence that being right
in the world should be correlative to winning, and since winning depends
on out-numbering the wrong people (the God of the Bible seems almost
always to favor the smaller number), U.S. cultural observers show a persistent fascination with the number of members in churches, the number
of votes for or against denominational legislation, and so on.

If we take Sacramerica seriously as a signifying practice of veneration
of national identity, as a social system, we can see a sort of performative
*mise-en-abîme* when politicians make a great show of their determination to display the Ten Commandments as integral parts of civil business.
The central figure in the Ten Commandments controversies has been Roy
Moore, a judge, politician, and columnist from Alabama.[34] Moore repeatedly insisted on the prerogative of displaying wooden plaques bearing the
Commandments in his courtroom, beginning from his appointment as a
circuit court judge in 1992. Once he was elected Chief Justice of Alabama—
arguably on the strength of his pro-God, pro-Commandments stance
against the American Civil Liberties Union—Moore commissioned and
installed into the Supreme Court building a granite monument crowned
by two tablets bearing an English translation of the Ten Commandments.
In so doing, he defied prevailing interpretations of the establishment

---

[34] Moore's career is amply documented in all major media of the U.S., and in his auto-
biography, co-written with John Perry, *So Help Me God: The Ten Commandments, Judicial
Tyranny, and the Battle for Religious Freedom* (Nashville: Broadman & Holman Publishers,
2005). Moore was re-elected as Chief Justice of the Alabama Supreme Court in the elec-
tions of November 2012.

clause of the Constitution (specifically the 'Lemon test')[35] and, eventually in 2002, the legal judgment of the U.S. District Court.

But while Moore repudiated the authority of any courts that did not acknowledge the God of the Commandments as the source of their authority,[36] he exemplified the signifying practice of Sacramerica. His integration of a pastiche of biblical and theological claims with the civil identity promulgated in the Constitution and selected quotations from canonical founding politicians captures both the feverish ardour of Sacramerican piety and the paradoxical affirmation of idolatry expressed when one of Moore's supporters decried the removal of the Ten Commandments monument by shouting 'Get your hands off our God, God haters!'[37] That supporter articulated the Sacramerican conviction that the love of God entails the love of the United States, made physically available in the form of a stone monument—a monumental stone tablet—on which are inscribed (in English) the very Commandments that forbid worship of, or construction of a sculpted representation of, any rival God.

Thus Moore and his constituency intensify anew the spiral of irony. In a world where the divine command that God's people not worship graven images is itself inscribed on a tablet of stone and unselfconsciously characterised as "our God", an extraordinary inversion of biblical interpretation has displaced any antecedent reading of the Second Commandment (or the First Amendment, for that matter).[38] And U.S. politics continues to

---

[35] In Glassroth v. Moore, Judge Myron H. Thompson observes that 'the Ten Commandments monument's primary effect advances religion is also self-evident. To satisfy the second prong of the Lemon test, the challenged practice must have a "principal or primary effect... that neither advances nor inhibits religion"...' and Moore's monument obviously promotes Jewish and Christian values over any other faith. Glassroth v. Moore, p. 27; http://fl1.findlaw.com/news.findlaw.com/hdocs/docs/religion/glsrthmre1118020pn .pdf, accessed 13 February 2013.

[36] As, for example, when he asserted (at the installation of the Ten Commandments Monument, 'It is axiomatic that to restore morality, we must first recognize the source of that morality. From our earliest history in 1776, when we were first pleased to be called the Untied [sic WSFA] States of America, our forefathers recognized the sovereignty of God.' "Speech by Judge Roy Moore at Monument Dedication," http://www.wsfa.com/ story/1056322/speech-by-judge-roy-moore-at-monument-dedication, accessed 13 February 2013.

[37] One might suspect that the quotation was concocted by unsympathetic observers as an illustration of preposterously self-contradictory Sacramerican national idolatry, if the report weren't published by Fox News, the 'fair and balanced' conservative media outlet: Wednesday, August 27: 'Put It Back!', http://www.foxnews.com/story/0,2933,95922,00.html, accessed 13 February 21013.

[38] The First Amendment to the U. S. Constitution begins 'Congress shall make no law respecting an establishment of religion, or prohibiting the free exercise thereof'; it is this

produce examples of such political idolatry; in January 2013, Indiana State Senator Dennis Kruse introduced a bill permitting a school to 'require the recitation of the Lord's Prayer at the beginning of each school day'.[39]

Such internal contradictions signal the sort of incoherence that ideology serves to render invisible. Critics of political theology from Hauerwas, Cavanaugh, and Budde to Crossley, Boer, and Sherwood can in near-unison flag up these glaring examples of malignant mutations of what Cavanaugh identifies as the theopolitical imagination.[40]

Activists political and theological, however, will have to struggle not only against state power and partisan demagoguery; the thrust of the century-old advertisement for Sapolio lies in its demonstration that the ideological amalgam of national idolatry and professed Judeo-Christian faith has deep roots and, most importantly, is ratified and nourished by the commercial usefulness of a pliably jingoistic, non-exclusive deity. In order to root out national idolatry, one will have to root out the displacement of eschatological hope from *both* the state *and* the market for consumer goods, and the latter is likely to constitute the more difficult obstacle. After all, when one of the most popular shows on television in the U.S. is candidly named *American Idol*, who's going to balk at a little idolatry in the national cause—especially if one wants bright, clean, and happy homes, and the powerful, peaceful, progressive nation that Sapolio produces?[41]

---

amendment that triggers lawsuits about public display of, or state promotion of, religious observance.

[39] "Senate Bill No. 23" http://www.in.gov/legislative/bills/2013/PDF/IN/IN0023.1.pdf.

[40] William Cavanaugh, *Theopolitical Imagination* (Edinburgh: T & T Clark, 2003).

[41] *American Idol* was based on the UK reality show more intelligibly named *Pop Idol*; *Pop Idol* was cancelled in 2004, however, while *American Idol* proceeds from strength to strength in television ratings. At a recent academic conference, my wife and I saw a cosmetics poster urging shoppers to "Be *Your Own* Idol"; it's hard to think that's a promising omen.

# MAKING AND UNMAKING THE WORLD IN THE BOOK OF JOB: READING *JOB* WITH HELP FROM ELAINE SCARRY, KURT VONNEGUT, AND DON LAFONTAINE

Abigail Pelham

## *Introduction: Rereading Job*

The Book of Job, with its unanswered questions, its textual complexities and its interpretive ambiguities, is particularly suited to being read and reread from different perspectives and with different lenses. In this essay, then, I engage in the activity of rereading to which the book so deliberately (it seems) lays itself open. Choosing the theme of the making and unmaking of the world, which appears in *Job*[1] in the dispute over what the world ought to be like, in which all the major characters participate, I bring the book into contact with other discourse in which this theme appears—opening up a kind of "space for thinking in,"—to see what happens, what new interpretive possibilities grow out of this cross-pollination. If these conversation partners—Elaine Scarry's book *The Body in Pain*, Kurt Vonnegut's novel *Galápagos*, and Don LaFontaine's famous phrase 'In a world where...'—are unlikely bedfellows, drawn from both 'higher' and 'lower' cultural contexts, so much livelier will the discussion be. As I introduce the Book of Job to its 'new friends,' I also think through commonly-held assumptions about how the book presents the making and unmaking of the world, tugging at the loose ends in those arguments, following them through to discover if they break down, and, if they do break down, where the flaws are. Dismantling assumptions in this way opens the book even more fully to new ways of reading and rereading. My goal is not, finally, to proclaim a definitive explanation of the Book of Job, nor to say anything definitive about the ideas raised by Scarry, Vonnegut, and LaFontaine, but to proliferate possibilities.[2] This, it seems to me, is how the book asks to

---

[1] In this essay I will sometimes use italicized *Job* as shorthand for the Book of Job; Job, without italics, will always refer to the character.

[2] David Clines writes that "There are two kinds of scholarly paper: one that offers answers to questions that have puzzled other people, and a second that tries to puzzle people by putting other questions." His essay "Why is There a Book of Job, and What Does it Do to You if You Read It?" he describes as the second kind of paper. David J. A. Clines,

be read and reread, and is what makes every fresh encounter with it so thrilling.[3]

## The World as Made Artifact

Don LaFontaine, "arguably the most successful Voice Actor of all time,"[4] was famous for introducing movie trailers with the phrase, 'In a world...': "In a world where robots have taken control of the United States government...;" "In a world where the earth has been hit by a meteor the size of Texas...;" "In a world where pinecones are as valuable as gold...," etc.[5]

---

"Why is There a Book of Job and What Does it Do to You if You Read it?" in *The Book of Job*, ed. W. A. M. Beuken (Leuven: Leuven University Press, 1994), 1. This essay, too, is of the second sort. In his article, Clines uses psychoanalytic theory as a point of access to *Job*. Here, I use the three 'texts' named above, which share with psychoanalytic theory the fact that their authors did not have the Book of Job in mind when they wrote what they did. Nevertheless, just as psychoanalytic theory, as used by Clines, opens up fruitful avenues of exploration within *Job*, so these 'texts,' too, allow valuable insights into *Job* that might not be available by other routes.

   [3] Carol Newsom opens her *The Book of Job: A Contest of Moral Imaginations* with the insight that "The book of Job lends itself well—perhaps too well—to being read in light of shifting philosophical and hermeneutical assumptions," going on to assess this characteristic as "truly not to be regretted, for it is what gives the book its perennial value." Carol A. Newsom, *The Book of Job: A Contest of Moral Imaginations* (New York: Oxford University Press, 2003), 3. Yet, her aside—"perhaps too well"—seems to reveal a certain niggling discomfort with the book's adaptability, and her pronouncement that it is "truly not to be regretted" suggests the opposite possibility—that it might very well be regretted. I am with Newsom on this one. *Job's* openness to a multiplicity of interpretative possibilities makes working with it both exciting and frustrating: exciting because the text seems ever new, and frustrating because, even after years of work, one (I) finds oneself (myself) in the position of still not really knowing it.

   [4] Don LaFontaine's website, http://www.donlafontaine.com/Index.html?p=Home. html&pt=, accessed 29 August 2012. Of course, LaFontaine most likely did not write the trailers he narrated, so the phrase 'In a world...' does not really belong to him, and, indeed, is used by other voice-over artists as well. I am using LaFontaine's name simply because, as the most well-known voice-over artist, the phrase is most associated with him.

   [5] These are my own made-up examples, and are not actual trailers. In fact, when I began to search for a trailer that would illustrate my point, I discovered that I could not find exactly what I was looking for. The trailer for *Mad Max 2* comes close. The narrator (not LaFontaine) says, "In a world without gas...this is a land that prays for a hero.... When it's every man for himself, and there's no place left to run...pray that he's still out there." *Mad Max 2* trailer, http://www.youtube.com/watch?v=kBrAh3OyYnI, accessed 29 August 2012. That such trailers must exist, however, is indicated by the prevalence of trailers that parody the form. The trailer for *The Hitchhiker's Guide to the Galaxy* begins with Stephen Fry's voice narrating, "Movie trailers are designed to give you an idea of the film in question.... Typically, they begin with the introduction of a main character, who will very shortly have something so fantastic happen to him that someone just had to make a movie about it.... Often this section is preceded by the words, 'In a world...'."

LaFontaine's phrase shows that human beings are world-makers, at least when it comes to the intentionally fictional worlds of movies. For movie-makers, making and unmaking worlds is all in a day's work. In LaFontaine's trailers, the opening descriptive declaration is frequently followed by something like a statement about "one man" who, acting as "an army of one," will unmake the movie's world and remake it in such a way that the opening "in a world" account no longer holds true. If the movie has begun with a world in which pinecones are as valuable as gold, by the end of the movie the hero will have "taken the ultimate risk" to remake that world as a world in which gold—and not pinecones—is supremely valuable.

It is noteworthy that the world with which the movie begins is unlike our own, whereas by the end of the movie it has been remade so that it is recognizable as our own world. A movie trailer would never begin with an announcement like, "In a world where gold is a valuable metal, one man will face his destiny to make it worth no more than a pinecone." It just doesn't work. That this is the case suggests that, although we may be world-makers when it comes to movies, we do believe that there is such a thing as the real world, a world which we have not made-up. In these kinds of movies, worlds are first made-*up* and then they are made-*real*, that is, they are remade so that they are like the real world.

In *The Body in Pain*, Elaine Scarry uses the terms 'made-up' and 'made-real' somewhat differently from the way I have used them above. In her usage, a made-up artifact is something that exists only in the human imagination and has no concrete reality, whereas when an artifact is made-real it exists in the external world and can affect human bodies. A chair conceived in the imagination is a made-up object. Once the chair has been built and can be sat upon, it has been made-real.[6] Although LaFontaine's trailers assume that there is such thing as the real world which can be

---

Fry's voice is then interrupted by LaFontaine's, explaining that these trailers are usually narrated by "a deep voice that sounds like a seven-foot-tall man who has been smoking cigarettes since childhood." *Hitchhiker's Guide to the Galaxy* trailer, http://www.you tube.com/watch?v=MbGNcoB2Y4I, accessed 29 August 2012. Other parodies include the trailer for *Jakob the Liar* (http://www.youtube.com/watch?v=RCYSRcBt9wg, accessed 29 August 2012), a Geico Insurance ad narrated by LaFontaine (http://www.youtube.com/ watch?v=ZJMGS7lowT8, accessed 29 August 2012), and the trailer for Jerry Seinfeld's film *Comedian* (http://www.youtube.com/watch?v=fVDzuTofXro, accessed 29 August 2012). This last trailer begins with a deep-voiced narrator saying, "In a world where laughter was king," only to be interrupted by Seinfeld who insists, "No 'in a world.'... It's not that kind of movie."

[6] Elaine Scarry, *The Body in Pain: The Making and Unmaking of the World* (New York and Oxford: Oxford University Press, 1985), 21, 280.

easily distinguished from the made-up worlds associated with the phrase "in a world," Scarry argues that, because it is a human-made artifact, the world, even what seems to be the real world, can be unmade to the degree that it was made in the first place. Even though, as noted above, we would never apply LaFontaine's "in a world" phrase to what we consider to be the real world, it is possible to apply the phrase to worlds that exist in the real world but which are different from our own and which do not conform to our understanding of the way the world ought to be. The following formulations, for example, do not strike us as ludicrous: "In a world where the economic system dictates that property ought to be owned in common, one man (or country) will make the ultimate sacrifice to guarantee private ownership." Or, "In a world where competition is rampant, one man (or country) will face his deepest fears to redistribute wealth amongst all segments of the population." That it is possible to apply LaFontaine's phrase to worlds that exist outside of overtly fictional contexts suggests that what we think of as the real world is actually a human-made artifact.[7]

Scarry argues that the body has a fundamental reality that goes beyond that capable of being possessed by any made object, no matter how real that object may seem. This is why, in some circumstances, the body must be used to substantiate the reality of made artifacts, which, otherwise, would remain imaginary.[8] Kurt Vonnegut, in his novel *Galápagos*, seems to agree with Scarry's assessment. There, Vonnegut tells the story of a world in the process of being unmade. Things that had previously seemed real have started to show their seams, to show that they are not really-real, but only made-up. The novel is set in Ecuador in 1986 and is narrated by the ghost of Leon Trout, looking back at the events of 1986 from a million years in the future. Reflecting on the world-wide economic crisis of a million years ago, Trout concludes that the human imagination deserves all the blame for the situation. He remembers,

---

[7] In fact, the trailer for the documentary about human trafficking, *Call + Response*, does just this. LaFontaine narrates, "In a world like nothing you've ever imagined, a hidden horror preying on the unsuspecting, the weak, and the powerless.... You believed it wasn't possible.... You were wrong." *Call + Response* trailer, http://www.youtube.com/watch?v=h6vTbtKjTUo, accessed 29 August 2012. Here, though, the corollary to the "in a world" beginning—the hero who will set things right—is missing.

[8] According to Scarry, the reason why war, which is fundamentally a contest, cannot be replaced by a bloodless competition like chess or ballroom dancing, is that the dead and injured bodies of the participants are necessary to substantiate the reality of the imaginary world which the winner wins the right to declare real. Scarry, *The Body in Pain*, 91–116.

Persons with anything life sustaining to sell...were refusing to exchange their goods for money. They were suddenly saying to people with nothing but paper representations of wealth, "Wake up, you idiots! Whatever made you think paper was so valuable?" There was still plenty of food and fuel and so on for all the human beings on the planet...but millions upon millions of them were starting to starve to death now.... And this famine was purely a product of oversize brains.... It was all in people's heads. People had simply changed their opinions of paper wealth, but, for all practical purposes, the planet might as well have been knocked out of orbit by a meteor the size of Luxembourg.[9]

A million years in the future the world has been remade, not through human making, but through the re-structuring of the human body itself. A million years in the future, humans have lost their ability to imagine and to bring their imaginings to life in the experienceable world, a development which Trout views as an improvement. If, in Scarry's book, it is the body which lends its reality to what humans have made-up, in *Galápagos* we are left only with the body and the world of nature, a world which needs no substantiation because it is itself fundamentally real.

The Book of Job, too, tells a story about the unmaking and remaking of the world. Job's world is first unmade when the bet between God and *hassatan* strips him of his wealth and health, possessions which he had previously believed to be inalienable. Then, throughout the dialogues, Job and his friends dispute the nature of reality, and Job calls God to task for perpetuating a world that is not real. In chapters 29–31 Job takes his stand for the world in which he believes, and, taking an oath which puts his life on the line, attempts to remake the world as it ought to be. When God responds to Job in chapters 38–41, he presents his own vision of the real world, one that is substantially different from that claimed by Job. Finally, in the prose epilogue, one reality is chosen and the world is remade. Questions linger, however, about the reality of this world, a world which is, fundamentally, a made artifact.

### The Bet as a Declaration of War

According to Scarry, a made-up artifact becomes real to us when we forget that we have made it. To be reminded that we have made the artifacts that together made up our world is, Scarry argues, intolerable. It is not,

---

[9] Kurt Vonnegut, *Galápagos* (London: Flamingo, 1994), 26–27.

of course, intolerable to be reminded that we are responsible for the reality of things like chairs, coats, and light bulbs, to know that before these
things became real things they were imaginary, made-up things. What is
intolerable is to be reminded that things like gods, laws, and economic
systems are also made artifacts. Scarry writes,

> Although at a distance human beings take pride in being the single species
> that relentlessly recreates the world, generates fictions, and builds culture,
> to arrive at the recognition that one has been unselfconsciously dwelling in
> the midst of one's own creation by witnessing the derealization of the made
> thing is a terrifying and self-repudiating process.[10]

It is this "derealization" of the world in which one lives, the forced recognition that one's world is not really real but has only been made-real,
before which it was made-up, which is, Scarry argues, at the root of war.
She writes, *"The dispute that leads to the war involves a process by which
each side calls into question the legitimacy and thereby erodes the reality
of the other country's issues, beliefs, ideas, self-conception. Dispute leads
relentlessly to war not only because war is an extension and intensification
of dispute but because it is also a correction and reversal of it."*[11] War "is the
declaration that 'reality' is now officially 'up for grabs.' "[12] What the winning side wins is the right to declare what the world is like, and the dead
and injured bodies of the war's participants serve to substantiate the reality proclaimed by the winning side.

The bet between God and *hassatan* in *Job* 1 bears some similarities to
Scarry's description of the meaning behind a declaration of war. What
is at stake is the nature of reality. Peggy Day argues that the interaction
between God and *hassatan* in the prologue involves "a challenge of world
order."[13] *Hassatan's* purpose, in calling attention to the fact that Job may
not worship God for nothing is not, she claims, an attack on Job, but a
challenge of "Yahweh's blueprint for world order; if the righteous always
prosper, how can it be ascertained that their behavior is not motivated
by material gain? The satan is...accusing the creator of perpetrating a
perverse world order."[14] Indeed, when God singles Job out for *hassatan's*
commendation, it does not seem to occur to him that Job's devotion
might be less than perfect. It does not seem to matter to God what the

---

[10] Scarry, *The Body in Pain*, 128.
[11] Ibid., her italics.
[12] Idem, 137.
[13] Peggy L. Day, *An Adversary in Heaven* (Atlanta: Scholars Press, 1988), 82.
[14] Idem, 80.

motivation behind Job's good behavior might be. At this point, God does not believe in a world where what is required for humans to be blameless and upright is that they are so for no reason, expecting nothing in return. God is perfectly happy to reward those who behave correctly. *Hassatan*, though, proposes another condition for goodness. He insists that goodness is not goodness unless it is engaged in *hinnam*, for nothing but its own sake. If God and *hassatan* have different ideas about how the world ought to work in this respect, it seems that they might find themselves in the same situation as nations whose beliefs call into question the reality of each other's beliefs, which, in Scarry's view, leads to war. Can the bet between God and *hassatan* over whether Job serves God for nothing be considered a declaration of war—a declaration that reality is up for grabs and will be defined by the upcoming battle?

There is something curious about the exchange between God and *hassatan* which will not quite allow us to answer this question in the affirmative. God's opening words assume that, in the world as it ought to be, reward follows right behavior. *Hassatan* argues that reward ought not to follow right behavior, but right behavior ought to be engaged in for its own sake, simply because it is the behavior that God prefers. What is curious is that, far from denying *hassatan's* claims about the nature of reality, God immediately accepts them. God says, "Look how good Job is," *hassatan* answers, "Actually, there's a higher standard of goodness than the one you have in mind, and by that standard Job probably isn't good," and, instead of saying, "What do you mean another standard of goodness? I'm God. I ought to know what reality is," or even, "Tell me a little more about it and let's see whether it makes sense or not," God says, "Oh. All right. Well, let's test Job according to your standard of goodness and if he doesn't pass the test I'll agree with you that he isn't good." *What*? *Hassatan* criticizes God's "blueprint for world order," the reality of the world that God has created, and God, instead of launching a counterattack, says, "Sure, I see your point."

Why is God so easily swayed? Why shouldn't God reward those who behave righteously? And why are we, the readers, as taken in as God seems to be by *hassatan's* question? If it is easy to overlook the strangeness of this scenario, at least for contemporary readers, I suspect it is because the idea that retributive justice governs the world has fallen out of favor. We know that, in life, reward does not always follow right behavior, so if a person is to be truly good it must be for nothing. Like *hassatan*, we are eager to criticize God's view of reality. "It just doesn't work that way, God," we might tell this naïve fellow. "That's not the real world." Yet, even as we disbelieve that life functions according to the rules of retributive justice, the question, "Why do bad things happen to good people?" still retains validity for us. We know that bad things *do* happen to good people, but that we ask why it should be so implies that, really, we believe it should not be so. Moreover, we do believe in laws of cause and effect and structure our behavior accordingly.

For example, although you may not call such behavior "retributive justice," if your new puppy does his business outside, you give him a treat; but if he goes on the carpet, you smack him on the nose. The right kind of behavior merits treats, and the wrong kind of behavior reaps punishment. If you smacked your puppy on the nose whenever he went outside and gave him a treat whenever he went on the carpet and then complained that he wasn't housebroken, everyone would think you had a screw loose.

Let us put the exchange between God and *hassatan* in these crude terms. God says, "Look at my new puppy. He's already housebroken. He never goes on the carpet!" *Hassatan* answers, "That's all very well, but is he only housebroken because you give him treats whenever he goes outside? Isn't it the case that if you never gave him a treat for going outside he would still be going on the carpet?" Listening in on this conversation, we would expect God to answer, "That's beside the point. Of course he wouldn't be housebroken if I never rewarded the correct behavior. What are you, an idiot? The point is he's housebroken. He does the right thing. He's a good dog, and I can let him run around the house without worrying that he's going to wreck the carpet." "Oh, I see. Right you are," *hassatan* answers, blushing for his foolishness and trying to melt into a corner. Yet, when we read this first conversation between God and *hassatan*, it never occurs to us to think that *hassatan* is missing something upstairs, and the reason for this, apart from any preconceived notions about retributive justice, is that God takes *hassatan's* question seriously. "You're right," says God. "If this were really a good dog, he would housebreak himself and wouldn't need treats and punishments to make him do the right thing."

So it is that God and *hassatan* set out to determine whether Job is good according to *hassatan's* definition of goodness. *Hassatan* proposes that the world as it is be unmade and remade in a different way, a way he thinks is better. According to *hassatan*, there is a higher standard of goodness to which human beings ought to be held, and they can only be held to that standard if the world is so constituted that reward does not follow right behavior and punishment wrong behavior. The goodness which *hassatan* requires is, arguably, a higher level of goodness than the goodness previously accepted by God. It is arguably better to do something for nothing than to do it for something, though, as I have already shown above, there is a certain insanity inherent in this kind of reasoning. If a dog is better who is housebroken without reward and punishment, who does not pee on the carpet *hinnam*, is it not also true that a dog who bites his owner's hand "for nothing" is better than a dog who bites his owner's hand "for some reason," such as that the owner has stepped on his tail? Behavior that is "for nothing," without cause or motivation is, fundamentally, insane. Yet, for whatever reason, God does not go to war with *hassatan* over the *definition* of goodness, which is, surely, the larger issue, but instead enters into a dispute with him over Job's personal, particular goodness.

Moreover, although *hassatan* may assail the world order put in place by God, it is not God who feels the effects of having his world unmade. God, it seems, can easily let go of previous realities, perhaps because, as creator, he never loses sight of the fact that it has all been made-up in the first place. God and *hassatan* do go to war—or, at least they play a "war game" which, because they are cosmic powers, promises to have real consequences in the world—but they go to war over whether or not Job is good, not over the definition of goodness itself. Strange as it is, God simply accepts *hassatan's* standard, accepts that *hassatan* knows better than he does about what constitutes goodness. The world that gets unmade by the bet between God and *hassatan*, is not God's world but Job's.

### Job in the Unmade World

If God does not recognize that the world proposed by *hassatan* is insane, Job certainly does. And if we, the readers, have not batted an eyelash at *hassatan's* claims that goodness "for nothing" is of a higher order than goodness for some reason, once we are launched into the book's poetic section and see the effect of the wager on Job's world we certainly have second thoughts. If the Book of Job were a movie introduced by Don LaFontaine we would have no trouble seeing that Job's world has been unmade and needs to be remade by a hero who will make things right. Here is the trailer for the Book of Job *à la* LaFontaine: "In a world where the blameless and upright suffer, one man will challenge heaven to bring an end to their anguish." Cue action-y music and a quick-cut montage of George Clooney as Job: first sitting on the ash heap in misery, his jaw set in an expression of fierce determination; then (before his troubles) entering the city gates as a revered nobleman, dispensing wisdom to the elders, among them Eliphaz (played by Peter O'Toole), Bildad (Kenneth Branagh), and Zophar (Cate Blanchett in a beard), who reappear in heated argument with Job as the scene shifts back to the ash heap, and finally to a shot of Job running through the desert, stopping as he comes to a swirling cloud of dust and raising his fist to the sky. To remake the world as it ought to be is precisely what Job proposes to do, and we cheer him on as he undertakes his mission. In fact, when we view Job's mission through this lens, we see that he cannot help but accomplish it. In the movies, the hero always succeeds in his efforts to smash the false world and establish the real world in its place.

When Job and his friends talk in the poetic section, they do not dispute the nature of goodness. They all assume that goodness is—or at least ought to be—rewarded. In the real world, reward and right behavior go hand in hand. The world is not chaos, for God's sake! The world is not chaos, but the unmade world in which Job finds himself *is* chaos. Job's cursing of the day of his birth in chapter 3, his wish that he had never been born or even conceived, has to do with the fact that his world has been unmade, turned from cosmos to chaos. He is not, as some interpreters claim, trying to turn the ordered world into chaos.[15] Such behavior would be insane, and Job is not insane. The world has been unmade and, in consequence, Job, quite sanely, wants out. The difference between the beliefs of Job and his friends is that the friends believe the world they and Job currently inhabit is the real world, while Job believes it is a fiction, a lie told by a God who has gone temporarily out of his mind.

In the poetic dialogues, *hassatan* is forgotten. The book becomes not an account of the battle between God and *hassatan*, but between Job and God.[16] Whereas the dispute between God and *hassatan* turned not on the

---

[15] See, for example, Fishbane's reading of Job 3 as a "counter-cosmic incantation," in which Job "binds spell to spell in his articulation of an absolute and unrestrained death wish for himself and the entire creation." Michael Fishbane, "Jeremiah IV 23–26 and Job III 3–13: A Recovered Use of the Creation Pattern," *Vetus Testamentum* 21 (1971), 151–67 (153). Fishbane's interpretation is widely, but not universally, followed. Clines, for example, disagrees, writing, "Job's concern is not with the created order as a whole but with those elements of it that have brought about his own personal existence." David J. A. Clines, *Job 1–20*, Word Biblical Commentary 17 (Dallas, TX: Word Books, 1989), 81.

[16] This detail may indicate that what happens between God and *hassatan* is only simulated war, a kind of chess game with living pawns, or, at least, *one* living pawn. As the pawn whose world is endangered by the game, Job fights back against the one he sees as responsible for the unmaking of his world—God. If Job knew about *hassatan's* role, he might declare him his enemy as well. It is because the perspective shifts, from the heavenly council to Job's earthly existence, that *hassatan* drops out.

nature of righteousness but on Job's righteousness, the dispute between Job and God returns to the question of the nature of righteousness. Job does assert his innocence—continually, repeatedly—but he does so because he believes that in the world as it ought to be, innocence merits reward, not punishment. For Job, the suffering visited upon him is evidence of both God's enmity and God's insanity. In identifying God as his enemy, Job is not only pointing to God as the source of his suffering but as a being whose view of reality differs from his own. God is Job's enemy in Scarry's sense of the term. In God's reality, the innocent *do* suffer. For Job, however, that this is God's reality is proof that God has lost his mind. Were God sane, he would not be Job's enemy. Were God sane, Job is convinced that he would share Job's beliefs about what the real world is like and would create and maintain that world. Job's task, in his speeches, is to describe the real world in an effort to call God back to himself. Job does not hope to win the war against God so that he may proclaim his own reality. Rather, he hopes to win God over, so that God will, once again, make the world as Job knows it should be.

Job's most compelling attempt to call God back to himself, to reawaken his right mind, comes in chapter 29, where Job describes in detail the way the world ought to be, which is the way the world really is. "O that I were as in the months of old, as in the days when God watched over me,"[17] (29:2) Job begins, and goes on to detail his activities of "fearing God and turning away from evil" (1:1b) and the rewards that attended his actions. The real world of chapter 29 is contrasted, in chapter 30, with the usurping lie, the present chaos in which Job currently finds himself. In chapter 30 Job laments, "But now they make sport of me, those who are younger than I, whose fathers I would have disdained to set with the dogs of my flock. . . . I am a brother of jackals, and a companion of ostriches" (30:1, 29). Certainly God ought to be able to see that this is insane. And just in case God is too busy foaming at the mouth, rolling in ditches, and dispensing blessing and curse willy nilly to pay attention to Job's depiction of the real world and its antithesis, in chapter 31 Job takes an oath designed to force God to sit up and take notice. "If I have done anything at all wrong," Job says, "then let me be punished by God in every way imaginable. 'Here is my signature! Let the Almighty answer me!' (31:35b)". One way or another, Job believes, God has to respond to this oath; God has to say something in return, either

---

[17] All Bible quotations are from the NRSV.

to initiate the fulfillment of the curses Job has called upon himself or to declare Job innocent of all accusations.[18]

What is interesting about this oath, of course, is that it presupposes a world in which wrongdoing is punished and righteousness, if not rewarded, is at least not-punished. It presupposes the world Job believes to exist but which is not the world of his present experience. The oath is intended, then, not just to get God's attention, but to reinstate the world as it ought to be—that is, the real world—as the world which actually exists. Job's oath is constituted as the ultimate intervention. Job has not only reminded God of what the world should be like, but his oath forces God to reinstate that world. By answering Job with either punishment or reward—and Job is certain that it must be reward—God is called back to his right mind and the real world is brought back into being. At least, this is what Job thinks must happen.

## The Whirlwind Speeches as the World A Million Years From Now

After Job has sworn his oath, God does appear, and from the whirlwind, God speaks about creation. It should be apparent that, although some interpreters have labeled it as such, this is no *non sequitur*.[19] What is at stake in the Book of Job is the nature of the real world. That God describes the world as he sees it is an appropriate response to what has come before. Contrary to Job's expectations, however, God does not appear to re-inaugurate the world Job believes to be the real world. He does not accept the blueprint for the real world Job has laid out in chapter 29.

---

[18] It was David Robertson who first proposed that Job's oath functions in this way, an interpretation which is now a commonplace. David Robertson, "The Book of Job: A Literary Study," *Soundings* 56 (1973), 446–469 (461). In fact, I contest this reading of the power inherent in Job's chapter 30 oath of innocence in my article "Job's Crisis of Language: Power and Powerlessness in Job's Oaths" (*Journal for the Study of the Old Testament* 36 [2012]: 333–354), but here I let it stand. What power Job believes his oath possesses is a matter for speculation. Does Job really believe that God must answer him, as I accept to be the case here? Or does Job set up his oath in such a way that it does not matter whether or not God answers him, as I argue in "Job's Crisis of Language"? I do not know. Yet, in any case, it does seem that Job expects his oath to initiate the remaking of the world as it ought to be, however, and by whomever, this is accomplished.

[19] As Edwin Good writes, "The divine speech is not so irrelevant to the issues of the dialogue as some interpreters have thought. Responding directly to those issues, it rejects them. Yahweh has decisively shifted the issue from the questions of morality, its rewards, its punishments, and its cosmic reverberations. Indeed, it seems that morality has no reverberations at all." Edwin M. Good, *In Turns of Tempest* (Stanford, CA: Stanford University Press, 1990), 356.

Job's innocence may be confirmed by the fact that God does not visit new punishments upon him,[20] but confirmation of his own innocence was not Job's primary objective in swearing his oath. Job has known all along that he is innocent. In order for his innocence to be evident to others, however, Job needs what he believes to be the real world to be reinstated. He needs the blessing that follows righteousness and removal of the curse that follows wrongdoing. This God does not give him, not from the whirlwind anyway.

From the whirlwind God describes a world that functions on principles different from those believed to be supremely important by Job and his friends. It is a world in which certain natural processes have been established and can be counted upon. Job can be sure, for example, that the earth is anchored in place and will not move from the place where God has laid its foundation (38:4–7). He can be sure that the sea will not overwhelm the dry land, claiming the land for its own watery depths (38:8–11). He can be sure that the sun will rise in the morning and that the light of day will follow the darkness of night (38:12–15). He can be sure that certain constellations will appear in the sky at certain times of year (38:31–33). He can be sure that the staggering diversity of living animals on earth will go on living: mountain goats will give birth (39:1), young deer will leave their parents and go off on their own (39:4), the wild ass will find something green to eat somewhere on the steppe (39:8), the hawk will find blood for its young ones to drink (39:29–30). Despite the ostrich's foolishness and lack of care for its young, ostriches will go on being born and growing to adulthood. Despite the horse's recklessness in charging into battle, horses will still survive. Life will go on and part of what enables it to go on is death. Some animals will be preyed upon by others. Some ostriches will be crushed underfoot. Some horses will be killed in battle and eagles will drink the blood from their corpses. In none of these cases can suffering and death be linked to wrongdoing. The antelope which finds itself the prey of the lion is not the antelope which did something wrong, nor is it not the antelope which did something right. Any antelope, good or bad, is fair game for the lion's hunger.

Although anyone can see that a master who punishes his dog for the behavior he wants to encourage and rewards him for the behavior he

---

[20] Norman Habel writes, "Job's innocence is affirmed. None of the sanctions given in Job's oath of clearance are imposed." Norman C. Habel, *The Book of Job: A Commentary* (London: SCM Press, 1985), 65.

wants to discourage is more than a few cards short of a full deck, it is not so readily apparent that the world God describes himself as having created is similarly incoherent and reveals its creator to be insane. Instead, it is a world that makes sense. There is a great variety of life, all of it important, and death functions in the service of life. Animals die, but new ones are born, and the death of the old makes way for the new. It is a world that makes sense, but only if it is amoral, that is, only if God is not trying to encourage certain behaviors and discourage others.[21] Even though there is some provision for the containment of destructive forces—the sea has its limit beyond which it cannot pass, the wicked have their activities curtailed by the dawn—these forces are not punished *per se*. God's setting of boundaries for the sea is not punishment of the sea for its wild raging, but a way of ensuring that both sea and land can exist, a way of making room for both. The wicked, too, are not punished, but are simply constrained so that their destructive actions do not destroy all the world and its creatures. Despite the raging of the sea and the machinations of the wicked, life goes on—not all life, to be sure, but Life with a capital "L," Life in the grand scheme of things.

The world described by God has much in common with the world "a million years from now" as described by Leon Trout in Vonnegut's novel, *Galápagos*. In that world, humans have evolved into furry, seal-like creatures, with small brains and flippers instead of hands. Humans no longer imagine anything, and if they could imagine, they wouldn't have the wherewithal to turn those dreams into "dreams-come-true," a phrase which, positive though it sounds, Trout uses negatively to describe the bomb which a Peruvian pilot dropped on Ecuador a million years ago and the "mortars and hand grenades and artillery" he himself experienced in Vietnam.[22] In the future, humans are animals like any other. Nature has corrected the mistake she made in allowing humans to evolve such big brains and hands with opposable thumbs. Trout describes the human situation of a million years hence as one of "perfect happiness."[23] Similarly,

---

[21] That the world presented in the whirlwind is amoral has been most famously propounded by Mattitiahu Tsevat, who writes, "God says: 'No retribution is provided for in the blueprint of the world, nor does it exist anywhere in it. None is planned for the nonhuman world and none for the human world. Divine justice is not an element of reality.'" Mattitiahu Tsevat, "The Meaning of the Book of Job," in *The Meaning of the Book of Job and Other Studies* (New York: Ktav Publishing House, 1980), 1–37 (31). Tsevat, though, does not reflect on the inherent insanity of a world in which effect does not follow cause nor does he address the question of how its amorality permits God's whirlwind world to be sane.

[22] *Galápagos*, 154.

[23] Ibid., 217.

what God presents from the whirlwind is the world of nature, a world free from human imagination and human making. The wild ass and the wild ox refuse to participate in the human dreams-come-true of agriculture and trade (39:5–12), and Leviathan will not permit himself to be made into a pet or a commodity (41:1–10).[24] What are humans in this world? They are simply part of the food chain, animals among other animals. At least, that is what God would like them to be. That humans refuse to be part of the natural world is perhaps evidenced by their absence, by and large, from God's depiction of the world. Humans are only there on the periphery, as the ones who will not be served by the wild animals, intimating that if God were to focus on them, his whole world would fall apart.

From the whirlwind, God invites Job to leave the world of his own making and to enter the world of nature. In this setting, his suffering can be explained. It is simply part of Life. Any criticism leveled against the amorality of the world presented by God can be countered by *Galápagos'* criticism of the human world. Trout asks, "What source was there back then, save for our overelaborate circuitry, for the evils we were seeing or hearing about simply everywhere?" and answers, "There was no other source. This was a very innocent planet, except for those great big brains."[25] Trout blames human brains, with their capacity for imagining worlds, and human hands, which were able to make human dreams into dreams-come-true, for all the ills of the former world. Slavery, for example, was caused by human brains and hands. Says Trout, "Now, there is a big-brain idea I haven't heard much about lately: human slavery. How could you hold somebody in bondage with nothing but your flippers and your mouth?"[26] Torture, too, can be blamed on big brains and skilled hands: "It is hard to imagine anybody's torturing anybody nowadays. How could you even capture somebody you wanted to torture with just your flippers and your mouth?"[27] The amoral world of nature is, God and Leon Trout would agree, more moral than the moral world of human making.

---

[24] This observation comes from Catherine Keller, who writes, "Much has been made of the ludicrousness of the trope of Leviathan as a pet for giggling girls. Little, however, has been said of its *economics*. Like Moby Dick, Leviathan makes a mockery of the whaling industry.... [I]n this deft parody of the ancient world trade and business class, the windy vortex mocks the powers of global commercialization; it puts in question the assumption of the exploitability of the wild life of the world—the 'subdue and have dominion' project." Catherine Keller, *The Face of the Deep: A Theology of Becoming* (London and New York: Routledge, 2003), 138.

[25] *Galápagos*, 16.

[26] Ibid., 143.

[27] Ibid., 118.

Countering Job's claims about what is real, God presents him with
the world of nature, a world whose reality can hardly be denied. It is not
made-up or made-real, as defined by Scarry. It is simply there, a given. Its
reality is like the reality of the body, described by Scarry as fundamentally
real, unlike the made-real. And yet, it is a world from which humans, as
they are now, must be excluded. To enter the world God presents as real,
Job must change. He must stop being a world-maker and become simply
a world-inhabiter. Is this what he does?

## Job's Answer and the Epilogue: the Remaking of the World

Much depends upon how Job's answer to God—a passage fraught with difficulty—is understood.[28] It is possible that when Job says, "I have uttered
what I did not understand...therefore I despise myself, and repent in
dust and ashes," he is accepting God's version of what the world is like and
relinquishing his own claims as fictions, recognizing that the world he had
insisted was an insane lie is not, after all, a lie, but a reality within which
he can live, just as the lion, wild ass, and ostrich do.[29] It is also possible,
however, that Job's apparent repentance is ironic and that he only seems
to accept the world with which God has presented him,[30] all the while
hiding his revulsion at a God who is "an amoral force of Nature, a purely
phenomenal personality which cannot see its own back."[31] Other interpreters suggest that the language of Job's response is purposefully ambiguous. Among these is Newsom, who argues that Job's final words function
as what Mikhail Bakhtin calls a "loophole," a purposeful withholding of
a final word so that many non-final words may later be spoken. That is,

---

[28] According to Newsom, the grammatical difficulties inherent in 42:6 make it so that
"No matter how hard we listen, we cannot be sure of exactly what Job has said." Carol A.
Newsom, "Cultural Politics and the Reading of Job," *Biblical Interpretation* 1 (1993), 119–138
(136).

[29] Good reads Job's final words along these lines, writing, "Job supposed that his pain
was punishment of guilt and asserted his innocence against it. Now he thinks that it was
the wrong question. Suffering has no connection with sin, and the world is not run by
deserving. He 'repents of dust and ashes,' gives up the entire structure of the world as mirroring moral retribution. He repents of repentance, even, perhaps, of religion." Edwin M.
Good, "The Problem of Evil in the Book of Job," in *The Voice from the Whirlwind*, ed. L.G.
Perdue and W. C. Gilpin (Nashville: Abingdon Press, 1992), 68.

[30] Robertson writes, "God's rhetoric, because Job has armed us against it, convinces us
that he is a charlatan god, one who has power and skill of a god but is a fake at the truly
divine task of governing with justice and love.... In 42:2–6 he [Job] has to entreat his
opponent; in order to calm God's whirlwinds he has to declare his guilt by his own mouth.
He makes his confession, then, tongue-in-cheek." Robertson, "The Book of Job," 464, 466.

[31] Carl G. Jung, *Answer to Job*, trans. R. F. C. Hull (London & NY: Routledge, 1954), 26.

Job's answer may mean one thing when he speaks it, but he is deliberately vague so as to keep open the option of having meant something else, the possibility of reinterpreting his position at a later time.[32]

If Job's answer functions as a loophole, however, in a way it simply pushes Job's decision about whether or not he will accept God's world as the real world out into the future, suggesting that later he might give a less ambiguous answer. Does the Book of Job show us what happens later? Actually, it does—in the epilogue. Unfortunately, the epilogue presents its own problems for interpreters, not because its language is difficult (as is the language of 42:6), but because it seems to make no sense in its immediate context. God has just finished telling Job that, in the real world, reward does not follow right behavior, but in the epilogue God rewards Job for speaking rightly and chastises the friends for their wrong speech. From the whirlwind God has shown Job that the world is a wild place, filled with a great variety of animals, many of which are indifferent to human beings and others of which endanger human life. In God's world, the wild animals are central, while humans occupy the periphery. The epilogue, by contrast, takes place inside the city walls, in the enclosure where humans are central, and the animals that are named have been domesticated to serve humans; they are Job's property. The epilogue goes so far as to say that the animals are given to Job by God, as part of the blessing for his right actions and right words. The world of the epilogue could hardly be more different from the world of the whirlwind speeches. Some scholars argue that this dissonance is the result of a clumsy editing job, either on the part of the author, who needed a way to end his book, but wasn't picky about how he did it,[33] or on the part of a saboteur, deliberately seeking to obscure the message of the book.[34] It seems to me, though, that the epilogue, despite its dissonance, can be understood as integral to the book.

The epilogue, it seems to me, is Job's answer to God. The real world, Job declares, is a world in which retributive justice is active, in which human

---

[32] Newsom, *The Book of Job*, 29–30.

[33] James Crenshaw, for example, writes, "The book of Job comprises a poetic dialogue which has been inserted into a narrative framework. As a result of this strange marriage of incompatible literary strata, tension between the prose and poetry mounts.... The epilogue ... can be dispensed with altogether, since the poem ends appropriately with Job's acquisition of first hand knowledge about God by means of the divine self-manifestation for which Job risked everything." James L. Crenshaw, *Old Testament Wisdom: An Introduction* (London: SCM Press, 1982), 100.

[34] So John Briggs Curtis, who claims that "The most important purpose of the prose ... is that of deliberately misleading the reader" from the real import of the book. John Briggs Curtis, "On Job's Response to Yahweh," *Journal of Biblical Literature* 98 (1979), 497–511 (510).

beings are central, and in which he, Job himself, is counted among the righteous and rewarded accordingly. The world proclaimed as real by the voice from the whirlwind is rejected as fantasy. Job, the "army of one," has accomplished the mission he set out to achieve—just like the hero depicted in a LaFontaine-style movie trailer—the reestablishment of the world in which he believes. How does Job win the right to declare what the world is like? The book doesn't say. But that he has won is evident. In fact, the God of the prologue has also won. Job's passing of the test set by *hassatan* results in the restoration of the cycle of good behavior and reward, which God originally claimed was basic to reality. Even though Job may have demonstrated that it is possible for a human being to worship God without promise of reward, in the epilogue both God and Job proclaim that such behavior is not necessary in the real world. As for the God who spoke to Job from the whirlwind, proclaiming a different kind of reality, he is left out in the howling wilderness where he belongs. Within the walls of the town, in the bosom of the human community, Job has no need of him. Job has sent him away with words of seeming submission and now builds his world without that God, a God so different from any God Job has ever known that he has no use for him.

Perhaps the epilogue, far from being an awkward and irrelevant ending, is how the book *had* to end. Could Job really have chosen the wilderness, being what he is, a human being? How could he have made himself into nothing more than an animal like any other animal? He is not that. He does not have fur and flippers and a small brain (at least not yet). To have accepted God's whirlwind world as the real world would have required an act of imagination and making-real beyond Job's capacity for making. Job may reject the real world—if that is what the world glimpsed in the whirlwind is—but he makes a world he can live in, as the kind of being that he really is.

There is one small, strange detail in the epilogue, however, which lingers as a reminder of Job's encounter with the God of the whirlwind. Job's daughters are given an inheritance along with their brothers, given the kind of freedom that God, from the whirlwind, described himself as giving to the wild animals. Here, Job follows in the footsteps of the whirlwind God, changing his world in this small but significant way, acknowledging, even as he forgets, that vision of another reality.

# SHARMANKA: ART, RELIGION AND IDENTITY IN THE WORK OF EDUARD BERSUDSKY AND TATIANA JAKOVSKAYA

## The Religart Group[1]

SHARMANKA (Russian for *hurdy-gurdy*) was founded by sculptor-mechanic Eduard Bersudsky and theatre director Tatyana Jakovskaya in St. Petersburg (Russia) in 1989. It relocated to Glasgow in 1996. It remains one of Glasgow's best-kept but most important art secrets, tucked away in a small space in the Merchant City. Bersudsky is not one of those big names in art criticism: there are no critical works on his moving sculptures which perform complex questions of art, identity, and religion. With titles such as 'Babylon' and 'The Tower of Babel', his kinemats evoke biblical themes and Jewish stereotypes, but also invoke the quasi-religiosity of the immense secular ideological edifice of Stalinism. They also refer to their now Scottish context, for example in 'The Last Eagle of the Highlands' or 'Jock's Joke', a tribute to a chimney sweep from the Borders who shared Bersudsky's scrap-metal addiction.

Born in 1939 into a Jewish family in Leningrad, Bersudsky was evacuated with his mother and brother before the Siege. He lived through the Khrushchev, Brezhnev and Gorbachev years, working as an electrical engineer, as a lorry driver, and in a military factory. In his late teenage years, he was sent to work as an engineer at the coal mine at Inta, in the far north, where he met survivors of the Gulags whose stories had a profound impact on him. In the 1960's he started carving and making his first kinetic sculptures; there was no possibility of becoming an official artist as this would have involved joining the Communist Party. During the stagnation (*zastoy*)[2] of the Brezhnev era, when the ideological stranglehold tightened and dissidents ran the risk of being sent to prison or psychiatric hospital, he became one of the many known as 'internal emigrants'—those who had left the Soviet Union psychologically if not physically—and he worked industriously on his machines. His working class credentials and

---

[1] Benjamin Morse, Yvonne Sherwood, Alastair Hunter and Brannon Hancock, The Centre for Literature, Theology and the Arts, University of Glasgow; and Alice Dansey-Wright, Glasgow School of Art.

[2] *Zastoy* is the Russian term used for the Brezhnev era. It literally means not just stagnation, but 'rot'.

the fact that he was dismissed as a mere toy-maker meant that he was ignored by the KGB. In 1988, he began his collaboration with the theatre-director and well-known critic Tatiana Jakovskaya, who began to turn his sculptures and machines into performance.

The following article is a collaborative attempt by the Religart Group to evoke and reflect on the experience of attending these performances in a combination of word and image.

### Begging for Words

> There is no link that could move from the visible to the statement, or from the statement to the visible. But there is a continual relinking which takes place over the irrational break or crack.
> (Gilles Deleuze)

How to translate? How to translate images, sounds, performance into words? Or how to airlift a piece of the former Soviet Union to Glasgow? How to make writing move, as Bersudsky's kinetic sculptures (or kinemats) move? How to translate the machines of a man never given much to words—who actually lost the use of words for much of his life—into words, without inadvertently suggesting that these machines, these a- or post-verbal noises, have always been crying out for translation back into words (as if the visual and the audible had only ever been required as words' docile servants and intermediaries)? As they perform the breakdown of well-known Communist soundtracks—as they grind, and creak in ways that bland onomatopoeic words like 'grind' and 'creak' can only struggle, childishly, to imitate—these sculptures seem to defy words. They convict lofty rhetoric and record the disintegration of language into silence and a scream. But in other respects they seem to be begging for words. Eschewing the word-defying 'untitled', they choose, instead, literate and literary titles: 'Master and Margarita', 'The Castle (1937)', 'Waterloo', 'The Autumn Walk in the Belle Epoch of Perestroika (Meta-Tinguely)', 'The Dreamer in the Kremlin'. Like chattering guests at a dinner party, they drop allusions to Bulgakov, Fellini, Herbert Wells, Kafka, Bergman, Bosch, Brueghel, Tinguely, Leonardo da Vinci, George Grosz, the Danish artist 'Storm P', Anna Akhmatova, Yosip Mandelstam, Isaac Babel, and the Bible. They garrulously attach parentheses and even explanatory text to themselves, as if wanting to spill everything and to speak, testify, witness. Sometimes the feeling is of being sent scurrying off into an intertextual labyrinth or of

Figure 1. Perestroika. (Images courtesy of the Sharmanka Kinetic Theatre, 103 Trongate, Glasgow; http://www.sharmanka.com/Home/Welcome.html.)

being dispatched on a referential treasure hunt. Sometimes—as in 'Time of Rats'—the explanation that 'The mole is like Russia: a very strong and but blind animal controlled by pretty clever rats enjoying themselves on his back', the moral is megaphone-clear.

There is another sense in which these sculptures beg for words; strangely Eduard Bersudsky (1939–) and his partner-collaborator Tatiana Jakovskaya, have had very few words attached to them in the world of art criticism. This piece of writing was prompted by a sense that here the unmentionable/unspeakable seemed to be crying out for public conversation, but that this need for conversation was met with a curious silence in the hallowed halls of art criticism. We do not believe that we have the ability to bring Bersudsky into the world of 'names', where the currency (in both senses of the word) of the name seems index-linked to aesthetic-market value. Indeed, that would be strange, for his art seems to belong to a different world entirely, a world of part-time, but viscerally necessary art, art that was non-lucrative and non-productive in any conceivable way, by definition. From his first kinemat in 1967 until his transfer to Glasgow in the early nineties, everything Bersudsky made was made alongside menial jobs as a skipper on a naval barge; a night watchman; an employee of the Parks department, making sculptures for the lofty exhibition space of a children's playground—his is not the typical artist's curriculum vitae.

The meta-edifice of (mostly) words that we are trying to create here does not dream of being the perfect translation machine. It has no illusions of processing the synesthetic overload of sound and colour that is 'Sharmanka' into neat, static, fully adequate script. It can only hazard links between the irrational 'breaks' or 'cracks' and between the visible/audible and the legible. And it knows too, that it flounders on linguistic and cultural difference. The very name Sharmanka comes from the Russian, 'barrel organ', which is itself possibly a derivation of Italian 'charmante Catherine', played by itinerant Italian street musicians. In Russian culture, the idea of 'sharmanka' implies both entrapment—in eternally recurring melodies, set forever in the careful, exquisite but repetitious patterns on the barrel pins—and diversion and momentary release. A typically sardonic barrel organ song proclaims:

> I can hardly walk
> More than an inch in five minutes
> How will I reach my goal
> When my shoes are so tight?
>
> Work is work
> There will always be work
> As long as I have enough sweat
> For all those years
>
> To pay for my errors
> That's work also
> As long as I have enough smiles
> When they hit me in the ribs

Before talking about *Sharmanka*, we perhaps should give, in advance, the same kind of apology that Edward Kemp gives to Mikhail Afanasievich Bulgakov by way of prologue to his 2004 stage adaptation of *Master and Margarita*. For us too, it is hard, "living in the comforts that we do", to find the tone for the "kind of humour that floats on deep despair", without "becoming either too heavy or too light and without resorting to English irony, which is a defence against the dark, rather than an acceptance of it".[3]

---

[3] 'A Letter to Bulgakov' by Edward Kemp, *Programme Notes to The Master and Margarita*, Chichester Theatre, 2004.

## Entering the Fifth Dimension

No, replied Margarita, 'what really puzzles me is where you have found the space for all this'. With a wave of her hand Margarita emphasized the vastness of the hall they were in.

Kororiev smiled sweetly, wrinkling his nose.

'Easy!' he replied. 'For anyone who knows how to handle the fifth dimension, it's no problem to expand any place to whatever size you please.[4]

The only visible sign of Sharmanka's existence is a door with a curious-looking sign on it. Beyond even the peripheral vision of the art world, tucked above the Glasgow eye-line, numerous people walk past it without ever noticing it. Entering feels like gate-crashing a party, attending the meeting of some clandestine underground resistance movement or visiting a secret lover. (Take a quick last check over your shoulder to see that you aren't being followed by a private detective or the secret police). You press the intercom buzzer (the last sound of modern Glasgow you'll hear for a while) and ascend through an echoey, tiled stair-well (wondering whether you're really in the right place). The harsh reverberations of footsteps give the impression that you are in the bowels of some giant stadium and that round the corner will be daylight and a vast sea of humanity. But instead you enter a room that has the air of a crammed, dimly lit basement. You are on the top floor, but where are all the windows? And if this is a windowless, secret, blackout place, is there a danger that we might be being watched, as well as watching? The small group of people who have assembled to watch the performance (who are they, and why have they come?) are offered opera glasses, as if making a spectacle of our spectatorship. As Behemoth the cat in *The Master and Margarita* knows, one wears opera-glasses to get oneself looked at, as well as to look; and we can't help but watch one another watching.[5] In this kind of secret space, it seems impossible to police the lines between surveillance and spectatorship (darkness and innocence).

Even if you read the 'real' history of Sharmanka's journey to Glasgow, as laid out in the gallery catalogue, it does not quite dispel the far more

---

[4] Mikhail Bulgakov, *The Master and Margarita* (London: Harvill Press, 1995 [1967]), p. 286.

[5] 'Why have you gilded your whiskers? And what on earth do you want with a white tie when you haven't even got any trousers?' 'Trousers don't suit cats, messire', replied the cat with great dignity. 'Why don't you tell me to wear boots? Cats always wear boots in fairy tales. But have you ever seen a cat going to a ball without a tie? I don't want to make myself look ridiculous. One likes to look as smart as one can. And that also applies to my opera glasses, messire!' (*The Master and Margarita*, 1995, p. 292)

believable scenario that some mischievous spirit, or muscular angel, suddenly took it on himself to airlift Eduard Bersudsky's original fifteen feet by nine feet room in Leningrad or the first Sharmanka theatre on 151A Moskovsky Prospekt, to Glasgow. Its relocation seems as curious as the relocation of the sugar-cake, ornate, Santa Casa—the house where the Virgin Mary was told of the miraculous conception—to Loreto, Italy, allegedly transported by angels. Unlike those pristine, crisp white galleries that feel like hospitals or churches (offering a view of 'art' as expansion of the spirit, and healing of the soul), it does not feel like a gallery space. It is claustrophobic and cluttered, calling to mind the caricature-crammed canvases of Breughel; the imp-crammed canvasses of Bosch's hell-visions; the mind-blowing impossibility of the intricate, labyrinthine structures of Escher—particularly his Babel Tower—or the clowns working on immense, elaborate structures in the work of the artist who could be seen as a contemporary Escher: Adam Dant. But there's also something wildly-coloured and exuberant about them, as if the elaborate black and white care of a Dant or Escher had been coloured over in crayon by a child who cannot stay within the lines.

Entered to the sounds of something like a cross between a bygone era sweet shop bell and burglar alarm, Sharmanka looks like a dream of toy-store shopping sprees turned into an evil nightmare of social commentary. Animal skulls are impaled atop mounds of junkyard scrap; wooden figures stand, lie, sit, and move with their arched backs, rounded bellies and behinds, protruding breasts and phalluses, beaked noses, outstretched arms, top hats and bells. Hunchbacks, ghouls, devils, bureaucrats, dictators, whores, skeletons, tortured Jews, hybrid animals, Columbines, Pierrots, jesters, angels, skulls, and cages tumble over one another in a world both Gothic and Grim[m]. Switched off, at rest, it looks like one of those marvelous and impossible collections: like the rare and delectable Victoriana that appears in the parking lot of the motel in Carmel, California in Brian Moore's 1975 novel, *The Great Victorian Collection*—as if the whole 'mind of the man who created it', had somehow tumbled out, for all to see.[6] Sharmanka's automata, generated out of found objects from the mind of a single individual, strangely move (as they strangely move)

---

[6] Brian Moore, *The Great Victorian Collection* (Flamingo: 1975) p. 213. Compare Edward Kemp's comments on Bulgakov's *The Master and Margarita*, as a 'personal museum (think *Ulysses* or *Tristram Shandy*), stuffed with artefacts from many ages and many places, some of which seem to have no more value than the fact that the collector happened to like them' (Mikhail Bulgakov, *The Master and Margarita* in a new adaptation by Edward Kemp (London: Oberon Books, 2004), p. 11.

the visitor to retrace his or her steps into a region of fantastic creatures, half animal half machine, which are only a moment away from buried but not forgotten dreams. Moore's fantasy hints at the risks the auteur takes of being consumed or destroyed by what s/he has conjured into existence. What is the relationship between this intensely personal creation and its creator? When there is no-one to orchestrate the *son et lumière* of Sharmanka does the great collection exist?

The effect of this particular collection is one of dissonance: the juxtaposition of amusement and angst, of light and dark, of rusted metal and organic matter, of toy and terror and motion and meaninglessness. The shock value of these 'toys' might make us think of Brit Art—the insects trapped in Damian Hirst's life-death-machines, the Chapman brothers' physical sculpture of Goya, or their Hell (1999)—but the effect is far more subtle. Whereas 'BritArt' has the air of celebrating the shit and detritus of life as a finger up to 'beauty', Sharmanka has the air of making something from the rot and stagnation of *zastoy*, and conjuring the fifth dimension from tiny tenement rooms. And it's really funny. All those phalluses and breasts protruding from human and animal forms look like the work of some ruder, wilder Beatrix Potter, as if a now well-endowed Mrs. Tiggywinkle were suddenly keen to show us her nipples.

### Machine-ations

$$work = force \times distance$$
$$(w = f \times d)$$

Children in elementary science classes are taught that the role of the machine is to amplify the effects of human labour, leaving human hands (and spirits) relatively free for other things (like making art). By adding the simple extra element of 'distance', for example, a simple lever decreases the amount of human effort and increases the total amount of work, according to the neat little formula above. But in the machines at Sharmanka, there is no extrapolation by distance because there is no room to move in this cluttered space. Therefore there is no effective work, or yield. The inbuilt axiom of these perverse machines seems to be that force will encounter counter-force as surely as an irresistible force meets an immoveable object. The machines absorb human life into solipsistic, self-sustaining structures of energy-dissipating 'wheels within wheels'. The machines manage to create the illusion of activity and movement and life. It seems as if these little carved figures work cooperatively to bring the machine to life, cranking handles, turning gears, tugging on chains, spinning wheels. And yet the figures do not drive the machine; rather, they are driven and consumed by the machine. Bound in repetitive motions, placed in contorted shapes so that they function like a piston, or a handle, they seem to be striving to perform some valuable task when in fact they are indistinguishable from the cogs and wheels.

As if mimicking the huge sense of break-down and entropy that these machines exude, the distinction between man and machine also breaks down. Bodies are merely parts within some larger massive machine, which is so vast as to be practically invisible to the tiny figures. As in Charlie Chaplin's *Modern Times* (1936), the overall mechanism, and function, is invisible to its human-instruments, who are absorbed back into it.

Unable to keep up with his tasks at hand, losing his battle with the speed of the machines, Chaplin is sucked into the machine, eaten up and consumed, passed through the digestive tracts of giant belts and gears. Incorporated into its inner-workings, merely another part on the assembly line, the producer becomes the product (but no product really exists). According to the instruction manual of the Industrial Revolution, the machine will take the strain, allowing the human spirit to stretch out, get airborne, fly free above the grinding force of necessity. In the machine is our redemption. But here, human life is food for the machine's life, food for its nourishment, sacrifice to its being.

But the machines are not Frankenstein's monsters—nemeses of the Faustian-creator whose vast creative energy has escaped and turned back on him. They wouldn't have the energy for mutiny in the Modern Myth of the Revenge of the Machines. Sharmanka is much more than another re-performance of the technological-Gnostic myth in which the machine-god, as evil Demiurge, seeks to trap our spirits in metal cages. It is more than a re-run of the hackneyed film plot where the Machine becomes an antagonist against the human (think *Forbidden Planet, Dark Star, Blade Runner*). Bersudsky will not permit us the luxury of sinking back into that conventional and comfortable Romantic armchair trope in which the human/the natural/the fleshy/the spiritual is juxtaposed to the machine. As you look closer, you see that the human is not just being sucked into the machine as its food, or victim, but that that the machine is the human. The machine's mechanisms and machinations are fundamentally social. They remind us of Durkheim's treatment of the social, as a kind of mysterious *deus ex machina*, possessing 'powers and qualities as mysterious and baffling as any assigned to the gods by the religions of this world'.[7] The

---

[7] Michael Taussig, *The Nervous System* (New York, Routledge: 1991), p. 119.

machines are attempts to parse different variations on the saying 'pulling one another's strings'. Trace the lines of the weights, pulleys, and strings that move a human creature's arms up and down, or tug at his penis, and you often find another human creature at the end, pulling him/her by strings of duty or desire. These monstrous edifices are made of flesh, wood and metal. Like modern artistic renditions of the Tower of Babel (see *Tower of Babel* by Stanislao Lepri (1965) or *Tower made of bodies* by Cobi Reise (1967)) the machine of the State is made of human beings.

## Antecedents and Affinities

### Bersudsky-Kafka

How Absurd then—in all senses of the word—and how Kafkaesque, this fruitless pursuit seems. Kafka's protagonists endure the stultifying retinues of endless servants and officials who demean them despite their efforts, prove them guilty despite their innocence, and enforce their dependence and fear so that they can never escape the borders of the sinister village.

Bersudsky writes how he remembered the torture machine in Kafka's 'In the Penal Colony' (1919) when making his own 'machine with needles', 'The Castle (1937)'—the date is important—made in 1983. The title of course recalls yet another tale by his tormented predecessor. Bersudsky's castle however has less to do with the maddening effects of prohibitive bureaucracy (an issue more potently illustrated in almost every other work in Sharmanka) than it does with the visceral realities of pain and death. 1937 was the peak of Stalin's repression, when the barbarism depicted in Kafka's story was actualized by arrests, forced testimonies, labour camps and executions. Bersudsky's needle-lined tower encloses chambers of persecution that churn and consume effigies of poets and artists who lost their lives to the murderous regime.

Elsewhere, Bersudsky's puppets give colour to Kafka's less violent but no less oppressive themes; they make ships run, bells chime, wings flap and organs grind, but they provide the thankless manpower that puts the parts in motion but tragically make the machine go nowhere. Page after page, K. in Kafka's *The Trial* (1922) discovers people to be naïve victims of a system that most of them only seem to understand in part. Confusion reigns as he attempts to establish identities and intentions, and his fate is determined by factors well beyond his control. Likewise, in Sharmanka, the eye wanders from one figure's performance to that of another, and it discovers relationships to be elusive—interdependent and yet unrelated. Their stone-faced stares give only the faintest hints of life. While they remain immune to the cacophony of noises and tunes that accompany their actions, we wonder like K., what that ringing (or that soundtrack), is all about. We view them as K. observes the peasants:

> ... in whose eyes he had lost none of his fascination and who with their positively tortured faces—the skulls looking as if they had been smashed flat on top and the features had taken shape in the agony of being struck—their lips, and their mouths continued to watch but then again were not watching because their gaze sometimes went wandering off and dwelled, before returning, on some trivial object...[8]

At the same time, many of Bersudsky's figures are animals, or humans who inhabit animal forms, like Gregor in Kafka's 'The Metamorphosis'. The viewer doesn't question the transformation. Such dualities of identity are further illustrated in the Jews who appear slung between the tiers of the system's precarious but iron-clad hierarchy in *Tower of Pisa* (1995–96), and crucified in *Victoria* (1994).

### Leonardo the Magnificent and His Flying Machine

Leonardo da Vinci, another mad dreamer to whom Bersudsky pays homage (not least in 'Homage to Leonardo'), once dreamed of making a machine to create heat to rival the sun, using cogs and gears and wheels. Bersudsky's machines, by contrast, seem to demonstrate that distinctly contemporary response to the myth of Icarus: the fear that little human bodies get scorched by flying too close to The Big Idea. In the 'The Great Idea' (an improbable edifice of hubs, and a weighing machine, and a music stand), a little Marx cranks the handle, and keeps cranking despite scenes of comic malfunction in which the machine threatens to break in pieces. The children's pioneer song that accompanies the machine, winds down into slurred, drunken, discordant slow-motion. If you understand Russian, you can hear fervent, angelic little voices becoming lower and lower and slower and slower as they fantasize about bringing the locomotive of Communism into the station with the aid of 'guns'.

In the fabulous wheel-cog-pulley-bicycle-wing-barrel contraption that Bersudsky calls *Titanic*, the effort of several little figures, working devotedly on their own little section, combines to climax in a desultory flap of little fan wings. This yearning, trying machine is a sad contrast to Leonardo da Vinci's fabulous flying machines, such as his Prone Onithopter (1486–90).

---

[8] Franz Kafka, *The Trial* (trans. J.A. Underwood; Penguin, 1997).

Figure 2.   Titanic. Images courtesy of the Sharmanka Kinetic Theatre, 103 Trongate,
            Glasgow; http://www.sharmanka.com/Home/Welcome.html.

And as you look around the gallery, you see that it is full of ineffective
wings. There are little wings made of mesh that the air will simply filter
through. There are fan wings, which create little puffs of air. There is also
a comic long phallic balloon-like object on the top of *The Autumn Walk
in the Belle Epoch of Perestroika (Meta-Tinguely)*, which suggests a parody
of the brief climax—and flaccid aftermath—of human desire. It's not that
transcendence is impossible but that it is improbable, and also dangerous:
the big visions that we need also threaten us. But paradoxically here the
transcendent vision is social and historical materialism: that which aspires
to eschew the transcendent, to be not so much beyond transcendence, as
safely beneath it.[9] The music that accompanies *Titanic* poignantly and
wistfully suggests the necessity of human dreaming—reaching/building
upwards—even as the name 'Titanic' suggests drowning in the immensity
of modern dreams.

---

[9] Compare contemporary attempts to think beyond transcendence and ontotheology,
for example in John D. Caputo (ed.), *Transcendence and Beyond: A Postmodern Inquiry*
(Indiana University Press: 2007).

*Bersudsky-Tinguely*

Three sculptures in the Sharmanka Gallery bear the heading, 'Proletarian Greetings to the Honourable Jean Tinguely from Master Eduard Bersudsky from the Cradle of Three Revolutions'. The Swiss kinetic artist died in 1991, and Bersudsky had only encountered his work for the first time in Moscow the year before. Thus the homage alerts us not to a dependency but to a discovered affinity.

Tinguely's sculptures adorn the fountains outside the Pompidou Centre in Paris, and his hometown of Basel has built a stunning museum to house his work. His rambunctious personality and occasionally anarchist political interests earned him legendary avant-garde status. But when one compares Bersudsky's constructions to works such as *Gismo* (1960), *Sculpture Destroying Machine* (1960) and other mechanized assemblages Tinguely made from junk metal and old bicycles, Tinguely's 'revolutionary' aims and his subversion of the fame-game of the art system can seem rather tame by comparison.

Inspired as he was by Max Stirner's *Der Einzige und sein Eigentum* ('The Ego and His Own', 1844), Tinguely's 'insouciant individualist' approach was further fostered by his unrestricted exposure to the work of Duchamp, Delaunay, Naum Gabo, and Alexander Calder. In 1960, he led a parade of his work from Impasse Rossin in Paris to the Galerie des Quatre Saisons. In contrast to the Communist-controlled context and cramped quarters within which Bersudsky worked, however, Tinguely's rejection of control appears almost decadent—the mere recycling of a consumerist collector who had grown insolent enough to poke fun at the death of tradition. 'Poor you', one is tempted to think.

Death and the carnival feature in both artists' works, but prior to emigrating Bersudsky had only limited access to the avant-garde of the West. To deconstruct in public, to parade about, and to raise the strains of anarchic festival were unthinkable in Leningrad. Bersudsky's use of transitory forms and his relationship to systems of control evolve from more pressing and compressed circumstances than Tinguely's. Accompanied by fairground tunes, ragtime numbers, and harpsichord soundtracks, his carved figures screech with mournful cries, without eliminating the comic/sardonic or subsuming it in lament. The tortured processes in which the Russian's subjects are inescapably embroiled show their cycles to be absurd and tortuous in their repetition—but, like Tinguely's, beautiful nonetheless.

## The Big Idea

Exposed and vulnerable, humanity itself can die. It is at the mercy of men, and most especially of those who consider themselves as its emissaries or as the executors of its great designs.[10]

To execute:
To put into effect; carry out: e.g. 'a government that executes the decisions of a ruling party'.
To create (a work of art, for example) in accordance with a prescribed design.
To put to death, especially by carrying out a lawful sentence.

If at first glance the kinemats seem to exude something of the hubris and ingenuity of the pre-industrial dream-machines of Leonardo da Vinci, on closer inspection they combine a sense of pre-industrial dreaming and industrial ruin. They seem cobbled together from the junk-yard and ruin of the machine-dream. Their materials combine the pre-industrial world—a world of wooden churches, folk crafts, and carved figures made lovingly, slowly, laboriously from wood—with blades, swords, cages and balls and chains, evoking all the cruel and unnatural punishments of epochs and regimes that have been graphically overt about methods of 'disciplining and punishing'.[11] But they also use twentieth century junk: weighing scales, lawnmowers, bicycle wheels, music stands, oil cans, old shoes, and soviet army helmets and gas-masks—the latter evoking not so much progress, but ever improved efficiency and ingenuity in means of mass destruction. The spectacle of shoes and lawnmowers alongside the detritus of war suggests the whole panoply of life in which music, a walk in the park, watching (select) films,[12] loving, having sex, indulging in local rivalries, empathies, hatreds, takes place alongside and despite atrocities. But it also has a sinister dimension. For as Elaine Scarry points out in her

---

[10] Alain Finkielkraut, *Remembering in Vain: The Klaus Barbie Trial and Crimes Against Humanity*, (Columbia University Press, 1992) p. 31.

[11] Drawing on Michel's Foucault's now famous argument that overt and graphic systems of public punishment—in grotesque scenes of dismemberment and torture—were not overcome by modernity, but transformed into internal technological systems of self-policing. (See Foucault, *Discipline and Punish: The Birth of the Prison* (trans. Alan Sheridan London: Penguin, 1991 [1975]).

[12] One of the kinemats, *Waterloo Bridge*, is based on the 1940's film starring Vivien Leigh and Robert Taylor—one of the few Western films mysteriously permitted within the Communist regime. The scene of dancing to "Auld Lang Syne" plays over and over behind rotating candles and mirrors. There is something poignant about the little shrine to this fragment of Hollywood film.

*The Body in Pain*, torture often utilizes domestic implements, precisely so as to disrupt the most private part of the self—the home.[13] Placed alongside knives, swords, gas masks, domestic appliances loom in a darker light. What might they be used for? They also imply punishment turned inwards—towards the individual life and psyche, and (and here we come back to the idea of surveillance) into the individual's own room.

Where/who are we when we are here? Are we the victims, the accused, or blameless, helpless spectators? The devices look dangerous. Parts could fly off and crack our skulls or lodge themselves in our eye sockets is we were to get too close. It feels as if we, the audience, are potential victims. But those lifeless eyes, which gaze blankly from bodies working so hard to create the illusion of life, seem to be staring straight at us, half-taunting, half-blaming. On a naïve—and important—level these are just toys/performances offering themselves as devices for our diversion. (After all, we have come here for entertainment). They also seem to absolve us of the need to act. By performing the futility of human action, they seem to excuse us. If you attempt to do anything, in this context where human agency means so little, what do you/can you achieve? But then, the act of looking down on the whole structure of the machines—with a vast all-seeing perspective denied to the Lilliputian figures trapped within them—makes us feel like God or Gulliver. And this omniscience, which is both the omniscience of God and of historical retrospect, begs questions of responsibility. When harpsichord music plays in ironic dissonance with the machines, evoking safer, pampered, times and the comfortable insularity of eighteenth century living rooms, it makes us feel like pampered western children, sitting in something like the equivalent of a chronological and geographical 'panic room'. Looking at those figures who, because someone is pulling their strings from above, respond by pulling the strings of those below, suggests that the infliction of pain comes not from morality play scenarios—as the effects of evils or the 'seven deadlies', easily abstractable and definable—but from competing obligations in the complexity of the human social machine. Sharmanka is frightening because it makes us think of what John Caputo calls obligation, beyond ethics, beyond principles, and categorical imperatives.[14] Such lofty moral prin-

---

[13] See Elaine Scarry, *The Body in Pain: The Making and Unmaking of the World* (New York and Oxford: Oxford University Press, 1985).

[14] John D. Caputo, *Against Ethics: Contributions to a Poetics of Obligation with Special Reference to Deconstruction* (Indiana University Press, 1993).

ciples have never been enough to stop us, when the situation demands, saving ourselves by tugging on someone else's strings. It suggests the push and pull of the immediate situation—down low—to which moral reasoning comes too late on the scene.

### The Raven, Carnival and Memory

The guardian of Sharmanka—presiding over the entrance hallway—is the raven: the bird who, in Russian folklore, signifies not death, but longevity, and long memory. Folk tradition has it that the raven lives to between two hundred and three hundred years. Sharmanka feels like the regurgitation of the memory of a particularly long-living Russian raven who has been flying over Russia, and Europe, for the last millennium. But how, from a small room in Leningrad, did this raven get its wings?

Julian Spalding and others have already commented on the curious medieval quality of Sharmanka—the feeling that a medieval clockmaker has somehow reappeared in the wrong time, having set his finely-tuned clock at the wrong century. From a context where Gothic does not exist, Bersudsky (magically?) creates an unheard-of Russian Gothic. Works such as *The Tower of Medieval Sciences* or *The Clock of Life* are suggestive of the fourteenth century astronomical clock in the Old Town Square in Prague or the riotous images in Western Christian medieval manuscript marginalia (as opposed to Russian Orthodox texts). The figures spilling out of the metal/wood structures look like those figures that cavort in, through, and around the black and white script of medieval devotional texts—even, sometimes, in mechanical fashion. Bersudsky's distended figures are reminiscent of those bawdy subversions around the sacred text: buttock-showing gargoyles, subversive 'bas-de-page' figures such as animals performing scenes from the life of Christ or a monkey suckling on the breast of a nun.

Carnival, coming from '*Carne vale*' means, ambiguously, 'flesh farewell'. It refers to the forty day period of fasting during Lent, mirroring Jesus's forty days in the desert. But it also means 'Flesh, fare well' in the sense of 'Flesh, may it be well with you'. So to take carnival literally is, at one and the same time, to celebrate and to confine/repress the flesh. *Festa stoltorum* ('feasts of fools'), *parodiae sacrae*, and mock liturgies like the 'liturgy of drunkards' point to an ancient fecund traditional counter-tradition where, in the words of Mikhail Bakhtin, 'yeast' is added to 'reality', life comes out of its 'legalized and consecrated furrows' and the 'icy, petrified seriousness' of official truth is allowed—momentarily—to thaw.[15] Carnival, famously, is one of the spaces invoked by Mikhail Bakhtin (1895–1975), a Russian of a generation prior to Bersudsky, who was arrested for his participation in the Underground Russian Orthodox Church in 1929 and sentenced to a Siberian labour camp—commuted, on the grounds of his fragile health, to six years internal exile in Kazakhstan. Bakhtin drew on Dostoevsky and Rabelais to open up his own internal imaginative space. Dostoevsky enabled him to theorize the so-called 'dialogic', which broke open 'monologic' textual and cultural spaces by allowing unorthodox voices to exist in intimate contact with the orthodox voice, without the tradition 'fusing with it', 'swallowing it up', or dissolving into itself the other's power to mean. Carnival and Rabelais opened up a space for flesh and allowed him to write in defence of earth-bound flesh. Carnival gave him the resources to oppose or at least momentarily suspend abstract (oppressive) hierarchies imposed from above, and open up a folk-communalism to counter the myth of the 'bourgeois atomized human being'.[16]

Sharmanka similarly draws on traditions of outburst—of colour, ambiguity, subversion—from the archive of the past. In the true tradition of carnival, the flesh bursts out but the flesh is also confined—often graphically, in chains and cages. Ancient traditions such as the *danse macabre* or the ship of fools are invoked. But the watchmaker scrambles his times, and sets the hour to the fourteenth and the twentieth century simultaneously. The ship of fools now has a name: 'Aurora' (the cruiser that fired the signal shot that began the October Revolution). Gothic-medieval modes of caricature traditionally applied to the 'Jew' and 'Turk' are now also applied to Stalin and Marx. *Victoria*—a crucified puppet in Jewish kippah, attempting a quirky jolting dance, or trying to raise his head, or release his hands amidst a machine of moving chains, swords and saws evokes that quintessentially twentieth century, post-Holocaust figure: the 'crucified Jew'. His futile attempts to dance, fly or escape are set to the sounds of a clarinet playing 'Jerusalem of God'. The effect is like placing fellow Russian émigré artist Marc Chagall's 'Introduction to the Jewish Theatre' (1920) alongside his now famous 'White Crucifixion', or his 'Study for the Revolution'. Dialogic/carnival exuberance co-exists with a clear monologic message. (There is little ambiguity about how to interpret *Victoria* or *Aurora*).

---

[15] Mikhail Bakhtin, *Rabelais and His World* (trans. Helene Iswolsky; Indiana University Press: 1984) pp. 73, 89. For Bakhtin's survey of medieval carnival ritual see pp. 1–58.

[16] Bakhtin, *Rabelais and His World*, p. 24.

As in Chagall's art, the strictures of socialist realism dissolve in a rebellion of form, an upsurge of magic and enchantment. It seems that facts, and the strictures and confines of historical events can in some sense be creatively changed. But this sense of creative transformation co-exists with a sense that, in Bulgakov's words, "a fact [or the strictures and confines of history and society] is the most obdurate thing in the world".[17]

## Fairytales

At first glance, Sharmanka looks as if it were made for children. Special matinee performances are even put on to cater for shorter attention spans. But in their overt sexuality and violence, this toy-shop disrupts twentieth century idealisations of the 'innocent child'. Images of a fool being repeatedly kicked in the backside, a donkey endlessly being lowered and lifted on a pulley elicit pleasure at a relative feeling of power; high spectatorship, from up in the 'gods'. The recurrent sexual embrace of a lascivious looking man and a voluptuous woman provokes snickers of delight. There is also wonder at an array of brightly coloured miniature figures who magically 'come to life' with lights and music and no apparent 'operator' in sight. The figures resemble Pinocchio or the shoemaker's elves, mischievous toys who awake from their dumb slumber to act out incredible stories and scenarios before returning to their posts, to be found inanimate on the workbench the next morning. Like little children, fantasising freedom from their parent-creators, the little imps move and work independently, for good and for ill. They also make us think of the invisible creator— Bersudsky—who one never sees, who is always in the back room. We might imagine him, perhaps, as a little Wizard of Oz, or a reclusive toy-maker, or even a mysterious Gepetto figure, who sees himself not so much as bestowing life as releasing life already in the wood.

In their charming whimsicality, anachronism and other-worldliness the puppets in the machines seem to be conjured from the world of fairytale—often set in dark continental forests and exotic far-off lands, such as 'Russia'. The famous tales of the (aptly named) Brothers Grimm and the macabre Hans Christian Andersen in particular come to mind. These writers never spare their readers from ogres, hags, witches, giants, torture and death—and this, is of course what is so thoroughly appealing

---

[17] Bulgakov, *The Master and Margarita*, p. 311.

to the child. The twentieth century Disneyfication of fairytale is a response to psychoanalysis's revelation of the violence, anxiety, destructiveness, and even sadism of the childish imagination,[18] and of the power of fairytales to feed that imagination. (Compare the sanitized circuses, purged of cruelty, discussed below). The U-certificate, saccharine fairytale, with cuddly talking animals and friendly dwarves caters to parental fears about letting dark images into the child's absorbent mind, and even worse, nurturing darkness already within them. Best not remind ourselves that Hansel and Gretel, in the original version, relish putting the witch in the oven she has prepared for them. But as Bruno Bettelheim argues, the morbid enchantment of fairytale does the child an important psychoanalytic service, because "learning that others have the same or similar dark fantasies makes us feel that we are part of humanity, and allays our fears that having such destructive ideas has put us beyond the common pale."[19] Paradoxically, over-analysis kills the fairytale, by rationalizing the ambiguity out of existence—an insight that would also apply to Sharmanka. As Bettelheim writes, "explaining to a child why a fairytale is so captivating to him [*sic*] destroys, moreover, the story's enchantment, which depends to a considerable degree on the child's not quite knowing why he is delighted by it,"[20] As adults we might be a little more guiltily conscious of how a darker shade of art, performance, film, writing, help us not just to shamefully live with—but also care for and indulge—the 'dark monsters residing in the unconscious'. We are comforted and given pleasure by the words of the author, or a character whom we have created, sharing internal shadows which we do not hide/enjoy alone.

But enchantment might also be dangerous in another sense: because it offers an escape route—a mode of displacement. Ogres, ghosts and witches can become a substitute for 'real' evils that do not necessarily occupy a 'real' part of children's minds. Children are often oblivious to the real dangers of the world—or tend to transform anything they overhear from it into fairytale terms.[21] Sharmanka seems to raise the question of this transformation/displacement by putting real figures, real events, real

---

[18]  See Bruno Bettelheim, *The Uses of Enchantment: The Meaning and Importance of Fairytales* (Harmondsworth: Penguin, 1976), p. 120.

[19]  Bettleheim, *The Uses of Enchantment*, p. 122.

[20]  Bettleheim, *The Uses of Enchantment*, p. 18.

[21]  One of us, as a child, remembers imagining the 'bad man' Pol Pot, with his manifestly unreal name, as a wicked giant; another remembers being totally sanguine in the face of real threats and evils, because she reserved her space for fear for the un-real enemies of fairytales.

dates, into the transformative machinery of fairytale. By making a crucified puppet Jew, the gallery poses a challenge that echoes A. S. Byatt's
incisive comments on the politically grim in Grimm: "It is important to
distinguish between the effects of tales of bludgeoned outsiders or glee-
fully tormented Jews and the folktale machinery of swallowed and regur-
gitated children, severed limbs magically restored, and even the dreadful
punishments of the wicked stepmother and sisters (such as red-hot iron
shoes and barrels full of nails)."[22]

By refusing the happy ending commonly believed to be its linch-
pin, Sharmanka subverts the idea of fairytale as, as A. S. Byatt puts it,
a "form... of hope", allowing us to live in daydream-world where happy
endings (and safety nets) "are not only possible but inevitable."[23] It closes
the gap between the adult and the child by suggesting that the adult world
of the political and the childhood mechanisms of fairytale are not so far
apart. By giving us more than of the 'real' than we can cope with, it pushes
Bettelheim's theory to the point where it perhaps breaks down: can so
much darkness, so much violence, still be, in some sense 'good' for the
adult or the child? Is it not impossible that adults, like children, would not
be forced to do some work of transformation on such a bloody history—
and isn't that what Bersudsky is doing? As with our childhood deflection
of fear in the direction of witches and monsters, is there not some kind of
poignant inevitability about the move that plays out the Stalinist purges
in a craftsmanlike retro-fantasy of music, colour, lights?

### Circus and Cruelty

At the St Petersburg Circus, you can watch the play of shadows on the
roof of the tent, as figures hang and spin high above the ground without
a safety net. You can see a huge brown bear dressed in shorts/nappies
ride a scooter around the auditorium, dance, walk a tightrope and walk
on his 'hands'. You can watch a clown abject himself and squall and shit
himself like a baby (his shit is sawdust). You can see a troop of monkeys ride round the auditorium on hobby horses, blurring the boundaries
between the human, the inhuman (material) and the inhuman (animal), and the mock-animal that is the 'toy'. In the grand finale (checking

---

[22] A. S. Byatt, Introduction to M. Tatar, *The Annotated Brothers Grimm* (London: W. W.
Norton and Co. 2004), p. 12.
[23] A S. Byatt, Introduction to *The Annotated Brothers Grimm*, p. 12.

yourself for effects of substance abuse) you can watch a dog and then monkeys ride on the back of a hippopotamus, and then a monkey dance on the back of a dog on the back of a hippopotamus. The effect is of absurd, grotesque pathos, and an indiscernible mass of life-forms: blurred boundaries between man and baby, dog and monkey and hippopotamus, real animal and mock animal.

With the overwhelming smell of shit and sawdust, the St Petersburg circus makes you gag and sneeze on a tradition of circus that has been banned from western circuses where, for all the best reasons, Russian circuses are for acrobats only, and EU standards of safety and non-cruelty must be observed.[24] The St Petersburg circus reminds us of a darker tradition that must, by definition, be unsafe, and by definition expose animals and clowns to cruelty and humiliation. In the tradition of the dancing bear, what matters is the pathos of the giant creature placed on a leash, dressed in silly knickers, and forced to do tricks for our entertainment. It is important that he looks for all the world like a giant man in a bear costume—for he is our scape-goat, our scape-bear. He is a figure for bound humanity but also an other for human beings who have, momentarily, unbound themselves, enjoying instead, the subjection of the bear. Helping us digest the noxious smell of sawdust, shit, sweat and the uncomfortable ambiguity of our response—the indigestibility of empathy-schadenfreude, and guilty pleasure—are the bright colours, the spangles, the stars. In short the St Petersburg circus feels like Sharmanka—with added smells.

The *balaganehic* (travelling circus) of Sharmanka is like the carnival/circus come to town out of time and in mysterious circumstances in Ray Bradbury's *Something Wicked This Way Comes*. Cooger and Dark's Pandemonium Shadow Show could be a shadowy image of Sharmanka drawn from the dark side. The sense of a dark side which is not far from the watcher's experience in Sharmanka—an evocation of goblins and faeries, of things which go bump—is foregrounded in Bradbury's fairground. But there are no real demons here, nor are there in Sharmanka. Such demons as there are come from our *own* imagining, but are none the less real for that. The fate that befalls vulnerable souls in Bradbury's worlds is no less horrifying for being an extension of their own weakness.

---

[24] The member of our group who visited the circus felt deeply uncomfortable and voyeuristic watching the spectacle of animal and human humiliation and we feel ambiguous about reproducing these images here, and repeating the spectacle—but we are doing so because it is precisely this discomfort that we want to explore.

*Something Wicked This Way Comes* offers the reader (and the people of Green Town) a carnival of grotesques, but with a difference: this is a carnival also of fools whose folly made them freaks. The viewer laughs at them, without pity, and is thereby lured into the fairground's hidden seduction which has the power to make freaks of them too. The Pandemonium Shadow Show exists in the end not for the viewer but for those who feed off the fears of those it ensnares. Its secret is the carousel:

> With a pop, a bang, a jangle of reins, a lift and downfall, a rise and descent of brass, the carousel moved.
> But, thought Will, it's broke, out of order!
> He flicked a glance at Jim, who pointed wildly down.
> The merry-go-round was running, yes, but...
> It was running *backward*.
> The small calliope inside the carousel machinery rattle-snapped its nervous-stallion shivering drums, clashed its harvest-moon cymbals, toothed its castanets, and throatily choked and sobbed its reeds, whistles and baroque flutes.
> The music, Will thought, it's backwards, *too*![25]

Later they realize that the music is the Dead March, and the carousel has the power to age or rejuvenate (but only the body, not the mind).

The eventual downfall of Cooger and Dark comes about when a key character realizes that their system cannot withstand genuine laughter.[26] Thus it comes close to Sharmanka: a fairground of mechanical freaks which is in many ways a long peal of mocking laughter in the face of the dark dehumanized systems out of which it grew, but which still prevail long after the downfall of their communist manifestations. Sharmanka's ubiquitous phalluses seem to be vulgarly 'taking the piss' out of the po-faced seriousness with which the Carnival of Freaks tries to seduce us. Here too the sense of fun is compounded by the real fear of both the unknown and the known. Death at the mercy of fairground rides is common enough, and yet the draw of the garish and ghastly, noisy and noisome, hyperactive and hysterical is famously irresistible. What lies behind the machinery? Who runs it?

---

[25] Ray Bradbury, *Something Wicked This Way Comes* (New York: HarperCollins, 1999), p. 77.
[26] See in particular the long passage (pp. 228–230) describing Charles Halloway's defeat of the witch.

## Light, Shadow, Christian, Jew

'You spoke your words as if you denied the very existence of shadows or evil. Think now: where would your good be if there were no evil and what would the world look like without shadow? Shadows are thrown by people and things'.[27]

What of shadows? Of the interplay of light and object that creates shadow? Is it a creation, or a negation? The shadow is nothing. It is an absence, the presence of an absence–a void space where light cannot penetrate. "Shadows," Mark C. Taylor writes, "cast their spell at twilight–that strange, enigmatic time between day and night, that strange, enigmatic place between light and dark. Does the interplay of day and night create twilight? Do light and dark join to cast shadows? . . . Are shadows the 'between' that makes light and dark possible?"[28]

In Bersudsky's kinetic sculptures, shadows function as an extension of the moving figures. The interaction of the coloured lights, the shapes and hues they create on the machines and their white wall backdrop is an integral part of the art event. And yet these figures, imprisoned in their mechanical world, seem strangely cut-off from their shadows, as if there were hardly any correlation between the two. Like Peter Pan, whose shadow is accidentally severed by a briskly-closed window, rolled up and stowed in a bureau drawer, and finally tenuously reattached with a needle and thread by motherly Wendy,[29] these shadows seem estranged, orphaned, prodigal. The figures' erratic movements are exaggerated in their shadowy reproductions, kinetic, frenetic, menacing. Or, perhaps, hollow, futile, lonely.

Shadows are both the thing and not the thing, a representation of the thing, yet actually the outline of an absence. They 'are' a thing created by a negation, for the light shines on and reflects off of the obscuring object which in turn blocks the passage of the light to the space. We tend to think of light as something, and darkness nothing: nothing more than the absence of light. Light, we believe, is stronger than darkness: if you flip a switch or strike a match in a dark room, the darkness is vanquished, for

---

[27] Bulgakov, *The Master and Margarita*, p. 405.

[28] Mark C. Taylor, *About Religion: Economies of Faith in Virtual Culture*. (Chicago: Chicago UP, 1999), p. 115.

[29] J. M. Barrie, *Peter Pan in Kensington Gardens; Peter and Wendy* (ed. Peter Hollindale; Oxford/New York: Oxford University Press, 1991) pp. 78–91. Interestingly, although Peter's shadow is returned to its proper place, it cannot be fully restored—the prodigal shadow remains creased, marked by the experience of this separation.

the two cannot coexist...at least not peaceably. Our metaphysical pre-
disposition in favour of light is interesting, and also, perhaps Christian:
'The light shines in the darkness, and the darkness did not overcome it'
(John 1.5). In Christianity, this light is the Word, the Word made flesh,
the Word that brings life, which is also light. The life/light of the Word is
the way, truth and life–the way to truth and life–the *via veritas*, the *via
vita*. Logocentricists and believers in Western Metaphysics that we are, we
tend to prefer these things to their negative correlates–silence, darkness,
deception, death. These are Evil, in direct contradistinction to Go(o)d.
But what if these opposites collided in a *coincidentia oppositorum*, held
apart and yet drawn together by a profound but necessary tension? Would
we recognize light if we did not have the contrasting experience of being
enveloped in utter darkness? Doesn't God have to create light and darkness together in Genesis 1? The fact is, the light needs the darkness–at the
very least to have something against which to appear, or to define itself.
In a Saussurean or Derridean understanding of language, no element—
even God or light—can exist independently of other words against which
it stands out by contrast. The God of Genesis seems to have anticipated
this Saussurean/Derridean understanding, since he creates by division—
separating sea and dry land, night from day. The lone word or concept
cannot exist if it absorbs all into itself. Light is never purely itself. The
introduction of light always illuminates certain things while casting dark
shadows over others.

   Bersudsky's figures toil on, some in the spotlight–or is it the heat lamp
of the interrogation chamber?–others in the shadows. What do the shadows hide? Perhaps sinister deeds, committed in secret (but still seen by
God, we are told)? (cf. Matthew 6.6) Perhaps noble deeds: acts of secret
construction? Perhaps the shadows hide nothing at all, and in doing so,
reveal nothing? Nothing is hidden, and no thing is revealed. The figures
labour, but for what? For nothing: nothing more than its own sake–to
refract a beam of blue light, to cast a shadow on an otherwise blank wall.
Gratuitous movement, gratuitous play—the aneconomic gratuity of shadows. The gratuitous play of shadows calls to mind the etymological connection between gratuity and grace. At the same time, it is impossible to
think about shadows, and not think about the catastrophic absorption of
the Jewish, the Old, as the shadow for Christian light. According to the
logic of supersession, the Jewish becomes the shadow cast by the figure of
Jesus, the true light, who comes to enlighten everyman (John 1.9) and who
declares 'before Abraham, I am' (8.58). The victory of Christ and Christian
time seems to be evoked by the trapped Jesus-Jew of *Victoria*. Perhaps

this figure is also trapped by the inexorable idea of progress that builds
on the radical destruction or transformation of the Old/the past: an idea
that is, as Kathleen Biddick argues, bound to the logic of supersession or
what she terms the typological imaginary which structures our very ideas
of time.[30] The explicit Jewish-Christian reference highlights the curious
but not unusual situation of Eduard Bersudsky and Tatiana Jakovskaya,
as assimilated Jews whose Jewishness appeared as an inescapable if intangible shadow, projected through persecution both Stalinist-secular and
Christian. Crude Jewish stereotypes, a few allusions to the Bible, and a
crucified dancing Jewish Jesus evoke this strange shadowy Jewishness, this
identity-shadow. Jewishness dances here, in the shadows, without being
something overtly religious, like 'Judaism'. Bersudsky's kinemats help us
to see how 'religion' can be articulated (or stumbles on) in complex ways,
and, in particular, how such articulation relies on a number of uncomfortable contradictions to remain in dynamic movement.

---

[30] See Kathleen Biddick, *The Typological Imaginary: Circumcision, Technology, History*
(Philadelphia: University of Pennsylvania Press, 2003).

# BY THE LIGHT OF A CLOUDY GLASS: BIBLICAL INTERPRETATION AND DISCIPLINARY SECURITY

A. K. M. Adam and Samuel Tongue

The field of biblical interpretation was forged in some of the most intense controversies of modern academia. Conflicts over blasphemy, secularism, modernism, historical integrity, and ideology (to identify but a few) have not only shaped, but also scarred the institutional practices of biblical interpretation. The outworking of these intellectual battles has affected almost all participants in related discourses; so much energy has been invested in upholding or assailing the legitimacy of one position or another that the preponderance of research in biblical studies tends to adhere resolutely to disciplinary mandates—or flippantly to flout them, observing a sort of *anti*-disciplinary regimen. At the heart of these predictable gestures lies an anxiety about the legitimacy of the interpretive repertoires that constitute biblical studies as a reputable discipline in the eyes of the university, the church, the government, or the general public. Only under very peculiar circumstances do biblical interpreters step out of the confines of the ominous shadow of interpretive security.

The essays in this collection constitute an offering toward a vision of biblical interpretation untroubled by the stresses of disciplinary (in)security. We are not so rash as to assert that none of these essays is coloured by the green shades of disciplinary envy, the red of heated polemic, the purple of bruised self-assertion; indeed, the very concern to have escaped disciplinary anxiety would betray the persistent effect of that anxiety. The collection gathered here aims not to have overcome anxiety (any more than a perceptive analysand presumes to have recovered from obsession or depression), but to demonstrate the possibility of recognising a problem, moving toward addressing it, and venturing forward with a measure of relief and chastened confidence.

Whether we frame our recuperation as intellectual maturation or as the *Aufhebung* of disciplinary self-justification—or attach any other label to it—the recurrent exuberance with which biblical interpreters embrace new *methods*, new *inter*disciplines, testifies to a restlessness close to the heart of the practice. Each newly-adopted supplement surges, plateaus, engenders conflicts over the true or correct or legitimate details of the approach, becomes tedious to onlookers who once thought it exotically illuminating, and gradually wanes to a core group of unwavering advocates. The new-then-old approaches do not, however, disarm the mechanism that produces securely unimaginative interpretations (on one hand) and fruitlessly fanciful interpretations (on the other); these conjoined twins of opposite disposition both owe their self-constitution to their reactive response to *security*.

Anxiety over interpretive security encourages practitioners to erect barriers to sequester proper, pure, legitimate textual behaviour from the disreputable conduct of outsiders. The higher the walls, the more extensive the concertina wire, the more saturated the minefield, the less room for growth and change within the citadel. To the extent that arbiters of interpretive legitimacy construct rigid criteria by which to recognise acceptable interpretation, they retard understanding. Anxiety over interpretive security tends to keep at bay just the sources of renewal and enrichment that might sustain the community of interpreters.

Such anxieties around secure modes of interpretive production are surely tied to larger contestations around what biblical studies *is for*; what the arts and humanities *are for*; and, in the broadest sense, what a university education *is for*. As Stefan Collini notes, asking what something is for is asking for trouble, a process of infinite regress in a hall of glassy mirrors.[1] Of course, such a question smacks of utilitarian economic frameworks: how are you going to argue that your explorations in Akkadian verb forms "has a direct impact on economic growth by encouraging innovation and providing new and cost-effective ways of meeting the needs of business, industry and services"?[2] The question is worth asking however, even if only as a starting point, pointing to broader questions around disciplinarity and its connotations. The recent debates between James Crossley and Larry Hurtado provide a very useful overview of the issues at stake, which

---

[1] Stefan Collini, *What Are Universities For?* (London: Penguin Books, 2012).

[2] Rick Rylance, "Innovation is about anticipating tomorrow's challenges." *The Independent* 10th May 2012. http://www.independent.co.uk/student/postgraduate/postgraduate-study/research-matters-innovation-is-about-anticipating-tomorrows-challenges-7733186 .html. Accessed 29th May 2013. The worrying thing here is that this is not written by a government official; this is Prof. Rick Rylance, AHRC Chief Executive and Chair of RCUK Executive Group, who, one surmises, must be caught between a rock and a hard place in trying to balance the perceived statuses between STEM and AHSS subjects in the current economic climate. As an aside, and perhaps protesting too much, it is worth counting how many times he uses the word 'innovation' to define the university's task, particularly striking in such a short article.

shall not be repeated here.[3] Broadly speaking, Hurtado raises the question of what should constitute disciplinary protocols in British New Testament PhDs, listing, among other things, a strong competence in Koine Greek, Hebrew, and Latin, an ability to read other important non-English NT scholarship, primarily produced by French and German scholars, and skills in using the Nestle-Aland apparatus on the Greek texts. Crossley is concerned that overemphasising such protocols restrains doctoral students from pursuing 'reception-historical' issues, maintaining disciplinary legitimacy at the expense of opening biblical studies to broader intellectual and political currents in the humanities and social sciences.

Although this is an oversimplification of both sides of an important debate, what is interesting is that both scholars see their proposals as a means of survival for biblical studies. Hurtado wishes to maintain strong and well-defined disciplinary identities so that biblical studies actually has a place at the table in the modern university without being diffused into myriad other departments and research programmes. On the other side, Crossley argues that "Biblical Studies has not really generated unique methods and ought rather to be conceived as a field of study which utilises methods from different disciplines. So we should perhaps begin by foregrounding interdisciplinary learning as standard [...]."[4] For both parties, Biblical Studies is still a 'useful' endeavour to pursue within a university setting.

Without denying such claims entirely (not least for our own employment, in all senses of the term), a reader might glimpse an important undercurrent in the articles presented in this book. Postdisciplinary work cannot, in the final analysis, settle on one discipline that trumps them all. Disciplinarity is like the lead came that holds the stained glass of the Glasgow Theology window in place; but if smashed, splintered, fragmented, it becomes useless or, at the very least, not useful in the same role that it had previously performed.

Perhaps, then, we might explore the fecund uselessness of biblical studies. Whilst probably a dangerous argument to make around a university management who are not versed in the subtle nuances of critical thinking, there might be something in this. As Tongue explored in his essay on

---

[3]  See James Crossley, "An Immodest Proposal for Biblical Studies," *Relegere: Studies in Religion and Reception* 2, no. 1 (2012): 153–177 and Larry W. Hurtado, "On Diversity, Competence, and Coherence in New Testament Studies: A Modest Response to Crossley's 'Immodest Proposal'," *Relegere: Studies in Religion and Reception* 2, no. 2 (2012): 353–364.

[4]  Crossley, "An Immodest Proposal for Biblical Studies," 157.

the Babel-complex, Gustave Eiffel responded to the charge that his tower was a useless monstrosity by scrupulously listing all the 'innovative' and notably scientific uses his creation could inspire: "aerodynamic measurements, studies of the resistance of substances, physiology of the climber, radio-electric research, problems of telecommunication, meteorological observations, etc."[5] But Roland Barthes went on to argue that "alongside the overwhelming myth of the Tower, of the human meaning which it has assumed throughout the world . . . [Utility is] nothing in comparison to the great imaginary function which enables men [sic] to be strictly human."[6] Indeed, the rhetoric of use "never does anything but shelter meaning."[7]

Uselessness in the Barthesian sense is, paradoxically, a way of freeing up a discipline, a concept, an architecture for other imaginary functions. Adam's article on how idolatry functions in 'Sacramerica' notes that Augustine distinguished between 'using' and 'enjoying' God in Book I of *de Doctrina Christiana*. The idolator, on these terms, fails to recognise that God is absolute, aniconic, and useless.

If 'use' implies control, restraint, objectification can a postdisciplinary biblical studies becomes 'useless' in this chastened sense? To the extent that these essays then make progress toward a goal, they mark progress not by advancing toward a disciplinary truth, nor by undermining the hegemonic domination of tyrannical disciplinarity, but by *not worrying or*, at least, not worrying for the duration of the essay's momentary stay against confusion. No biblical interpreter will ever defeat the need to undertake study of grammar and semantics, or to accede to others' conclusions. No interpreter will ever deploy unarguable premises from disciplines outwith the discourses associated with biblical studies, with which to dislodge problematic impediments to interpretive clarity and truth. No interpreter will attain universal assent by hewing so assiduously to conventional interpretive gestures that no one dares to ask them any more questions. Interpreters cannot buy security simply by doing exegesis the right way (whatever that right way may be). The only way to elude the perils of interpretive vulnerability lies by way of not aiming at an impossible invulnerability, but by moving beyond the constraints that define disciplinary conventions. Past the borderline of anxiety, they offer interpretations whose qualities themselves warrant respect (or not, as the case may be).

---

5 Roland Barthes, "The Eiffel Tower," in *A Barthes Reader*, ed. Susan Sontag (New York: Hill and Wang, 1983), 239.
6 Ibid.
7 Ibid.

Such interpretations can and will be contested, most vigorously by the enforcers of disciplinary tedium. As we have been insisting, no interpretation escapes contestation and resistance, and such interpreters as venture outward in non-anxious disregard will encounter various sorts of disincentive for their temerity. Under such circumstances, one should not be surprised if any particular convergence of postdisciplinary interpreters soon disperses again. We can still notice the possibility, however; we can observe that intelligent readers can learn from disciplinary discourses while still venturing interpretations that pass beyond those conventions.

The murky windows in the Theology Window of the University of Glasgow's Memorial Chapel may be designed to transmit the vibrant tones that would suggest the twists and illuminations one might encounter in the Bible; the dull cast to the window may indicate the simple effects of years of exposure to the elements without efforts toward support, maintenance, or preservation. On the other hand, the dull tones may be deliberate, casting the study of Bible and theology as less exciting than Literature and Art, History, Law, or Medicine. At least here, in this collection from the Glasgow School, Biblical Studies catches and refracts some of the rare Glasgow sunlight into vibrant colour.

# INDEX OF NAMES

# INDEX OF SCRIPTURE

# INDEX OF ANCIENT SOURCES
## (Judaic, Christian, Islamic)